Corporate Governance of Sustainability

ESRI STUDIES SERIES ON THE ENVIRONMENT

In April 2000 the Japanese government launched a series of comprehensive,
interdisciplinary and international research projects called 'the Millennium
Projects' and as part of this initiative the Economic and Social Research Institute
(ESRI) of the Cabinet Office of Japan initiated a two year project entitled 'A Study
on Sustainable Economic and Social Structures in the 21st Century', which focuses
on ageing and environmental problems in the Japanese and international context.

The *ESRI Studies Series on the Environment* provides a forum for the publication
of a limited number of books, which are the result of this international
collaboration, on four main issues: research on solid waste management; the
analysis of waste recycling and the conservation of resources and energy; research
on the compatibility of environmental protection and macroeconomic policy; and
the analysis of problems related to climate change. The series is invaluable to
students and scholars of environment and ecology as well as consultants and
practitioners involved in environmental policymaking.

Titles in the series include:

Corporate Governance of Sustainability

A Co-Evolutionary View on Resource Management

Edited by

Raimund Bleischwitz

Wuppertal Institute for Climate, Environment and Energy, Germany and Visiting Professor, College of Europe, Bruges, Belgium

ESRI STUDIES SERIES ON THE ENVIRONMENT

Edward Elgar
Cheltenham, UK • Northampton, MA, USA

Published by
Edward Elgar Publishing Limited
Glensanda House
Montpellier Parade
Cheltenham
Glos GL50 1UA
UK

Edward Elgar Publishing, Inc.
William Pratt House
9 Dewey Court
Northampton
Massachusetts 01060
USA

A catalogue record for this book
is available from the British Library

Library of Congress Cataloguing in Publication Data
Corporate governance of sustainability : a co-evolutionary view on resource
management / edited by Raimund Bleischwitz.
    p.   cm.—(ESRI studies series on the environment)
    Includes bibliographical references and index.
    1. Corporate governance.   2. Corporate governance—Case studies.   3.
    Sustainable development.   4. Sustainable development—Case studies.   I.
    Bleischwitz, Raimund.
    HD2741.C77656 2007
    658.4′08—dc22

                                                                2006101922

ISBN 978 1 84720 228 4

Printed and bound in Great Britain by MPG Books Ltd, Bodmin, Cornwall

Contents

PART 3   CASE-STUDIES ON SUSTAINABILITY
         AT THE MESO-LEVEL

PART 4   CONCLUSIONS

Contributors

Bettina Bahn-Walkowiak   Research Fellow at the Material Flows and Resource Management Research Group, Wuppertal Institute, Germany

Raimund Bleischwitz   Co-Director of Research Group Material Flows and Resource Management at the Wuppertal Institute, Germany, and Visiting Professor (formerly Toyota Chair for Industry and Sustainability) at the College of Europe, Bruges, Belgium

Oliver Budzinski   Habilitated Economist and Research Fellow at Marburg University, Germany

José Acosta Fernandez   Research Fellow at the Material Flows and Resource Management Research Group, Wuppertal Institute for Climate, Environment, Energy, Germany

Oliver Karius   Chief Executive Officer and Co-Founder of VantagePoint, Zurich, Switzerland, former Manager Research Services and Senior Sustainability Analyst at SAM Research (Sustainable Asset Management), Zurich, Switzerland

Michael Kuhndt   Head of the UNEP/Wuppertal Institute Collaborating Centre on Sustainable Consumption and Production (CSCP), Wuppertal, Germany

Thomas Langrock   Former Research Fellow at the Wuppertal Institute, Germany, now with German Emissions Trading Authority within the German Federal Environment Agency

Stephan Ramesohl   Co-Director of the Future Energy and Mobility Structures Research Group at the Wuppertal Institute, Germany

Ulf-Manuel Schubert   Former Research Fellow at the Environmental Policy Research Centre, Free University of Berlin, Germany

Burcu Tunçer Project Manager at the UNEP/Wuppertal Institute Collaborating Centre on Sustainable Consumption and Production (CSCP), Wuppertal, Germany

Holger Wallbaum Director of triple innova, Wuppertal, and Senior Consultant at the Wuppertal Institute and Assistant Professor of Sustainable Construction at the Swiss Federal Institute of Technology, Zurich, Switzerland

PART 1

Analysing corporate governance of
sustainability: insights from research
and policy analysis

1. Scope and main thesis

Raimund Bleischwitz

Environmental policy can claim some success considering the state of the environment in the 1980s, and it certainly remains important for efforts towards sustainable development. More recently acknowledged problems such as climate change, land use, and management of natural resources and material flows are some of the most challenging environmental policy issues. They are challenging because:

- the complexity of causes and effects prevails, though science is able to increase its understanding of them;
- potential disasters resulting from cumulated impacts cannot be excluded;
- the international dimension is vital both for analysis and for action;
- the need for action is acknowledged by some actors, whereas others prefer a 'wait and see' position;
- any action taken needs to be coordinated among different policy fields (geographically as well as sectors) and private actors (such as business, consumers and green non-governmental organizations – NGOs) across local, regional, national and international levels;
- any action needs to be weighed against social and economic concerns, because sustainability requires an integration of those dimensions.

These challenges differ from those which led to the emergence of environmental regulation in the 1970s and 1980s. At that time, policies had to tackle immediate risks where the polluters were relatively easy to identify. It was almost natural that the policies of those days focused on what were later called command-and-control efforts, that is, legal instruments such as quality standards and pollution targets formulated and decided upon by governments.

In contrast to those early years, contemporary environmental policy is characterized by a shift from governments to governance, meaning that institutions and actors outside the state become more important. It is claimed not only that the acceptance of those actors is pivotal for any implementation of policies, but also that corporate and societal actors play a role in policy formulation and precautionary measures. General driving forces of the change from governments to governance can be seen as follows (Jordan et al., 2003, pp. 202–6):

- Dissatisfaction with environmental regulation. Concerns about implementation costs in bureaucracy, compliance costs in industry, and the inability to get through to small and medium-sized enterprises as well as to private households were raised in most OECD (Organisation for Economic Co-operation and Development) countries during the 1990s. These concerns were raised in forerunner countries (such as Germany) and the laggard countries alike.
- Shift in the regulatory debate. Previous arguments about the merits of state-driven policies were perceived less attractive than before. A governance 'turn' in most OECD countries spurred privatization programmes and enabling of private activities alike. Not only neo-liberal ideas, but also ideas of communitarianism and a 'third-way' beyond capitalism and socialism paved the way for a context outside environmental policies in which governance ideas could thrive. Importantly, the sustainability paradigm has not been directly aligned to these debates, but has highlighted some limitations of traditional regulation while emphasizing an equal weight of economic and social considerations (Berkhout et al., 2003).
- Market integration and influence of the European Union. Most OECD countries, and in particular the European Union, have intensified their efforts towards market integration, that is, a harmonization of legal institutions with the aim of reducing transaction costs for international business operations while coordinating economic policies. These efforts have almost automatically required more systematic thinking about appropriate levels of action and the interface between corporate actors, politics and society. As regards international sustainability policy, the European Union (EU) seems to have accepted its role as a forerunner region. Interestingly, however, the EU's regulatory toolbox is not yet designed by a clear concept but rather experiments in different directions of economic incentives, voluntary agreements, eco-labels and formalized planning tools. With the EU enlargement since May 2004, one can expect further steps towards governance structures, be they in the form of indirect pressure, or in the form of market facilitation for environmental purposes.

The following study starts from the assumption that any governance[1] for sustainable development requires further analysis on a) how to include corporate and private actors and b) what to conclude for policies and the role of the state. In that research area, our book will seek to test the following thesis: governance of sustainable development goes well beyond traditional, state-centred policy-making because it aims at proactive changes of private actors' behaviour at different levels. It necessarily involves different levels of policy-making as well as business, individuals and NGOs in policy formulation and implementation. Innovations are key to facilitating action by private actors. Innovations generate positive externalities, enabling corporate actors to play a public role while doing good business on competitive markets. For reasons of outreach and power, corporate actors play a particular role. Our notion of 'responsible corporate governance' identifies this pursuit as a driving force towards relieving environmental pressure and the internalization of some externalities. Motivated by self-interest and by soft incentives, corporate actors transform areas previously perceived as part of the public domain into new markets for sustainable development. The state, however, retains the responsibility for reforming the framework conditions, for monitoring of public concerns and for innovation-inducing regulation. The latter in particular is bound to lower levels of policy-making, that is, it is characterized by the EU principle of subsidiarity. 'Co-evolution' characterizes such a dynamic relationship of private and public actors and institutions towards sustainability. In order to test this thesis, the book addresses the following questions:

- What exactly is the function of governance systems for sustainable development? What exactly is their role in decoupling the use of natural resources from economic well-being towards more sustainable production and consumption patterns?
- Suppose that networks driven by corporate pioneers become important: how can those networks enable corporate actors while permanently keeping an eye on public concerns? How can those networks be assessed?
- Which conclusions can be drawn for policy analysis? What conclusion can be drawn for policy instruments and programmes?

Methodologically, the book applies recent theories from social science with a particular focus on economics to the sustainability debate. A particular emphasis is given to institutional analysis. Political science analyses the governance system with emphasis on the role of the state and public administrations (Héritier, 2002; Young, 1999; Sabatier, 1999); economics offers findings on firms, market failures and regulatory theories (Williamson, 1999; Dixit, 2000; Nelson, 2002; Stiglitz, 2000). The interdisciplinary approach is worthwhile because an interaction between actor-centred institutionalism (political science) and new institutional economics helps to explain the role of responsible corporate governance and political governance towards sustainability. New institutional economics seems helpful in analysing firms' behaviour, their internal procedures, markets and competition. The analytical framework derived from those theories to an extent departs from models of rational choice, that is, it does not assume a fully rational actor with perfect information (Ostrom, 1998; Mantzavinos, 2001; Bleischwitz, 2003c). Recent literature on 'corporate governance' is of special importance here as it provides insights into the motivation and self-interest of firms, which in turn is helpful for the design of policy reform.

It is interesting to note that such an approach still is relatively new for sustainability research. Many economic studies have a background in welfare economics (and the ensuing concept of 'internalization of externalities'). For that reason, many studies tend to distinguish between legal and economic incentives. Our book attempts to cut across such a distinction because – following the literature on law and economics[2] as well as that on institutions – actors receive economic and legal incentives alike and have to address both in their strategies. In that regard, networks can be regarded as laboratories of policies to be formulated later on, which integrate different types of incentives with motivational aspects and self-interest. Seen in that way, our book analyses possible sustainability policies from a micro- and meso-perspective.

The next chapter of Part 1, Chapter 2, will introduce the concept of 'responsible corporate governance' and give a short survey of how it may fit into recent theories of firms, markets, competition and regulation. This is followed by a chapter on recent concepts of competition. The study assumes that those concepts are important for balancing sources of innovation with price signals and possible externalities. After this, three further chapters discuss consequences for regulatory tools on an analytical level. Part 1 concludes in stating the importance of networks among private actors as well as between private and public actors.

Part 2 provides more in-depth analysis into those networks among private actors as well as between private and public actors. It develops an assessment methodology of those activities, which stems from literature in Part 1 as well as from the emerging European policies of 'regulatory impact assessment'.

Part 3, certainly a key section of our book, explores certain case-studies where the interaction of political and corporate governance is illustrative, and where corporate action is a strong driving force. Resource management, eco-efficiency and energy are the physical dimensions of those case-studies. The case-studies have been selected from a European perspective and should illustrate different types of networks.

Part 4 draws conclusions on how the results might be used for policy analysis and draws some lessons from using the assessment methodology. Because policy-makers will have to respond to weaknesses of networks, Chapter 19 outlines a programme on material efficiency.

This book fits well into a broader frame of policy research activities. Besides the Millennium Collaboration projects from the Japanese Economic and Social Research Institute (ESRI), it certainly is worthwhile referring to the Johannesburg Earth Summit 2002, which has clearly addressed the need for more public–private partnerships towards sustainability (called 'Type II commitments'). There, a need for policies of sustainable production and consumption as well as policies for decoupling resource use from economic well-being has also been formulated. This book analyses the role states and private actors may play as well as potential network-based strategies in regard to climate change, eco-efficiency and energy. In doing so, it contributes to analysis on global change from a micro- and meso-oriented perspective. Though it does not explicitly address theories of international relations (such as international climate policy research), it surely would be interesting to connect our research on co-evolution and networks of sustainable development with this strand of research.

NOTES

1. For the purpose of our book, 'governance' is understood as the capacity of a country's institutional matrix (in which individual actors, firms, social groups, civic organizations and policy-makers interact with each other) to implement and enforce public policies and to improve private sector coordination; see Ahrens (2002, p. 128); this book is recommended reading by the International Society for New Institutional Economics (ISNIE).
2. Faure and Skogh (2003), one of the first books systematically addressing the law and economics of environmental policy, nevertheless argues largely within the paradigm of rational actors, whereas our book analyses actors and institutions under the assumptions of imperfect information, uncertainties and bounded rationality; see also Bleischwitz (2003c, 2004).

2. Sustainability as a business challenge: the concept of responsible corporate governance

Michael Kuhndt and Burcu Tunçer

MOUNTING COMPLEXITIES AND INTERDEPENDENCIES ALONG GLOBAL PRODUCT CHAINS

Along with the liberalization of trade and the broad diffusion of information and communication technologies, economic activities have extended beyond national borders. Globalization is leading to a delivery of products constituted by large numbers of inputs from numerous intermediate producers. The extension of product chains between countries and sometimes among several continents has become possible. For example, the life-cycle stages of a laptop – that is, design, manufacturing, marketing, use and disposal or take-back – can all take place in numerous countries. Overall, product chains linking consumers to producers of products are dominated by complex and international relations (Moltke and Kuik, 1998, p. 1).

Surging complexities around the globe are associated with increasing international resource[1] dependencies. As the extraction of materials for a product occurs miles away from the site of its final use and disposal, the manufacturing of a product becomes heavily dependent on imported supplies, often from the developing countries.[2] Hence, the environmental load may shift to the actors in the upper parts of the product chains. For example, the depletion of tropical forests in the developing world can be an environmental aspect of a corporation located in the developed world utilizing timber in its products that are marketed in the Northern markets. In this respect, the importance of achieving eco-efficiency improvements becomes central not only in the First World, but also in the developing countries.[3]

In fact, economic development in the developing countries is in line with the capability and resource availabilities along global product chains. In the developing countries, while the proportion of manufacturing industries stays high, the proportion of service industries, which are normally related to the concept development and design stages of product chains, is still low. On the other hand, service industry is surging in the developing world, reaching 70–80 per cent of the economic share. Higher innovation potential (build-up of innovation capabilities) in the First World is a major factor in shifting economic wealth to the lower points in the life cycle. Hence, added value concentrates more and more on the parts of the chain which have the capacity to develop the image and social meaning of the final product rather than the parts involved with production or extraction of raw materials.

Increasing complexity of environmental problems is not only reflected along the structure of global product chains, but also in the management of global environmental problems such as climate change or ozone depletion. In the case of mitigation of and adaptation for climate change, multinational action is required, since no single country or small group of countries can reduce emissions sufficiently to stop greenhouse gas (GHG) concentrations from continuing to grow and, also, wherever the emissions originate, they affect the climate globally. Primary responses to address concerns about climate change range from international initiatives, particularly through the United Nations Framework Convention on Climate Change (UNFCCC), such as the adoption of the Kyoto Protocol, or international scientific organizations, such as World Climate Conferences by the World Meteorological Organization (WMO) and United Nations Environment Programme (UNEP); to national or local public responses, such as assessments of climate science and abatement strategies, implementation of legally binding policies; and also to initiatives taken by environmental non-governmental organizations, such as climate change campaigns or partnerships; and private business action, such as facilitation of trading of permits for carbon emissions or schemes to help manage CDM transactions (Schneider and Sarukhan, 2001, pp. 87–8). As regards policy analysis, these initiatives from corporate, political and societal actors co-evolve, that is, various actors participate in policy formulation (see also Chapter 17).

THE NEW FACE OF CORPORATE RESPONSIBILITIES

In the current state of the world, where dependency and complexity are major factors, managing sustainability problems faced at both the global and the regional level requires shared responsibilities. Among all societal actors, corporations face extended responsibilities, as they are major constructors of global product chains and contributors to global environmental and social

concerns. As the impact areas of their activities extend, governance implications become inevitable, leading to a dramatic shift in the balance between
private actors and government agencies in international product chains
(Moltke and Kuik, 1998, p. 11). As decisions taken and operations run by
corporations may affect a wide range of communities and cultural back-
grounds along product chains, their responsibilities extend beyond the
culture, social networks and geography of their headquarters. Due to their
economic and political influence, specifically high-impact sectors (such as
mining, chemicals, automotive industries) are continuously facing expectations to assume stricter responsibilities for their management decisions and
activities in developing countries (Sullivan and Frankental, 2002, p. 80).

Stakeholders'[4] agendas for corporate responsibility have extended as
their perceptions of corporate impacts have widened and their capabilities[5]
are developed in time. As the new economy and resource dependencies
has enhanced information-sharing around the globe, outreach capabilities
of non-governmental organizations (NGOs) and pressure groups have
extended and made them a major driver in the wave of change towards
social accountability and equity (Zollinger, 2001). With the formation of a
'global village', instantaneous media coverage has become extensive, allowing local problems to be listened to and shared at a global level. In this vein,
more pressure can be placed on corporations to contribute to environmental resource preservation and social development alongside economic
development of regions (Korten, 2001).

The financial sector is slowly extending its perception of corporate risks to
a combined social, environmental and economic performance beyond single
bottom-line financial performance.[6] Firstly, the criteria for eligibility for
financing are gradually extending, as the financial sector realizes the materi-
ality of environmental and social risks associated with the operations of high-
impact sectors.[7] Among global environmental concerns, climate change is
becoming a major factor for investments, as it is realized by the investment
community that corporate exposure to the risks of climate change can vary
according to, for example, companies' 'greenhouse gas intensity' (Innovest,
2002). Secondly, ethical and social funds in the European and US markets are
growing. Socially responsible screening concentrates on evaluation of how
well companies manage to integrate corporate social responsibility[8] issues
into strategic business development process, in order to identify sustainability winners (Mistra, 2001) (see also Chapter 18).

The sensibility of shareholders to corporate responsibility has also
stemmed from the recent corporate scandals. In particular, problems associated with the scale and structure of corporations are becoming more pre-
eminent, whereby trust has to be continually earned. Following the collapse
of the multinational oil giant Enron at the end of 2001 and corporate

scandals from World-Com to Halliburton, Tyco and other corporate giants, loss of confidence by the general public and investors has increased dramatically. These failures usually signify a crisis in the large 'command and control' hierarchies dominating the organizational structure, that is, a top-down corporation with a single unitary board. Hence, corporations now face pressure to become more accountable for their operations. In this respect, they are continuously asked to change from being giant mechanical structures towards being locally adaptive flexible organisms.

In response to stakeholder demands, many corporations, particularly multinational corporations (MNCs) have gradually taken action and adapted various sustainability concepts to respond to stakeholder expectations (Schmidt-Bleek, 1994; Weizsäcker et al., 1997; Zadek, 2002; Elkington, 1998). However, it is a common belief that 'corporate responsibility, as presently constituted, is a fairly fragmented and uneven affair' (Utting, 2000). The potential of corporations to support sustainable development and to attain a role in supporting public policies still remains untapped.

Currently, companies' rhetoric on corporate social responsibility (CSR) communication is likely to outpace their performance. Companies might tend to concentrate their CSR efforts on activities that have an external rather than internal focus, that is, producing reports, publicly issuing codes of conduct or signing up to external principles. Some call it 'greenwashing' of public awareness. Popular tactics also include striking partnerships with pressure groups and convening discussions with 'stakeholders' (Litvin, 2003). Thus, the result is that companies' attention might often be diverted from the internal task of actually implementing the policies set out in their codes of conduct for public relations activities. The conclusion for an analytical framework is that real cases ought to be assessed against criteria derived from research; such empirical analysis contributes to progress in research.

RESPONSIBLE CORPORATE GOVERNANCE: A STAKEHOLDER-ORIENTED AND POLICY-RELEVANT APPROACH

The success of recent policy mechanisms depends on the ability to match the mounting complexities and interdependencies along global product chains. Respectively, coordination of economic activities and societal interactions shall allow corporations to remark their expanding responsibilities and encourage corporations to put them into practice. In this respect, the question, 'What kind of policy structures is required to make corporations understand and implement their social, environmental and economic responsibilities?' is highly relevant.

Our study proposes that policy networks, as collaborative forms of problem-solving among corporate, political and societal actors, have considerable potential to address increasing complexities and resource dependencies. Central to network cooperation is the existence of resource interdependency among the network members. Coordination is realized through the use of capabilities and exchange of resources. As the fair participation of many societal actors is encouraged, the outcome of a build-up of social capital such as trust and reciprocity can be expected (National Economic and Social Forum, 2003). Such forms of policy-making also provide flexibility in the sense that they can include various levels of interrelation or scales of interaction. Hence, the extent of involvement in a network can range from global actors or from national actors to local community-level actors.

According to the network approach, our proposition is that cooperative structures and inclusion of actors enables governments to mobilize resources that would not otherwise be under their hierarchical control. In this way, policy networks give governments the ability to solve policy problems that they would not otherwise be able to solve.

In the context of policy networks, beyond public institutions, both global and local stakeholders of large corporations can play a significant role in driving corporate accountability. By making effective use of resource interdependencies, corporations can be coordinated to act responsibly. Hence, coordination of corporate accountability does not become a question of neither governance nor government, but rather becomes an issue of setting up the right stakeholder networks of coordination.

An innovative form of coordinating corporate action would assign stakeholders to encourage and monitor responsible corporate action. This book perceives responsible corporate governance (RCG) as a stakeholder-oriented and policy-relevant concept that can encourage the involvement of many societal actors – hence, multiple capabilities – to drive corporate accountability. However, this concept shall not aim at substituting for other policy mechanisms. Instead, we believe that it needs to be considered in the context of research on policy instruments. The following sections of our analytical framework explain our thesis in more detail.

All in all, the definition of RCG can be given as follows: 'RCG is a stakeholder-oriented policy approach allocating responsibilities to societal actors, who will drive corporate accountability'[9] (Kuhndt et al., 2004, p. 16).

As in all cases of policy-relevant networks, RCG shall provide a clear understanding of the principles it supports in line with its objective of corporate accountability delivery, while recognizing globally complex relationships and resource interdependencies. Despite the fact that the degree of involvement and types of stakeholders involved can vary, the principles of corporate accountability shall universally stay common. Hence, this analytical approach consists of two pillars: (1) the principle of encouraging corporate responsibility; and (2) a framework to set up routes for the stakeholders to drive corporate accountability.

First Pillar: Principles of Encouraging Corporate Responsibility

Collective action in a policy-relevant network has to be driven towards common principles (whose formulation is part of the network's activity), since in the absence of a collective vision the purpose of coordination will hardly be reached. Actors in the network shall have shared responsibilities to exercise these principles by utilizing resources, which stay unique to each.

We suggest as a core principle of RCG that all actors involved in the policy-relevant network shall encourage the corporation to exercise the following elements:

1. stakeholder-empowered corporate governance;
2. management and performance evaluation systems;
3. transparency enhancement;
4. stakeholder verification (Kuhndt et al., 2004, p. 17).

These elements have been deducted from the initiatives of environmental NGOs (ENGOs), intergovernmental organizations (IGOs), financial institutions, research institutions and multi-stakeholder organizations. These actors support one or more of these elements for corporate accountability, while RCG, as a supportive policy instrument, aims at gathering all these principles under one roof.

The element of 'stakeholder-empowered corporate governance' means that corporations need to realize the stakeholder demands beyond responsibilities to their shareholders. As Jeucken (2001, p. 39) suggests, corporate governance shall also concern issues related to the actors upon whom corporate actions can have an influence. The International Corporate Governance Network (ICGN) Statement on Global Corporate Governance Principles (ICGN, 1995), Commonwealth Association of Corporate Governance (CACG) Guidelines (CACG, 2003), the OECD Guidelines for Multinational Enterprises (2000), OECD (1999), the King Report on Corporate Governance (2002), the Global Corporate Governance Forum (World Bank/OECD, 2006) and the United Nations Global Compact (United Nations, 2006) are among the major corporate governance codes of conduct encouraging stakeholder involvement.

Involvement of stakeholders can be based on the codes of conduct, which emphasize procedures for stakeholder engagement in corporate decision-making and operations. The spectrum of stakeholder involvement can range from one-way communication to stakeholder coordination. Forrest and Mays (1997) offer a typology on the level of interaction with the stakeholders, namely creation of an ongoing dialogue (collaboration), formation of a more interactive but ad hoc dialogue (ongoing consultation), limited two-way communication (occasional consultation) and, finally, absence of any communication. Additionally one-way information exchange (communication) can be incorporated in this typology. The Responsible Care initiative by the chemical industry, which is taken as a case-study in this volume, demonstrates an ongoing consultation of the industry with its stakeholders (see Chapter 16). Though it is voluntary, several chemical companies organize Community Advisory Panels, where the surrounding communities are involved in the discussion of the environmental, health and safety aspects of their operations. On the other hand, the national chemical associations in several countries organize National Advisory Panels (see also Chapter 16).

Transparency is about the willingness of each business unit of the cooperation to reveal information on their activities. 'Transparency enhancement' aims at a healthy set-up of informal institutions among the societal actors. Transnational corporations (TNCs) can make use of a diverse range of information disclosure instruments such as preparing corporate reports (for example so-called environmental, social or sustainability reports beyond financial reporting), compiling site reports (pollutant release and transfer registries), making environmental product declarations (for example Type I, II and III eco-labelling schemes), or taking part in sustainability indices (for example Business in the Community) or internationally binding or voluntary transparency agreements (for example Aarhus Convention, Extractive Industries Transparency Scheme).

Commitments for stakeholder empowerment shall follow up by the set-up of 'management systems' and 'performance evaluation systems', which is about integrating demands with the daily business routines. Management systems are required to review the priority action areas, develop goals for environmental, social and economic bottom line improvements, compile relevant tools or instruments to reach set goals, develop routines and action plans, assign responsibilities to business units, departments and personnel and, finally, review the performance of these systems.

Finally, the aim of 'accountability verification' is further to enhance the informal institutions both internally and in relation to the stakeholders. Transparency is not sufficient to build a credible environment, since it indicates a one-way process. Another requirement is that when corporations disclose information, they shall also be answerable in terms of its quality and sufficiency. Accountability verification can be conducted as independent environmental, social and ethical audits. These audits can be conducted by multi-jurisdictional authorities (for example AccountAbility, Social Accountability International), financial auditing companies (for example PricewaterhouseCoopers, Ernst&Young, KPMG), sustainability indexes, (for example Dow Jones Sustainability Indexes, FTSE4 Good UK Corporate Responsibility Investment Index Series, Oekom, Domini Social Index) or by local stakeholders such as NGOs or trade unions (for example Social Observatory in Brazil). Decisions on the form of verification shall be made considering the credibility of the verifier, cost burden, scope of the verification (all environmental, social and economic aspects or with a focus on a certain aspect due to potential expertise) and feedback loops for further corporate performance improvements (Kuhndt et al., 2004, p. 32).

Second Pillar: Institutional Framework to Construct Routes for the Stakeholders to Drive Corporate Accountability

The second pillar of responsible corporate governance shall aim at developing an institutional framework to arrange routes of interaction for the external stakeholders to shape corporate accountability. As the goal of RCG, corporate accountability refers to a process by which individuals or organizations are made answerable for their actions and the consequences that follow from them. In this study, we propose that corporate accountability can be achieved by urging corporations to apply the four elements defined above at the first pillar. A variety of actors ranging from public institutions, intergovernmental organizations, financial institutions, nongovernmental organizations and research institutions to private consumers can take place in a policy network with the aim of enhancing the practice of these elements by the corporation.

Each societal actor relates to a corporation with respect to the role and function they assume in the society (preferences and perceptions) and according to the capabilities (human, social, physical and financial capital) they possess. It can be proposed that stakeholders can influence the practices of corporations by changing their orientation (perception and capabilities) in line with the principles of RCG (Kuhndt et al., 2004).

The activities of a given actor are influenced by other stakeholders' strategies and choices according to the analytical concept of 'stakeholder constellation' (Coleman, 1990 in Scharpf, 1997, p. 44). This concept emphasizes the fact that the involved stakeholders are interdependent, where the strategy decision of one stakeholder will influence the other stakeholders' strategy decisions and vice versa. Hence, based on the

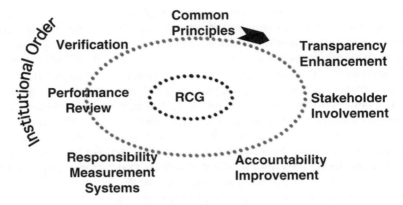

Figure 2.1   The institutional order should support the elements of RCG

expectation of other stakeholders' strategies, an actor will choose the strategy with the highest individual pay-off.

The study proposes that a change in the institutional setting around TNCs towards implementation of the elements of RCG will alter the relationship between societal stakeholders and contribute to the integration of social and environmental interests in the development of TNCs (see Figure 2.1). The elements of RCG can be seen as a complementary institutional development in an already existing institutional setting of norms, traditions, policies and so on.

CAPABILITIES AND ACTIVITIES

The following section will briefly review the capabilities and activities of two major stakeholders, namely financial markets and international environmental non-governmental organizations, with regard to their potential to influence the practice of corporate social responsibility by TNCs. We will try to discuss the shortcomings of the current constellation and in brief try to illustrate how it can be altered for the implementation of the four major elements of RCG.

Financial Markets

Today, globally integrated financial markets and institutions have considerable potential and capabilities to influence and, in some cases, exert control over corporate investment and management decisions (Delphi and Ecologic, 1997). They can exercise their power to steer corporations by supplying capital and developing innovative financial products to encourage sustainable development, evaluating triple bottom line risks of corporations, investing specifically in sustainable corporations as shareholders and striving for their own sustainable performance as role model responsible institutions. Therefore, they significantly influence the pace and direction of corporate and overall economic growth.

The core activities in the financial markets can be separated into three major categories: risk management, asset management and engagement policy (Busch and Orbach, 2003). Risk management is a central element in banking, insurance and investment industries. The functioning of the banking industry is based on calculating the technical risk of borrowing and reflecting it in the credit rates. Insurers also deal with many kinds of risks ranging from the settlement of all sorts of environmental losses and natural catastrophes to the provision of prevention advice to their customers and to the general public (UNEP, 2002). On the other hand, capability in assessing risks might differ between industries. While banking and insuring industries have the ability to obtain first-hand detailed information on the practices of TNCs, investors often have to rely on secondary data such as corporate reports.

Despite being a core activity in financial markets, risk management activities have not yet realized the whole range of risk. Environmental risk assessment activities can exert a demand on some corporations for performance improvements; however, corporations would still not be pressurized to improve many other corporate social responsibility aspects such as worker rights, human rights (Busch and Orbach, 2003, pp. 35–7) or product responsibility. Additionally, in failing to communicate the significance of associated risks to corporations, banking and insuring industries especially fail to exercise their capabilities to change corporate practices. Furthermore, Jeucken (2001, p. 69) mentions that financial institutions may even inhibit sustainability, focusing only on government environmental policy in judging financial risks, especially in cases where the public policy is actually weak or passive. Risk management also rates poorly in grasping the efforts of corporations for sustainability or their misbehaviour, missing the link between environmental, social and financial performance (Kuhndt et al., 2004, p. 41).

Another core activity in financial markets is asset management. In the area of asset management, socially responsible investment (SRI) can be seen as a major drive for corporate accountability. SRI is based on investing in corporations which are selected according to analysis of their performance with respect to a set of sustainability criteria defined by the financial institute. Asset management companies and fund managers can adapt different screening methods promoted by a wide variety of screening companies to decide the range of companies which shall be included in their funds. The issues included in screening activities may range from the avoidance of certain sectors (such as tobacco and alcohol) to the assessment of product and service innovation, corporate leadership, shareholder and society commitments, environmental and human rights records. However, the market size of SRI is currently quite small (for example the assets under management of SRI funds in Europe are just 0.4 per cent of the total assets managed by UCITS[10] (SIRI, 2002) (see also Chapter 18).

Even though in theory both private and institutional investors' capability to affect TNCs' sustainability decision-making or management systems is quite high, the instruments used for evaluation are often weak compared to risk assessments. The current constellation of information acquirement via questionnaires is considered to be cumbersome by many companies. On the other hand, results of the assessments are very rarely utilized for the mitigation of impacts or for performance improvements via the provision of advice. Hence, the capabilities in the asset management industry are not fully utilized.

Engagement policy is seen as the third main area of activity in financial markets. In the area of sustainability, financial institutions can develop environmental funds, environmental advice services and climate products, or engage in shareholder activism to engage with the corporations in which they invest. Recently, the development of an engagement policy by the financial institutions on the issue of climate change is gaining considerable importance following the acceptance of an agreement in June 2003 on the EU emissions trading scheme, which came into operation in January 2005. Moreover, there are awareness-raising activities such as the 'Carbon Disclosure Project', which was an initiative of 35 institutional investors demanding information from corporations regarding greenhouse gas mitigation (Innovest, 2003). Shareholder activism can happen via corporate engagement or dialogue (communicating with management on particular issues), shareholder resolutions (filing or supporting shareholder proposals on social and environmental issues), proxy voting (establishing policies for voting shares on social and environmental issues) or divestment (selling of shares) (O'Rourke, 2002, p. 3).

Engagement policy can be considered to be potentially the most effective way among all three activities to steer corporate activities. In particular the common concerns raised by the sector deliver coherent messages to corporations and have started to be taken seriously for a change. However, the potential of shareholder activism is still in its infancy, as stakeholder resolutions may not urge corporations to change their decision-making mechanisms, stakeholder engagement or management practices, but may rather make them focus on transparency such as gathering reports. Hence, replies of corporations to shareholder activism may in the end turn into a public relations exercise, making them non-instrumental to corporations.

In order to strengthen the effect of interaction between financial markets and TNCs towards sustainability improvements, extension of traditional risk assessment to triple bottom line (TBL) risk assessment would first be required. For this, the development of new evaluation tools would be necessary. On the asset management side, one can suggest collection of information on TBL performance from sources which are considered to be more insiders to the corporations, and later, use of the evaluations in order to derive suggestions of performance improvement and follow-ups. In this way, a change in corporate behaviour might be initiated. On the other hand, in order to increase the effectiveness of engagement of financial institutions with markets, a change in the legal set-up might be required, which is beyond the capabilities of financial institutions. For shareholder resolutions to be legitimately taken into consideration by a corporation, only the willingness of the corporation is perceived as a major factor. In most countries, resolutions directed to the management systems of corporations can be omitted with the permission of stock exchange commissions.

International ENGOs

Environmental NGOs (ENGOs) can be considered as the linkage between the economic and production-oriented world of business with social and civil society (Brown, 1993; Waddell, 2000, p. 205). On the one hand, ENGOs provide insight into the sustainability implications of complex business operations for society; on the other hand, they can make business aware of aspects that might be regarded as beyond mainstream business operations. International ENGOs have the financial and human resources together with time to specialize in certain aspects of sustainability, becoming sources of new ideas and critical thinking (Waddell, 2000, p. 195) and inducing learning.

A wide range of instruments is used by the ENGOs to urge corporate accountability. These activities of ENGOs are rather fragmented and uneven in nature, particularly geographically. This wide range of activities can be considered as being scattered between conflict management and collaboration management (Kuhndt et al., 2004, p. 44). Collaboration management usually takes the form of voluntary engagements of which the major forms are: long-term partnerships to manage sector-wide impacts (for example Marine Stewardship Council); project-based collaborative action to handle specific environmental or social impacts (for example Clean Clothes Campaign); consultations on management systems (for example pilot project of the Fairtrade Foundation to develop codes of practice to guide supplier relationships); shareholder activism (for example Friends of the Earth's campaigns); and voluntary verifications (for example the Other Shell Report). Confrontational actions can be observed in the form of resolutions on 'binding corporate accountability' and activist campaigns. 'Binding corporate accountability' aims at the enhancement of public enforcement to realize corporate responsibilities (ToBI, 1997).

Voluntary engagements by international ENGOs can be effective instruments to enhance corporate accountability, as they lead to information-sharing activities and the set-up of new routines in the organizations. Through partnerships and voluntary initiatives undertaken with NGOs, which are often entitled as 'civil regulation', business comes under pressure to comply with norms and standards defined to some extent by civil society institutions (Murphy and Bendell, 1999; Utting, 2000, p. 8).

On the other hand, it can be said that collaborative engagements with TNCs are still not carried out effectively. For example, partnerships may fail to involve Southern NGOs in their decision-making and consultation processes (Murphy and Bendell, 1999). Furthermore, when the conditions for setting up effective networks such as transparency, independent verification, monitoring and local stakeholder participation and internationally binding standards are missing, claims of 'greenwash' (Corporate Watch, 2001) and non-compliance come into the picture (ToBI, 1997).

At the confrontational end, ENGOs call for more enhanced international and national public agency responsibilities, as they believe other societal actors may not have similar capabilities to steer globally effective corporations. Some campaigns such as the 'International Right to Know' in the US demand regulatory frameworks which would force TNCs to disclose their overseas operations to 'empower communities with information' (International Right to Know, 2003) and to hold companies accountable to US citizens and customers as well as to local people being employed or neighbouring facilities. However, dependence only on the capacity of public institutions might urge reactive rather than proactive strategies, meaning that the real grounds of corporate action may not be changed. In this way, ENGOs would be disregarding their capabilities and their social, human capital.

In order to strengthen the role of ENGOs in influencing corporate behaviour towards a more sustainable direction, ENGOs can research the possible corporate routines, which they can influence by utilizing or transferring their environmental and social knowledge and skills. They can develop intelligent collaborative strategies, which would give them the opportunity to develop continuously applicable tools and instruments (for example tools for triple bottom line (TBL) aspects management, third-party verification and improvement) for sustainability management by corporations. In order to expand their outreach and capabilities, the set-up of global networks, which would include both local and global partners, would still be a valid action route. Through strong partnerships, supported when needed by public institutions (such as the sanctioning power of government), ENGOs can engage with the corporations and be involved in their daily activities rather than tracking the results of their actions.

Consequently, during the development of policy networks, stakeholder constellations should be carefully analysed. Each actor might have different perceptions of corporate responsibilities, and have different capabilities to steer them. The success of the network would depend on working towards common principles and the delivery of common messages and understanding. On the other hand, the effective use of capabilities will directly relate to the effectiveness of the networks for corporate responsibility management. The potential to change corporate behaviour cannot be realized fully by one actor, and most often capabilities of other societal actors would be utilized.

RESPONSIBLE CORPORATE GOVERNANCE AND THEORIES OF THE FIRM

Having introduced the concept of responsible corporate governance, one might ask how the notion of profit-maximizing firms fits into such a concept. The following section tries to lay down explanations derived from theories of the firm. Recent economics (Nelson, 2002) reveals a shift in the connotation of 'profit maximization'. Previously, businesses were quite naturally assumed to be motivated by profits and striving toward optimization along a sharply defined set of opportunities. Firms were not thought of as groping, experimenting and gradually innovating toward incremental improvements. The idea, rather, was that the predefined set of average total cost, marginal revenues due to market demand, and technological choices predetermined profits. Management in this view aimed at an optimization toward market equilibrium. Such companies would obviously have no interest in providing for common goods or internalizing externalities.

This standard model, however, can hardly account for the dynamics of competition and knowledge generation. More recent views therefore have established an analytical model of knowledge-based firms (Leonard-Barton, 1995; Langlois and Robertson, 1995; Grant, 1996; Nonaka and Toyama, 2002). Firms are assumed to act under uncertainties and information deficits. They rely on permanent knowledge generation provided by outside sources, experiments and internal implementation processes. Firms can also create markets from scratch, by coordinating with others along vertical or horizontal lines. In doing so, firms establish communication with stakeholders in order to learn about changing demand, developing useful

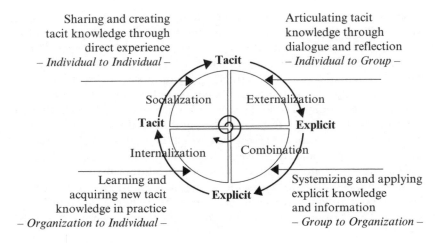

Sharing and creating
tacit knowledge through
direct experience
– Individual to Individual –

Articulating tacit
knowledge through
dialogue and reflection
– Individual to Group –

Learning and
acquiring new tacit
knowledge in practice
– Organization to Individual –

Systemizing and applying
explicit knowledge
and information
– Group to Organization –

Source: Nonaka and Toyama (2002).

Figure 2.2   The spiral of knowledge generation

goods and services, and in order to avoid the stunning blows of hostile reaction. Figure 2.2 illustrates that firms make use of a spiral of knowledge generation, helping them to transform information generated elsewhere into useful knowledge and, moreover, into transaction cost-reducing routines.

The question now is whether such a model overcomes prevailing assumptions about corporate approaches to sustainable development and involvement in governance structures. What are the implications for the questions outlined here if the model is acknowledged to reflect competitive markets? Keys to an answer are: (1) our proposition that there is no fixed borderline between common and private goods; and (2) that there are potential low-cost or even profitable options ('low-hanging fruit'). Knowledge-based firms basically do two things toward sustainable development while serving their own interest. They develop technologies and/or services that are private but contribute to public goals; renewable energies and clean water technologies are examples. Firms also work on demand creation, be it by marketing or other professional forms of doing business. Examples are services like leasing, renting, pooling and sharing goods that contribute to the commons, such as the organization of car-sharing by the industry in order to save parking costs. Moreover, firms in their internal processes can switch to integrated management and value chain management. These efforts help combat free-riding.

A point that is relevant in our context is that firms participating with stakeholders in the evolution of new market rules can profit from that

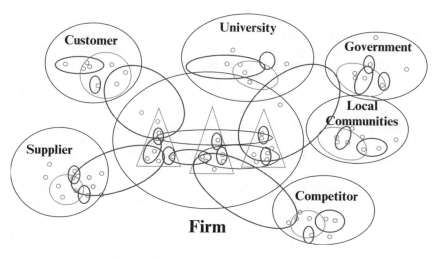

Source: Nonaka and Toyama (2002).

Figure 2.3   Firms as part of social environments

exercise. This is not only because they can influence the outcome. The main reason as derived from our analytical framework is the learning advantage of being a forerunner or fast adopter. Adaptation times are significantly shorter for participating firms. Learning during times of governmental reframing can trigger competitive advantages. In other cases, any further regulation has to rely on experiences gained by pioneering firms because they can draw on precise data about the costs and benefits of various institutional mechanisms. Governance systems can thus rely on exploration and experiments undertaken by corporate actors. The free-riding position of simply waiting for market rules to come because of the costs of their development is only one choice for firms.

It is worth noting that not only TNCs but also small and medium-sized enterprises (SMEs) are analysed as knowledge-based firms. Some theories (Langlois and Robertson, 1995) even suggest that SME networks (like Silicon Valley) have more innovative thrust than the big companies. Such networks among SMEs are quite often associated with local or regional clusters of innovation, involving local municipalities, universities, and so on. In a wider horizon its relevance for market development and stakeholder concerns mean that innovative business increasingly requires the understanding of local issues beyond regional or national borders. Figure 2.3 shows a firm as part of a social environment, interacting with numerous outside stakeholders.

The conclusion for an analytical framework is not that the model of the knowledge-based firm reflects the only or dominant form of doing business. Many firms struggle to survive and spend hardly any time on learning and exploring new opportunities. Others still demonstrate their ability to externalize social costs to the public. Though such firms may be seen as laggards in terms of sustainability, they are certainly relevant for any analysis. One also has to keep in mind that firms do not necessarily act with total consistency. Some operations may become more sustainable than others where asset-specific investments hinder rapid change. But our book suggests that firms tend to imitate pioneers and their successors through benchmarking processes, so that incentives for improvements towards sustainability are easier to understand if they come from markets, and not only from governments or the law. These processes of imitation lead to both a vertical and a horizontal diffusion of best practices, which is pivotal for sustainable development. In contradistinction to Hart (1995) and Gabel and Sinclair-Desgagné (1998) who try to develop 'green' business models, our model nevertheless reveals a stronger emphasis on knowledge generation as an explicative variable of firms' behaviour and underlines a rational explanation for responsible corporate governance.

NOTES

1. Resources can be divided into several categories: economic, human, social and environmental.
2. For example, the macro-indicators in the UK demonstrate this fact. 'Although the proportion of goods consumed in the UK which come from overseas is around 33 per cent, up from 23 per cent in 1985, for some resources the proportion is much bigger. Some 77 per cent of the UK's timber and 70 per cent of its food are imported' (ENDS Report, 2003).
3. In fact, making product chains more resource-efficient is not in itself sufficient, if the current trends of consumption of products continue. The improvements in efficiency are being cancelled out by economic growth – caused in part by those very efficiency gains (Fabian Society, 2003).
4. A stakeholder is 'any group or individual, who can affect or is affected by the achievement of the organization's objectives' (Freeman and McVea, 2001). Based on this definition stakeholders exist both internally and externally to the TNCs. Employees and workers are the internal stakeholders, while the communities, public authorities, shareholders, financial institutions and the media can be counted among external stakeholders.
5. The term 'capabilities' describes all action resources that allow a stakeholder to influence an outcome in a certain respect and to a certain degree (Scharpf, 1997, p. 43). These include personal properties like physical strength, intelligence or human and social capital (Coleman, 1990 in Scharpf, 1997); physical resources such as money or land; technological capabilities; privileged access to information and so on (Coleman, 1990 in Scharpf, 1997).
6. On the other hand, it is getting more common that financial performance is evaluated in terms of intangible assets such as creation of brand value or reputation management. Reputation of corporations has become a key managerial concern in many sectors (especially in high-impact sectors, as in the Brent Spar case of Shell in the North Sea or the

ABN AMRO Bank's involvement in hazardous mining activities in West Papua New Guinea), as the public valuation of corporations can drastically change the return on their particular products.

7. For example, disregarding responsibilities for land use or human right impacts at mining sites may lead to social or political disruption of operations and this, in turn, can cause labour conflicts, restricted access to land and other local services, or delays in delivery of products (Sullivan and Frankental, 2002, p. 84).

8. Although there is no commonly accepted definition, 'most definitions describe it as a concept whereby companies integrate social and environmental concerns in their business operations and in their interaction with their stakeholders on a voluntary basis' (European Commission, 2001, p. 8).

9. As the goal of RCG, corporate accountability at its simplest definition refers to a process by which individuals or organizations are answerable for their actions and the consequences that follow from them (Kovach et al., 2003, p. 3). Our assumption is that when all stakeholders of corporations can operationalize the same principles, then the behaviour of corporations can be altered towards sustainability.

10. UCITS stands for 'Undertaking for Collective Investment in Transferable Securities', which is a collective investment fund that can be marketed in all EU countries.

3. Competition and responsible corporate governance

Oliver Budzinski

CONCEPTS OF COMPETITION IN ECONOMICS

The cradle of competition theory in economics lies – just like the cradle of market economics itself – in Scottish moral philosophy of the eighteenth century and is connected to the works of David Hume, Adam Ferguson and, above all, Adam Smith (1761, 1776). The revolutionary thing about it was to view competition as a method of coordination of individual behaviour, which leads to overall social benefits. If competition is implemented effectively, every participant of the market process can act according to its own goals and desires without harming society's welfare. Like an invisible hand, the competitive interaction of the individuals alters their individual plans and induces such modes of behaviour which – in the complex sum of all individual actions – bring about significant improvements of social wealth. In particular, it is the allocation of production factors and the division of labour which become optimized by competitive markets, allowing for an increase in output. However, Smith emphasizes that an institutional and moral framework is necessary in order to exclude anticompetitive and unfair (immoral) modes of behaviour which could – in the end – destroy the benefits of competition. Altogether, the original concept of market competition (classic competition) represents a concept of social coordination of free individuals, improving the wealth of society.

In the following decades and centuries, this original concept of economic competition has been developed, altered, specified, improved, distorted, abused, misinterpreted, ideologically misused, and much more. Consequently, there is no consensual, united theory of competition in today's economics. Instead, a pluralism of (at least partly) incompatible concepts of competition theory and policy characterizes the state of the art (Budzinski, 2003b). Among them, the currently most influential concepts are neoclassic competition, workable competition and Chicago competition.

Neoclassic competition theory is first of all price theory. Since its beginnings in the 1870s it has dealt with the mathematical formalization of market structures and equilibrium situations, originally using predominantly the mathematics of differential calculus and nowadays focusing on mathematical game theory and modern methods of econometrics. Its central concept is the equilibrium of (market) forces, derived from Newton's physics (traditional mechanics). Different from the classic view, competition is not analysed as a dynamic process of rival interaction of individuals but as the stationary state of an equilibrium where all interaction and all changes have been finished and the market process has stopped.[1] The homogeneous polypoly with its heroic assumptions (homogeneous products, no transaction costs, perfect information and complete market transparency, objectively rational agents, absence of innovation, and so on) emerged as the ideal of competition and, therefore, was called 'perfect competition'. This shift in analysis came not as a purposeful alteration of the notion of competition but, instead, was a by-product of the introduction of mathematics and the subsequent focus on mathematical feasible problems – in regard to which numerous important insights have been achieved. In doing so, however, other important features of classic competition like innovation, mutual learning or rivalry, but also the analysis of institutions, became neglected. Although game theory at least partly allows for a reintegration of such kinds of problems into modern industrial economics,[2] the crucial concept of neoclassic economics, the notion of equilibrium, inevitably remains a inherently stationary concept which is why any integration of dynamic and evolutionary aspects of competition always comes as a more or less smooth add-on. Nonetheless, neoclassical price theory remains the most influential ingredient in industrial economics.

In the times of the Great Depression in the late twenties and thirties, the widespread trust in the self-healing forces of market economies became shaken. This also influenced competition theory and induced the development of concepts that seek to use competition as a device to realize politically defined (economic and non-economic) goals (instead of relying on laissez-faire and the self-healing capacities of free markets). The common ideas of the different concepts of workable competition (including the Harvard School and traditional Empirical Industrial Organization) is a strong (linear) relationship between market structure (S), market conduct (C) and market performance (P), the latter indicating the degree of fulfilment of political and social goals. According to the SCP-paradigm, an appropriate design of the market structure is sufficient to make competition work towards the defined goals. As soon as market structures allow enterprises to act in independence from the competitive constraints, the achievement of social goals becomes jeopardized. Therefore, market power (that is, the power to act independently) represents the central problem in these concepts of competition and has to be prevented and/or destroyed through political intervention. Consequently, these concepts can develop a tendency towards an incremental increase in interventionism, eventually eroding the dynamics of competition. Altogether, the Harvard School represents a more sceptical view in regard to business and big enterprises and, instead, highlights the roles of public intervention and political influence.

Since the 1950s, the Chicago School of Antitrust Analysis developed a completely contrary concept of competition, which has become increasingly important in antitrust policy during the 1980s. They emphasize efficiency as the sole effect of competition and, consequently, the sole adequate goal of competition policy. According to the Chicago view, liberalized and deregulated markets represent the best way to enhance consumer welfare,[3] whereas political interventions only favour powerful interest groups at the expense of society. Market structure is less important in this concept because the forces of competition (if left undistorted) self-organizationally select more efficient solutions and, vice versa, results of free market processes always represent superior solutions in regard to economic efficiency ('survival of the fittest'). Therefore, any market structure which is produced by free competition is efficient – even (apparent) monopolies. The meaning of potential competition represents another important line of argument. Even if an enterprise apparently has a powerful market position, it cannot act anticompetitively because in that case other enterprises would enter the market, thereby eroding the powerful position. According to the Chicago view, the threat of entry itself is sufficient to discipline apparently powerful enterprises – as long as the market is contestable. In the world of the Chicago School, the vast majority of barriers to market entry can be traced back to political interventions whereas free competition is unlikely to produce incontestable markets. Altogether, the Chicago School represents a highly sceptical position towards politicians and policy interventions and, instead, highlights the self-governing role of business and enterprises in competitive markets.

Although all these concepts also deal with innovation and change, neither provides an endogenous explanation of such phenomena. However, the challenge of sustainable development represents a problem in which change is inherent and at the heart of the discussion. A governance concept for sustainable development, like RCG, both represents an innovation and seeks to induce innovations, albeit with specific characteristics (markets for sustainability). Therefore, it is useful to introduce economic competition concepts which focus on the creation and diffusion of innovation in competition, or, in other words, address innovation-inducing competition.

EVOLUTIONARY COMPETITIVE MARKET PROCESSES

Introduction

The concept of evolutionary competition as a knowledge-generating process[4] is rooted in a couple of process- and innovation-oriented competition theory traditions. This includes Austrian market process theory in the tradition of Friedrich August von Hayek, dynamic competition theory in the tradition of Joseph A. Schumpeter, ordoliberalism (particularly Walter Eucken) and ordoliberal-inspired German market process theory (Erich Hoppmann and others). According to Schumpeterian concepts, competition is viewed as a dynamic process of rivalry in which the interplay of creative (innovative) and adaptive (imitative) forces produces and reinforces permanent dynamics.[5] These dynamics create new structures by destroying old ones (creative destruction), and change is the main characteristic of competition rather than an exogenous force which from time to time 'distorts' the market equilibrium (like in neoclassic competition). The creation and use of knowledge and, thus, learning processes are central to the Austrian concept of competition as a discovery procedure (Hayek, 1968) which claims the unique competence of market competition to coordinate free economic behaviour of individual agents and enterprises rather than assuming the relevant knowledge given (like in the perfect competition concept). The institutional framework of the market process plays an important role in shaping the direction of the competition process and, consequently, is systematically integrated into the evolutionary concept of competition.[6] Altogether, from an evolutionary perspective, competitive market processes are permanently evolving, everlasting, endogenously innovation-generating and principally open in results (Langlois, 1994).[7]

The Creation of Knowledge

According to Hayek (1937, 1945), the unique superiority of competition as a device to coordinate (otherwise independent) individual economic behaviour can only be understood via an appropriate treatment of the knowledge problem. In doing so, Hayek at the same time goes back to the classic tradition[8] and beyond it. The fundamental problem every coordination mechanism of economic activities would have to face is the decentralized character of market-relevant knowledge. No central planner or organization, neither human nor computerized, can ever centralize the knowledge necessary to coordinate the individual economic plans of the market agents, which is why only decentralized procedures (like competition) can cope adequately and satisfactorily with the coordination task.

This line of thought stands in accordance with modern insights into the mechanisms of cognition, perception, knowledge creation and rational individual behaviour, which become increasingly adapted in economics.[9] One of the most important characteristics of the process of knowledge creation is the fundamental subjectivity of cognition and perception. Individuals create their context of economic (competitive) action by subjectively interpreting the perceived signals from their environment. In doing so, they develop cognitive theories (also called mental models) which consist of causes–consequences hypotheses about the real world. Due to the constructive character of the human cognition process and due to the unique past experience of every individual agent (against which new signals are interpreted), these cognitive rules are completely subjective and differ among individuals.[10] The cognitive theories are connected to rules of action, that is, if a context of action is identified as belonging to a specific causes–consequences hypothesis, the individual derives a promising disposition to behave based on his individual and subjective cognitive theories.

If an individual agent faces an economic context of action (a decision to consume, to produce or to change his individual patterns, and so on), he develops an individual plan to behave based on his interpretation of the context of action. This plan is the outcome of a process of classification, that is, the individual looks for cognitive theories which, against his subjective background of experience, seem to be an adequate representation of the situation, and carries out the connected modes of behaviour. Some contexts of action fit relatively easily into the existing cognitive theories (routine situations) and the individual can successfully behave in experienced ways. However, since each situation is (historically) unique – and thus does not perfectly fit into past experiences – the process of classification leads inevitably to a loss of information.[11] In routine situations, this loss is marginal and the chosen mode of behaviour adequate. In cases like these, the behaviour of the individual in reaction to a specific type of situation is relatively stable and can be anticipated by interacting individuals.

However, some situations an individual faces when doing business or acting as a consumer do not successfully classify as routine situations. In such problem situations, the individual agent has to: (1) change his prevailing pattern of (re)action (because it yields no more satisfying results); or (2) develop or create a new mode of behaviour (because the situation is not yet represented in his cognitive theories). This is when the individual agent creates new economic knowledge. In such cases, interacting agents cannot adequately anticipate the way the individual agent will react to this problem situation. The crucial aspect, however, is that no external observer,

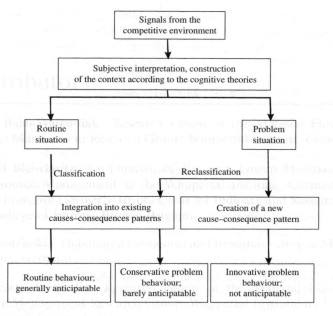

Source: Budzinski (2000), p. 138.

Figure 3.1 Dimensions of subjective-rational action

irrespective of his amount of knowledge, can know in advance how the individual agent will react in the face of a problem situation.[12] The reason is that even the individual agent himself does not know in advance how he will react to a specific problem situation. Only if the situation occurs does he start to search for an alternative; it may be the switch to another mode of behaviour he disposes over, or it may be the creation of a totally new one.

Only competition as a decentralized process of the interaction of individual agents can collect and use this kind of relevant economic knowledge. According to this fundamental knowledge problem, solutions to market problems can hardly be designed in advance and subsequently implemented top-down by politicians or any other centralized institution.[13] According to Hayek (1975), any such attempt represents a 'pretence of knowledge'. Instead, competition has the character of a procedure to discover and create workable market solutions. Since this knowledge cannot be obtained otherwise, competition is a process with an unpredictable outcome. The fundamental and never-ending openness is essential since, according to Hayek (1948, 1968), the coordination mechanism 'competition' would be completely useless and a complete waste of resources if the result was or could be known in advance. However, this does not imply that policy (intervention) is always and inevitably harmful, as modern applications of evolutionary competition economics and economic policy theories have demonstrated.[14]

Evolutionary Competition as a Test of Hypotheses

Against the background of Hayek's fundamental knowledge problem, enriched by the insights of modern cognitive economics, an evolutionary theory of competition as an endogenously knowledge-creating process can be described.[15] Competition in evolutionary market processes can be analysed as a research process in which the competitors try to improve their always limited, situational and fallible knowledge on economic problem solutions and subsequently to utilize it in the course of market interaction (Kerber, 1997, pp. 49–50). From their (subjective) cognitive rules and theories, the individual participants of the market process derive hypotheses about successful modes of behaviour in regard to market interaction. Generally, such hypotheses are directed towards the market, that is, they represent hypotheses (entailing the individual's knowledge) about price, quality, performance, relations[16] (in the case of producers and sellers) and about the potential of buyable goods to contribute to the fulfilment of the individual's needs (consumers and buyers).[17]

If an individual agent carries out his favorite hypothesis, he experiences reactions from the market or from any other interacting market participants respectively. This feedback can either confirm or disappoint the expectations of the agent. In doing so, the individual gains knowledge about the appropriateness of his initial hypothesis. In the case of confirmation, the agent becomes encouraged to stick with his chosen mode of behaviour, whereas in the case of disappointment, the agent experiences incentives to change his behaviour. By testing their hypotheses in competition, the individual agents obtain new and improved knowledge due to the (expectations-confirming or -disappointing) reactions of interacting agents. Thus, competition leads to the creation of additional knowledge about market opportunities and it does so through a decentralized process of market interaction of individuals. Consequently, the new and improved knowledge is decentralized itself: it is represented only in the changes of the cognitive theories of the individual agents which have participated in the market process.

The fact has to be emphasized that the agents' efforts to create hypotheses about successful modes of behaviour does not necessarily imply a process optimization or maximization. Instead, the less ambitious concept of 'satisficing' suffices to explain individual behaviour in

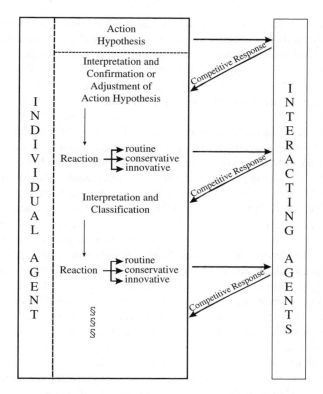

Figure 3.2   Evolutionary competition as a test of hypotheses

competition. If the results of economic action satisfy the expectations of the individual agent, he will most often not search for alternative modes of behaviour and, instead, stick with this satisfying option, even though it may not be the (theoretically or objectively) optimal alternative and the agent could improve his performance by changing his modes of action. This waiver of searching for even better alternatives in the case of satisfying market feedback is rational because, by doing so, the individual can concentrate his scarce and limited cognitive capacities on problem situations in which his current modes of behaviour do not yield satisfying results.

Although evolutionary competition is a process of the permanent creation of additional knowledge, this does not imply that some kind of a knowledge-optimum (which could match the equilibrium theory's notion of omniscience) can ever be achieved. Firstly, the knowledge improvements are situative, that is, they offer the opportunity to adjust the individuals' cognitive theories in order to perform more adequately under the same or sufficiently similar circumstances. However, situations can change and some parts of the situations always do change. If, for instance, an individual agent has experienced negative feedback from his market behaviour (due to the reactions of interacting agents), he most probably will change his behaviour to achieve more satisfying results. This change of behaviour, however, represents a change of situation for the agents that are interacting with him. They, again, will have to respond. It may be that the change of behaviour of our agent does not require them to drop their cognitive representation of this context as a routine situation. However, it may also be that the change of behaviour of our agent leads to sufficiently severe disappointments of expectations for the interacting agents. Thus, they will (re)classify this situation as a problem situation and, consequently, choose a different mode of behaviour or even create a new one. Both lead to a change of circumstances in regard to the decision to act of our agent. The knowledge he has obtained before in competition may have been an improvement (under the modes of behaviour of the interacting agents at that time) but can be obsolete now. This line of argument emphasizes the openness and never-ending evolutionary character of competitive market processes. The economic interaction of agents on markets permanently produces incentives (and requirements) to change one's own behaviour or, in other words, to look for and create new modes of behaviour.[18] Only this permanent force to adjust one's own individual economic plans to the reality of the market and the state of interacting agents' individual plans allows competitive markets to be superior to any other device in regard to the task of coordinating millions of free-acting individuals. However, this superiority is inevitably connected to the non-equilibrium character of market processes, particularly the endogenous creation of change and evolution (in the sense of variation and selection).

Next to devaluations of individual economic knowledge caused by market interaction, the imperfection of the learning process itself represents the second obstacle for knowledge optimization. To act within a market context requires the combination of a multitude of parameters. A 'mode of behaviour' is itself a complex phenomenon. The supply of a good, for instance, consists among other things of the quality of the good, the cost of production, the marketing strategy, the choice and organization of distribution channels, and so on. And the same is true for the demand side since the satisfying of needs is also a multidimensional problem. Therefore, any market behaviour does not represent one clear-cut hypothesis but a (more or less) complex bundle of hypotheses (Kerber, 1997, pp. 52–6; Budzinski, 2000, pp. 122–5). In order to identify the real cause for success or disappointment, the individual agents have to engage in a process of interpretation. They have to determine which part of the bundle of hypotheses has been responsible for the feedback experienced (confirmation or disappointment).[19] Since this process has to rely on the subjective and fallible cognitive theories of the agents, the process of learning is imperfect and errors occur.

Altogether, evolutionary competition is an open-ended process of experimentation. By testing divergent hypotheses, the participants in the competitive market process create situative and fallible knowledge about the market and competitors. The adjustment of their individual behaviour according to their knowledge improvements improves the coordination of the interacting agents, albeit imperfectly, since the creation of new (innovative) problem solutions permanently renews the necessity for coordination.

Enterprises as Agents

The concept of evolutionary competition as laid out in the previous section refers to 'individual agents' as the units which are interacting in market competition. Obviously, humans acting economically belong to this category. However, in real-world markets, a lot of important 'agents' are enterprises. They are not individuals but can be viewed as 'collective agents' (organizations). According to North (1990, p. 5), organizations are 'groups of individuals bound by some common purpose to achieve objectives'. They perform as agents in the competitive market process and, thus, belong to the players of the 'game'.

On the one hand, enterprises can be viewed as being similar to individual agents, that is, they act on markets similarly to individual agents. This is how most interacting agents perceive enterprises in most of their market interactions with them, for example when buying a product. Therefore, the analysis of the previous section also applies to enterprises as agents.

On the other hand, however, the internal learning mechanisms of enterprises differ significantly from those of individuals. It is important to imagine that enterprises as organizations do not act themselves but only through individual agents which are members (employees) of it. These agents act on behalf of the enterprise, trying to pursue a mixture of the goals of the enterprise and their individual goals.[20] Like the individual agents, the organization as a whole learns through the feedback of market interaction, but this process is much more complex and indirect. Signals from market interaction influence the enterprise through their member agents and, consequently, are available within the organization only in an interpreted form. Thus, the cognitive theories of the member agents play an important role in the learning process of the enterprise. Furthermore, the internal structure of communication and decision systems within the organization has a decisive influence on the rate and quality of the organizational learning process. The interplay of organizational structures and member agents can improve the learning from market feedback because there is more potential for creativity and the generation of alternatives. However, it can also hamper the learning process and represent a source for misinterpretation and errors.

It is because of this second aspect that the theory of the firm matters for evolutionary competition. Unfortunately, an integrative theory, which combines evolutionary theories of the firms with evolutionary competition theory, is still missing. Although such a theory could provide valuable insights, the interpretation of enterprises being 'similar to individual agents' in competitive interaction represents a useful assumption in regard to the context of this chapter.

Competition, Institutions and Governance

Evolutionary competition cannot be analysed without its institutional framework. There is no such thing as a free market or free competition, if 'free' is meant to describe the absence of institutional influence.[21] Competitive market processes always and inevitably take place within an institutional framework. Sustainable market interaction even requires a minimum of institutional arrangements like legal rules about property rights and contracts and their enforcement. 'If one views the world as consisting of self-interested agents unconstrained by rules or norms, or norm-like phenomena, there exists no explanation for why the world does not degenerate into a Hobbesian war of all against all' (Field, 1984, p. 685).

The meaning of 'institution' in economics is commonly described as 'sets of rules that allow a plurality of persons to coordinate their behavior and to routinely solve typical problems that arise in social interaction' (Vanberg, 2002; see also North, 1990). This distinguishes them strictly from organizations (see above). Contrarily to organizations, institutions do not belong to the players but, instead, represent the rules of the 'game'. For instance, environmental laws are institutions, whereas the European Commission is an organization. However, organizations have an internal institutional structure (organizational rules or routines) through their governance structures.

Institutions can be differentiated into external and internal ones (Lachmann, 1963). The former constitute a framework of laws and moral rules – external to the market sphere – in which individual economic action takes place, whereas the latter are generated within the market sphere such as, for example, standardized contracts or organizational rules. Institutions may be formal (that is, codified, such as constitutions of states and companies, or written law) and connected to explicit public enforcement or informal (that is, non-codified, such as moral codes of behaviour, manners and customs, or rules of zeitgeist) and enforced through social sanctions (North, 1990). Additionally, one can distinguish designed institutions which are purposefully created and intentionally implemented by authorized human agents (governments, parliaments, religious leaders and so on) from undesigned or spontaneous institutions which emerge unintended as a result of human action but not of human design (Hayek, 1967) and evolve self-organizationally over time (Horwitz, 1993). From a normative point of view, one can identify functional, afunctional and dysfunctional institutions (Mueller, 2000). This classification corresponds to the adequacy of institutions to solve the problems they are created for.

The economic effects of institutions are largely connected to their guiding character compared to individual behaviour. Institutions reduce the complexity of decision-requiring situations, thereby decreasing transaction costs and facilitating market transactions. Moreover, institutions facilitate interaction of both individuals and collective agents, since they restrict the agents concerning their dispositions to behave. Hereby, expectations about the behaviour of other market participants become more secure (albeit not absolutely) and rational systematic economic behaviour is promoted. Institutions lead to regularities in behaviour and, by doing so, their reductive character develops an enabling function. Without an institutional framework, the reality of ordinary decision-making situations would be much too complex for a human mind to cope with (Langlois, 1998). Only because institutions reduce this complexity are agents able to develop competence (or contingency) to construct cognitive theories about the world and act purposefully. Altogether, institutions guide individual behaviour (without determining it) and, thereby, order the market process.[22] Otherwise, the latter would be an irregular and accidental process (Field, 1979).

Within the concept of competition as a test of hypotheses, institutions have two different implications for the direction and rate or pace of evolutionary competition. This corresponds with two different types of competition-relevant rules.[23]

Firstly, institutions define the content of competition processes. The institutional framework determines which modes of economic behaviour are allowed or prohibited. Alongside very general legal rules (which are not only directed towards the economy) such as law against larceny and fraud as well as rules in regard to liability, contracts and so on, specific competition rules are addressed. Competition laws usually include rules against unfair competition, prohibition of hardcore cartels, merger control rules, and rules against monopolization and the abuse of market power by dominant enterprises. These types of institutions devaluate specific modes of behaviour, thereby restricting the participants of the market process. At the same time, the institutional arrangements induce the market agents to search for and create modes of behaviour which lie within the permitted range. If the institutions are effectively enforced, it is not rational for the market participants to engage in or create prohibited modes of behaviour. Thus, the institutional framework channels the direction of the competitive market process, particularly the direction of the creation of innovative problem solutions. The rules of the competition game define the content to which the knowledge-generating competition between interacting agents is related.

Secondly, institutions govern the dynamics of competition, that is, the intensity and pace of the experimentation process by the market participants. Evolutionary market processes inherently produce incentives both to innovate and to conquer innovations through imitation and/or counter-innovations. This permanent and never-ending interchange of action and reaction drives competitive market evolution. The institutional arrangements of an economy shape the incentive system in regard to its intensity and effectiveness, which can be demonstrated by the following issues:

- It is indispensable for creative innovation dynamics that new modes of behaviour are allowed to be carried out in competition. This implies that the institutional arrangements restrict themselves to the prohibition or devaluation of behavioural dispositions, which are well known to be harmful. New and to date unknown modes of behaviour generally have to be allowed.
- Creative and innovative agents always devaluate previous market positions and options of interacting agents. If they are forced to compensate the (temporary) losers, the incentives to be creative and innovative are reduced and the evolutionary market process becomes handicapped.
- Similarly, subsidies in order to preserve specific industry structures reduce the welfare-enhancing capabilities and potential of competitive market processes.
- Cartels and cartel surrogates aim at the alleviation and/or elimination of the devaluation of the cartel members' economic dispositions through competition and market evolution. In doing so, they handicap creative and innovative agents and deter them from challenging their market positions. Thereby, market evolution is hampered by the reduction or exclusion of incentives to innovate. Strictly speaking,

this is very clear only for hardcore cartels like price-fixing, market division and agreements about production quotas or supply quantities. As far as these parameters of competition are concerned, any other kind of inter-firm arrangement or cooperation, irrespective of its degree of informality, produces the same negative outcome as a hardcore cartel. If collaborative inter-firm arrangements cover other parameters of competition, the effect on the incentive system may not be so clear. For example, and under specific circumstances, standardization arrangements may produce pro-competitive outcomes.[24]

- Patents and similar institutions play an ambivalent role. On the one hand, they strengthen the incentive to innovate because they temporarily delay the devaluation of innovation profits by imitation.[25] On the other hand, if they sweepingly protect the innovative agents of the past and, thus, sustainably preserve their market positions, the future dynamics of competitive market processes become handicapped.

Altogether, institutions shape evolutionary competition in two ways. The first type of competition institutions demarcate permissible from prohibited modes of behaviour. Thus, they guide the avenues along which new knowledge becomes created, thereby selecting which (kinds of) hypotheses are generated and tested in evolutionary competition. Different designs of the institutional framework lead to different evaluations of opportunities, that is, a specific mode of behaviour is more or less promising, depending on the design of the institutional arrangements. Market participants choose and create modes of behaviour according to the incentives set by the institutional framework, which therefore can create path-dependencies. To choose, search for or create sustainable or responsible modes of behaviour can be unattractive under one institutional framework (therefore few agents engage in such strategies) but very attractive under another, channelling the strong innovation power of evolutionary competition. An intensive competition for more sustainable and/or responsible problem solutions would be the result.

The second type of competition institutions influences the pace of the innovation process in evolutionary competition. Those institutions shape the extent of the generation of new hypotheses and, thereby, the rate of the dynamics of competition (see Figure 3.3). This influences the intensity with which obsolete hypotheses are devaluated and eliminated. Institutions of the first type shape the path of the evolutionary market process, whereas institutions of the second type contribute to determine how fast and how vigorously this path is pursued.

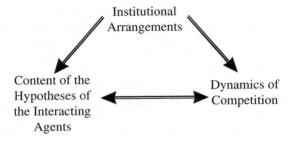

Figure 3.3   Institutions and evolutionary competition

The Meaning of Diversity

The evolutionary process of competition is characterized by a never-ending interplay of creative and adaptive modes of behaviour, the first implying innovations which devaluate previous hypotheses and permanently regenerate the need for coordination and the second, being equally important, eroding the profits of previous innovations, thereby regenerating the incentive and pressure to be creative and innovate. Adaptive behaviour can also be viewed as being imitative as the creative ideas of others are copied. However, additional to the incentive-preserving character of imitation (forcing the creative agents to remain creative), adaptive behaviour and imitation are beneficial because they generally also include elements of improvement. A successful imitator must: (1) copy the creative idea but organize it more efficiently (for example producing the same product at lower costs); or (2) make incremental changes to the creative idea which make it even more attractive for the market.[26]

Diversity and plurality play a crucial role for the endogenous 'production' of innovation through evolutionary competition. The more hypotheses are tested independently from each other at the market, and the more diverse these hypotheses are, the higher is the speed of the creation of knowledge and the smoother and more effectively the process of decentralized mutual learning works. Consequently, diversity is a most important driving-force for evolutionary competition and yields benefits in terms of knowledge creation and mutual learning. Different from non-evolutionary concepts of competition, diversity possesses a value of its own (Budzinski, 2003b). If diversity, and especially the emergence of new diversity through creative actions, is reduced or has even expired, the evolutionary market process becomes hampered.

The beneficial effects of diversity of hypotheses cover the market. On the supply side, this implies a diversity of products, but also a diversity of technologies, forms of organization and production, marketing strategies and so on, as well as governance systems. If different hypotheses about all these dimensions of economic activities are tested in competitive markets, mutual learning is promoted, for instance in the form of benchmarking strategies and the derivation of best practices. In particular the latter becomes more efficient if the pool of practices which can be comparatively evaluated – the yardstick being the performance in market competition – comprises a large assortment of ideas and problem solutions. However, it has to be emphasized that benchmarking and best-practice strategies can develop a tendency towards monocultures, for example if there is a common benchmark which all market participants aim to copy or a dominating best practice. Yet, two objections against such a 'benchmark harmonization' and in favour of sustainable diversity have to be considered (Kerber and Budzinski, 2003; Budzinski, 2004a, 2004b):

1. It is rather improbable that one problem solution is superior in all circumstances. Market activities take place in an ever-changing environment and that means that today's superior hypotheses may be obsolete and inferior tomorrow. Moreover, even the stationary market environment is heterogeneous and, therefore, demands different solutions. For example, a best practice for an industrialized country may be inferior in regard to developing countries. Other dimensions of heterogeneity include (among many more) diverging cultural, legal and social traditions.
2. The value of diversity is not temporary. As it has to be concluded from the line of thought in this chapter the benefits of evolutionary competition do not lie in a 'competition' between an *ex ante* defined set of problem solutions which is stopped after the superior solution is identified. If benchmarking and best practices are understood in that way, this is misleading from an evolutionary perspective and it disregards the fundamental nature of the knowledge problem.[27] Instead, benchmarks and best practices have to prove themselves under the permanent challenge of alternative and innovative hypotheses.

Additionally, it has to be recalled that adaptive competition, like aiming at an observed benchmark or best practice, is only one element of dynamic rivalling competition. The endogenous generation of innovation (creative competition) is the indispensable counterpart which implies that creating new benchmarks and, thus, challenging prevailing best practices instead of adapting them, belongs to the core of the benefits of evolutionary competition.

BENEFITS OF EVOLUTIONARY COMPETITION

From the perspective of evolutionary market process theory, competition represents the best available coordination device. In general, competitive markets develop the following beneficial outcomes:

- Allocative efficiency: competition leads to an efficient allocation of factors of production. The factors tend to be employed in their most productive way, thereby generating a higher level of output of goods than any other coordination device. Inefficient production processes and goods tend to be driven out of the markets by competition. This causes a minimal level of waste of resources, labour and capital (given the achievable output level).
- Consumers' sovereignty: the composition of the produced goods basket follows the needs of the consumers. Market participants who offer problem solutions (goods) which are superior in the eyes of the consumers, gain, whereas the suppliers of inferior products (which do not benefit or benefit less the needs of the consumers) lose. Without competition, producers would not have sufficient incentives to adjust their supply according to the changing demand.
- Distributive efficiency: the competitive income distribution follows the individual performance in competition. This sets incentives to perform successfully in economic interaction and to search for better problem solutions. However, some market participants cannot perform as successfully as others even if they want to (children, old people, sick and handicapped persons, and so on); therefore, the competitive income distribution has to be complemented by social policy.
- Economic freedom and erosion of economic power: competition means freedom of choice, that is, the freedom of consumers to choose between suppliers, the freedom of producers to decide what they want to produce, the freedom to innovate, and so on.[28] Furthermore, competition implies the freedom to challenge the positions of other market participants, thereby eroding market power. Powerful market agents can exercise their power (monopoly rents, exploitation of the market and so on) only if no competitors are available to erode their dominant position by offering lower prices, better service or more innovative products.
- Dynamic efficiency: competition provides stronger incentives to innovate than any other coordination device. Only competitive pressure forces market participants to choose the less comfortable route of engaging in the creation of new and superior problem solutions.

If financial potential for research and development is high (for example because of monopoly rents) but competition is restricted, both individual agents and enterprises will most probably concentrate on preserving their rents and cut out the risky and uncertain undertaking of 'innovation'.[29]

- Adaptive efficiency: competitive markets offer a higher flexibility in regard to changing conditions of economic activities than other coordination devices. This includes external shocks, recessive and depressive tendencies, the evolution of technology and (intended or unintended) changes of the institutional framework. Adaptive efficiency does not imply that any kind of crisis is avoided, but competitive markets can better and more flexibly react to and cope with challenges and, therefore, overcome the crisis more smoothly.

The beneficial effects of competition can only be reaped if competition is not restricted by the private agents (hardcore cartels, predatory strategies and so on), and/or by public policy (monopoly privileges, political barriers to entry and so on). Thus, the institutional framework of the market economy plays a decisive role concerning the effectiveness of evolutionary competition. However, some goods cannot be subject to competition (public goods) and society may opt to exclude some markets from evolutionary competitive processes. The latter may be the case if the restriction of competition yields the intended results, which more than compensate for the inevitable inefficiencies emerging from alternative coordination devices. Drawing on economics, this might be realistic only in regard to very few markets like education or health care – and even there it does not include all features of those 'industries'.

The challenges of sustainable development provide a high necessity for economic change, and the same is true for an institutional evolution towards higher importance of social responsibility. Therefore, in particularly the dynamic and adaptive efficiency of the economy plays a significant and important role in regard to the implementation and sustainable diffusion of the intended changes. Consequently, evolutionary competitive market processes represent the best available design of economic coordination to cope with these challenges.

RESPONSIBLE CORPORATE GOVERNANCE IN COMPETITION

Competition as a test of hypotheses represents an approach which thoroughly analyses competition as a process of mutual learning and puts weight on the response mechanisms with which market participants are confronted when experimenting with their individual and subjective hypotheses in competition. Prices play an important role in this process of learning through interaction, because price changes bundle reactions of other agents and signal their combined effects to the agent, thereby further reducing complexity. However, prices are not the only medium of communication, albeit they are a very important one. Consequently, price theory becomes complemented by institutional and cognitive approaches, which all together fuel the evolutionary approach. The institutional focus is on the meaning of the institutional framework as a process-ordering factor. Through the institutional reduction of the complexity of choice situations, agents with scarce (instead of unlimited) cognitive capabilities become enabled to act purposefully because a manageable context of action is defined. Besides, the cognitive perspective provides an analytical framework which views limited and interpretative-constructive perception and cognition not as an imperfection or even a failure (in the sense of a deviation from the optimum) but as driving forces of permanent coordination, including creativity and innovativeness. Just like the new sustainability debate, which is discussed in the preceding chapters, complexity, uncertainty and the fundamental knowledge problem play decisive roles.

Changes in relative prices are signals for market participants to adapt or alter their individual plans in order to (unintendedly) contribute to coordination. However, price changes are nonetheless a matter of interpretation. Enterprises have to develop hypotheses about the causes of price changes and about promising reactions. It is important to understand that price changes devaluate previous knowledge but do not reveal new knowledge in the sense that they tell the enterprise what it must do. Instead, price changes induce a process of learning (problem situation), which generates new (situative and subjective) knowledge through a process of interpretation. In the end, adaptive or creative changes in the enterprise's market behaviour result.

Enterprises cope with the need to interpret and subsequently react to market signals by developing internal institutions including network structures. One of the major tasks of an enterprise's internal governance system is to increase the resonance ability of the enterprise towards market signals, that is, to develop a high sensitivity in regard to the slightest changes in the competitive environment. This has to be combined with competence to develop promising hypotheses out of the resonance. In comparison to rather narrow short-term profit-oriented governance approaches, responsibility broadens and enriches a company's resonance ability. By widening the focus of attention, more signals from the competitive environment are allowed to enter the internal learning process of the enterprise. This leads to a knowledge creation which has a more multidimensional character compared to narrower governance approaches. Consequently, the built-up competence is richer and allows for a better adaptive flexibility, that is, that with RCG the enterprise is better suited to cope with varying challenges from the competitive environment. From the perspective of evolutionary competition theory, RCG offers the potential to enhance long-term competitiveness, particularly if the challenges and demands from competition change significantly and at high rates over the course of time. Altogether, responsibility in the sense of its application in this book is likely to contribute to the generation of multidimensional competence and, thus, work as an instrument both for long-term profit generation and for innovation.[30]

However, both the quality and the rate of competitive knowledge creation depend on the institutional framework. Consequently, incoherent institutional arrangements, contradictory institutional incentives and requirements, regulatory loopholes and distortions of the system of relative prices may cause handicaps for the process of knowledge generation. We can also discuss this in terms of increasing costs of learning. It has to be emphasized that any institutional framework can never be completely free of incoherence and distortions,[31] especially in the face of the ever-evolving character of competition and the business environment. Consequently, institutional reform at the level of governments remains a permanent task. Furthermore, a co-evolution of political and corporate governance concepts can offer the potential to improve the institutional framework of competition in regard to both the content of the competitive discovery procedure and the dynamics of change.

NOTES

1. The change in the meaning of 'competition' becomes very clear in Friedman's (1962, pp. 119–20) description of the notion of neoclassic competition: 'Competition has two different meanings. In ordinary discourse, competition means personal rivalry, with one individual seeking to outdo his known competitor. In the economic world [Friedman actually refers to the world of neoclassical price theory], competition means almost the opposite. There is no personal rivalry in the competitive market place . . . The wheat farmer in a free market does not feel himself in personal rivalry with, or threatened by, his neighbor, who is, in fact, his competitor. The essence of a competitive market is its impersonal character. No one participant can determine the terms on which other participants shall have access to goods or jobs. All take prices as given by the market and no individual can by himself have more than a negligible influence on price . . .'
2. Modern industrial economics is predominantly oligopoly theory, focusing on Cournot- and Bertrand-competition equilibria instead of perfect competition equilibria. However, the equilibrium of a polypolistic market remains the benchmark with other (including oligopolistic) competitive equilibria – typically enough – often denoted as imperfect competition.
3. Strictly speaking, the Chicago benchmark is total welfare since the sum of consumer and producer surplus is addressed. However, Chicago economists argue that an increase in

producers' surplus eventually benefits private households (and thus consumers) since the additional profit increases the income of the shareholders.

4. Kerber has developed this concept (1994, 1997). See also Vanberg and Kerber (1994), Kerber and Saam (2001), and Kerber and Budzinski (2003, pp. 417–24), Kerber (2006).

5. See for example Clark (1961), Müller (1974), Metcalfe (1998) and Langlois (2001).

6. See Langlois (1986a, 1986b), North (1990), Vanberg (1994), Budzinski (2000, 2003a) and Dulbecco and Dutraive (2001).

7. They represent non-deterministic phenomena (Budzinski, 2000, p. 85).

8. Most emphatically, Hayek (1948, p. 92) argues in favour of a realistic, original notion of competition as a lively process of rival interaction. Consequently, he fiercely attacks the equilibrium notion of competition: '[W]hat the theory of perfect competition discusses has little claim to be called "competition" at all and (.) its conclusions are of little use as guides to policy. The reason for this seems to me to be that this theory throughout assumes that state of affairs already to exist which . . . the process of competition tends to bring about (or to approximate) and that, if the state of affairs assumed by the theory of perfect competition ever existed, it would not only deprive of their scope all the activities which the verb 'to compete' describes but would make them virtually impossible.'
   Hayek (1948, p. 94) extends this criticism to the general attempt to focus economic analysis on the notion 'competitive equilibrium', that is, he includes models of monopolistic competition as well as equilibrium theories of oligopoly (like Cournot- and Bertrand-'competition' in oligopoly price theory). Especially therefore, his critique is still very topical since modern industrial economics predominantly builds upon Cournot- and Bertrand-oligopolies.

9. This is symbolized by the 2002 Nobel Prize in economics, which was awarded to Daniel Kahneman. See for seminal contributions for example Denzau and North (1994), Vanberg (1994), Searle (1995, 2001), Kahneman and Tversky (2000) and Kahneman (2003). A couple of decades earlier, Hayek (1952) has developed quite compatible ideas. The following discussion follows Budzinski (2003a). Other contemporary surveys and analyses provide for example Rizzello (1999), Egidi and Rizzello (2003), Kaisla (2003) and Van den Bergh and Stagl (2003).

10. However, social and cultural interaction (communication) leads to the development of a minimum compatibility of individuals of the same group. Without this incomplete compatibility, no reasonable expectations about the interaction with other individuals would be possible.

11. Due to the subjective and interpretative character of human cognition, the individually constructed context or situation will always differ quantitatively (incomplete information) and qualitatively (distorted information) from the objective one. For more details see Budzinski (2000, 2003a).

12 This is convincingly analysed by Wegner (1996, 1997).

13. This does not influence the design of simulations and scenarios about possible future solutions of economic problems as long as they are part of a competition of ideas and as long as it is not intended to model the market reality according to the scenarios in a centralized, top-down way.

14. See for example Wegner (1996, 1997, 2003), Vanberg (1999), Budzinski (2000) and Okruch (2003).

15. For the following see Kerber (1994, 1997, 2006) and Budzinski (2000, pp. 165–70; 2003a, pp. 225–8).

16. This may for example be a hypothesis about consumer preferences that are carried out by firms through new products, new marketing techniques, and so on. In addition, new technologies or new forms of (internal) organization, governance systems, and so on may be viewed as hypotheses about more efficient ways of producing and supplying. We will readdress these aspects later.

17. This process can be analogously modelled for seller–buyer relationships on downstream markets (for example component markets), implying for instance that buyers can also be wholesalers or retailers. See more elaborately Kerber (1997, pp. 59–61).

18. Competitive interaction introduces a permanent threat of devaluation in regard to market-relevant knowledge. This is the main driving-force of evolutionary market processes since it forces the competitors to permanently struggle for improved knowledge. Devaluation of previously successful market behaviour thus represents an inevitable and, at the same time, indispensable element of evolutionary competition. See Langlois (1986b), Loasby (1993, pp. 204), Kerber (1997, p. 55) and particularly Wegner (1996, pp. 131; 1997).

19. This task becomes further complicated by the fact that the bundle of hypotheses also includes tacit knowledge.

20. According to both standard economic theory and cognitive science, agents cannot waive completely taking their own 'egoistic' goals into consideration when deciding and acting.

21. Or, as the libertarian philosopher Karl R. Popper (1997, p. 312) puts it: 'in a complex society, anything approaching a free market could only exist if it enjoyed the protection of laws, and therefore of the state. Thus the term "free market" should always be placed in inverted commas, since it was always bound, or limited, by a legal framework and made possible only by this framework.' See on the indispensability of institutions for any kind of market competition Vanberg (1999), Loasby (2000), Dulbecco and Dutraive (2001) and Budzinski (2003a). Differing from other radical libertarians, Hayek (1973) emphasizes the meaning of institutions for the market process.

22. See for example Langlois (1986b), North (1990), Horwitz (1993), Vanberg (1999), Budzinski (2000, pp. 139–51), and Dulbecco and Dutraive (2001).

23. See Kerber (1994, pp. 300; 1997, pp. 63–8).

24. A particularly difficult subject are cooperations in regard to innovation. We will address this in the next section on 'The meaning of diversity'.

25. However, patents do not protect market participants against additional (counter-)innovations that challenge their market positions without imitating the initial solution.

26. This is also a nice example for the intricate interdependence of free behaviour in competition and the institutional framework. Patent laws prohibit specific kinds of copying for a defined amount of time. This can be justified because: (1) the innovator has to spend costs to develop his idea, which may not arise during the process of copying and (2) the innovator gets a reward for his creativity, which – in terms of the use of scarce cognitive resources – is always more demanding than routine behaviour. But note that a lot of important types of innovations, like new forms of organization, governance and marketing, but also some kinds of products, cannot be protected by patents and their relatives.

27. The idea of a best-practice process towards an 'ultimate' solution is confronted with an internal problem of logic. If it is beneficial to have a diversity of practices (hypotheses, products, problem solutions, and so on) to 'discover' superior ones through competition, why should one waive making use of these efficiencies permanently by skipping diversity after the current best practice has been 'discovered' – or is thought to be discovered if the limits and working properties of human perception and cognition are considered.

28. In this sense, competition is an expression of economic democracy.

29. This is supported by cognitive economics because it is rational to save scarce cognitive resources (which are needed to be creative) for problem situations and a situation without competitive pressure does not qualify as a problem situation (since it yields satisfying results without changing one's modes of behaviour). Additionally, recent insights of experimental industrial economics demonstrate that in the face of a choice between increasing profits through exercising market power versus exploiting efficiency potentials, most market participants tend to engage in power strategies (Martin et al., 2001; Elliott et al., 2003).

30. Responsible corporate governance itself represents an innovative hypothesis (about adequate governance) that has to be tested in competition. The competitive response will evolve and improve a concept such as RCG. Only the long-term evolutionary competition can ultimately tell whether RCG will develop to become a best practice (benchmark), or whether it will prove to be inferior compared to other concepts (which are not yet developed).

31. Of course, Hayek's fundamental knowledge problem also applies to institutions.

4. A co-evolutionary view on market and government failures

Raimund Bleischwitz

Following the introduction of the notion of 'responsible corporate governance' and the analysis of competition, this chapter will discuss market and government failures alike. The reason stems from the discussion in the previous sections. If companies change and if competition can serve as a source of innovation, the questions are: (1) how prevailing market and government deficits would hinder processes of diffusion; and (2) how mechanisms of governance can counteract those deficits.

Beginning with markets, one can start with the insight that coordination of economic activities via markets works dynamically and powerfully, but imperfectly. Markets work extremely well in regard to the provision of private goods for average, well-informed consumers. But they have some trouble when those conditions do not exist or still have to be set up by any external authority. The following categories of market failures have been analysed extensively by research (for example Stiglitz, 2000); the recent debate is summarized for the purpose of our book (see also Bleischwitz, 2004):

- the provision of public goods;
- positive and negative externalities;
- adaptation deficits;
- information deficits;
- natural monopolies.

Any market provision of public goods can be regarded as difficult because their attributes of non-rivalries in use and non-excludability make any production unattractive. Once provided, everybody is able to enjoy the benefits without paying a fee (Olson, 1965; Ostrom et al., 1999). Usually, therefore, the state has to play a role in providing the legal or financial framework for the production of public goods. National defence is a case in point, where living in a protected area has to be guaranteed by any national authority able to raise taxes that finance defence. By and large, this conceptualization has been extended to several other fields such as disaster relief, stability and environmental protection.

The standard conceptualization of public goods can, however, be problematic (Nelson, 2002). Attributes may change due to technological progress; harbours and lighthouses illustrate such a conversion from a public to a private good due to technological improvements and better pricing possibilities. Another point relates to citizens' preferences. Though citizens are usually taken as one aggregated unit, they benefit from public goods in quite enumerable ways. Preferences are often heterogeneous and change over time. Even in the case of national defence it is not likely that each inhabitant is protected at the same order of magnitude. This unequal benefit applies even more with regard to global environmental public goods. Earth's atmosphere yields differently favourable climate conditions in different regions. When climate change continues, winners and losers will differ between regions and within societies. The assumption of a fixed borderline between private and public goods no longer seems tenable; in fact the borderline is rather blurred.

The conclusion for an analytical framework is as follows: any governance structure has to develop mechanisms that accurately reflect the true demand for public goods over time in different regions, taking into account inter-regional and intergenerational fairness. Looking from this angle, governance comes closer to the people, to the rules of their interaction, and to market processes.

With the notion of externalities, economists refer to by-products of activities having negative or positive consequences that are not reflected in market prices. Environmental pollution is an obvious example for both a negative externality and the ensuing price distortion. It too leads to the observation of private markets producing negative externalities, whereas society as a whole struggles with the impacts. Not all externalities can successfully be tackled with the programme of Ronald Coase (1960), where a limited number of affected parties would be able to agree upon appropriate property rights, thus leading to an internalization without governments. With many of today's externalities, impacts are widespread, the number of affected people is large, and producers are heterogeneous if not hard to identify. Globalization truly extends these difficulties. Each of these criteria makes bilateral negotiations costly and ineffective; a demand for more general rules and the involvement of governments seems obvious. The more recent debate about internalization of externalities clearly reflects such a demand (Stiglitz, 1998; Nelson, 2002; Young, 1999).

Again, there are some problems associated with the standard conceptualization. Internalization efforts may come at the expense of third parties that have not been involved in the formulation of policies. Governments have to serve their respective voters and may tend towards decision-making in favour of certain vested interest groups. This might lead them to over-looking vulnerable, underorganized groups inside and outside society. The different schemes of an ecological tax reform, for instance, offer exemptions and postponements for certain industry groups. Some environmental fees protect domestic industries and are a barrier to trade with developing countries. This is not to deny that a second-best internalization is better than doing nothing. But who cares for third parties if their voice is too quiet? Participation, which also has merits in other areas of sustainability, certainly becomes a topic in internalization strategies. Its relevance becomes even clearer when one looks at the openness of technological change (Freeman, 1998), where mechanisms of absorbing new knowledge and actor coordination are crucial. Acknowledging that firms pursue these interests of transforming common knowledge into business concepts creates scope for an endogenous internalization of externalities (Beckenbach, 1998).

Our conclusion is that any governance structure needs to co-evolve with endogenous internalization efforts. In doing so, it ought to involve quite a number of enterprises and civil society actors because of the need to discover previously unknown solutions and to choose among various internalization strategies. Any approach of 'setting the framework conditions right' therefore needs to set incentives for continuous improvements emerging through learning processes among actors. Assuming that those activities may generate positive externalities and are to be pursued against the persistence of barriers, the design of policy instruments and public programmes may be reformulated.

The category of adaptation deficits refers to the speed at which markets and firms adapt to new circumstances arising from new legislation and new business conditions. While it is clear that adaptation always takes time and adaptation costs cannot be zero, real processes of change are sometimes extremely slow, have to deal with prevailing path dependencies and inertia, and may thus lead to new inefficiencies. Firms usually specialize and may oversee new opportunities arising at the horizon. According to Figure 4.1, firms behave differently with regard to innovation.

In particular, the empirical literature on energy efficiency has shown evidence for the following types of adaptation deficits (Nilsson and Wene, 2001; Jaffé et al., 2002):

- Split incentives where the owner, designer and user of any technology are not identical. Coordination costs are high.
- Biased calculation when payback times used by either firms or consumers in savings calculations are too short.

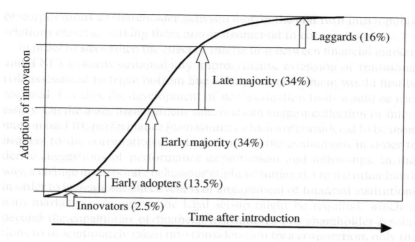

Laggards (16%)

Late majority (34%)

Early majority (34%)

Early adopters (13.5%)

Innovators (2.5%)

Adoption of innovation

Time after introduction

Source: Nilsson and Wene (2001).

Figure 4.1 Different firms' behaviour towards innovations

- Costs of equipment when investments for small volumes of new technology cannot compete with incumbent technologies.
- Market power because established companies guard their market position and market share. Newcomers need to establish a critical mass of supply to emerging markets.

Moreover, some markets are characterized by an oligopoly rather than by competition. A minimum response to adaptation deficits, therefore, is the establishment of effective antitrust and competition policies by governments. Competition needs to be protected against firms' interest in raising their rent by lowering the degree of competition.

Consumers are relevant in this process because their demand for collective goods often starts vaguely and needs to co-evolve with market development. The point here is that a typical sustainability market evolves over time, driven by changing corporate behaviour as well as by stakeholder activities. Our point easily applies to consumer goods such as energy-efficient light bulbs. In addition, infrastructures and other network goods could be seen as dependent on consumers' choices too.

Our conclusion for governance structures starts from the observation that sustainability markets are created step by step, created by pioneers and early adopters from a variety of firms (Witt, 2003; Pelikan and Wegner, 2003). Adaptation moreover refers to principles of sustainability and ensuing market development, not only to market demand. Looking from this angle, incremental corporate change towards accountability and responsibility as well as stakeholder involvement become as essential for adaptation processes as appropriate policies. Taking adaptation seriously means that policies ought to recognize the emergence of dynamic processes, and should avoid the *ex ante* design of overly precisely defined obligations.

Information deficits are serious. Economic textbooks for undergraduates often assume perfect rationality based upon perfect information. The magic of the invisible hand strongly relies upon those assumptions. Both hardly exist in the real world. 'Asymmetric information' complicating the work of markets has become an established field in the realm of economics (Simon, 1992; Stiglitz, 1999; Mantzavinos, 2001). In particular it is:

- lack of information on superior investment options as regards sustainability concerns;
- transaction cost for decision-making, viewing different options;
- uncertainties as to what extent the performance of innovation develops, and what regulatory changes might come.

What seems important for the purpose of our book is the necessary involvement of individuals and organizations in problem-solving efforts to balance information deficits. Though open access to information may lower the costs of learning processes, the mere providing of information cannot replace real learning efforts. This is why publicly financed agencies and research institutes ought to be involved in permanently monitoring and assessing the quality of certain public goods (Dixit, 2000): it is not only information supply that matters, but rather the transformation of information through learning processes. Knowledge creation moreover essentially depends on individual and organizational learning. Again, stakeholder involvement as described in the concept of 'responsible corporate governance' appears as a means for those learning processes.

One may conclude for a governance structure that it should stimulate learning processes, including private research and development (R&D), above a level that might be perceived as optimal. Exploitation of existing knowledge is one side of the medial, exploration into the unknown the other. By necessity, these learning processes are undertaken de-centrally by individuals within organizations or networks. The more importance policy places on precautionary measures and innovations, the more important become such processes of individual, organizational and social learning. Guidance and rules developed by collective action in networks appear as a means to regulate those processes with least-cost bureaucracies. It is also to be concluded that quality of public goods should be monitored separately, and governance structures have to create the pathway through which such information finds its way into those learning processes.

One can add one additional category of market failures, which has become an essential part of economic policies since mid the 1980s and 1990s: natural monopolies. Their characteristics lie in indivisibilities as well as in permanently declining average total costs, resulting from large investments in their establishment compared to low costs for running the system. Well-known examples are the electric grid and the railway system. The strive for deregulation in the 1980s and 1990s resulted in cost reduction and innovation on the one hand, and additional problems on the other. Sometimes it was overlooked that natural monopolies had close ties to public goods and externalities, namely regarding security of supply and safety. After discovering these mistakes, a wave of 're-regulation' (Majone, 1998; Héritier, 2002) has started, most notably in the European states. This re-regulation takes the course of opening markets for those parts that can be considered mainly private goods, and establishing standards and other forms of regulation for natural monopolies in the narrow sense.

Looking at market failures overall, the conclusion for governance of sustainable development is that to function properly markets need not only appropriate institutions, but also participation and learning processes among and beyond market actors. If markets' efficiency is to be maintained and improved, and if responsible corporate governance is to play a major role, markets need incentives for stimulating participation and learning. Nobel laureates such as Douglass C. North (1990), Mancur Olson (1996) and Joseph Stiglitz (1998, 2000) would support our conclusion, which is generally supported by New Institutional Economics and the German Ordnungspolitik (Ahrens, 2002; Grossekettler, 1997; Mantzavinos, 2001). The Japanese tradition of 'administrative guidance' (*gyosei shido*) also entails wisdom towards that perspective (Bleischwitz, 2003b). Following the new dimension of environmental change from Chapter 1, the new challenge is to stimulate continuous participation and learning processes rather than undertake heroic efforts and set an everlasting frame. Such co-evolution of responsible corporate governance, other actors and different rules will lead to more dynamic processes for coping with information and adaptation deficits than the traditional division of labour, where governments were supposed to determine the structural conditions and businesses to comply. This conclusion is particularly relevant when complexity is high and a variety of actors need to coordinate their actions.

Recent theories on government failures have yielded similar findings. Beyond the often too simplistic general view of public choice theories, it makes sense to assume that self-interest is an important motivating factor for politicians and bureaucracies (Buchanan and Musgrave, 1999; Olson,

1982). Most politicians strive for re-election rather than long-run problem-solving; this is particularly true in political systems characterized by low stability and corruption (Rodrik, 2000). Bureaucracies tend to look for maximization of their budgets and power, which does not necessarily coincide with fulfilling their various tasks. Regulatory agencies are exposed to the lobbying of powerful actors, leading to the 'capture of the regulator' phenomenon (Dixit, 2000). Clearly, control is the best check to self-interest and capturing endeavours. Such control may come from parliaments, competing parties and other levels of policy-making (for example the European Union – EU), newspapers, non-governmental organizations (NGOs) and agencies for budget control. Too much control, however, increases the regulatory costs and can seriously hamper innovations and learning.

Government failures put the development of both markets and society at risk by:

- slowing down dynamics of progress;
- causing high regulatory costs ('deadweight losses');
- creating incentives for rent-seeking and lobbying activities that favour established interest groups against new businesses and small and medium-sized enterprises (SMEs);
- 'crowding out'[1] voluntary action and other non-paid civil activities; people rely on the government to take action and flinch from voluntary action even if public programmes turn out to be ineffective;
- causing new externalities created by unforeseeable market responses to any regulation;
- causing cognitive overload due to dense regulation;
- causing orientation deficits about the long-term direction of development beyond the usual uncertainties.

Ubiquitous information deficits suggest a departure from rational choice approaches that often underlie environmental policies. No matter how extensive the competences pooled in their various administrations are, governments hardly possess the knowledge to be able to steer business and society in a certain direction. They can acquire new knowledge through hearings, studies, expert committees and advisory councils. One may remember that the 'Global 2000' report to the US President at that time, Jimmy Carter, definitely had a severe impact on the environmental debate of the late 1970s and 1980s. The German Bundestag's Enquête Commissions were able to influence the climate change debate. Various councils of economic advisors play their role with remarkable success, though they sometimes feel upset with hard-headed politicians (see, for an insider story, Stiglitz, 1998).

A success story, at least in the long run, can be traced from observing the European Union. It can be regarded a miracle that after a World War and a long-lasting period of nationalism, a few countries started to transfer some sovereignty to a newly established body which was able to evolve over time and to attract many other European countries. Who would deny that European countries, after all, profit from burden-sharing and the internal market regime? Like the USA in the late nineteenth century, the mid- to late twentieth century in Europe has been a period of unification driven by some good governments. While it is certainly true that much needs to be done to reform European institutions, there will be no way back to a *status quo ante*.

Nevertheless, there is no occasion for any general optimism about governments' steering capacities. Moreover, public budgets are loaded with huge deficits, so financial capacities are low. Governments depend heavily upon knowledge generated in the decentralized activities of research organizations, companies and society. Governments' comparative advantage in knowledge generation can, rather, be seen in terms of setting a tentative institutional framework, arriving at a consensus where conflicts among different groups arise, and formulating an overall orientation based upon people's heterogeneous views. Overcoming knowledge deficits by acknowledging different roles and by setting incentives for knowledge creating is thus a key to improving governments (Dror, 2001; Rodrik, 2000; Pelikan and Wegner, 2003; Young, 1999). In the environmental debate, this has been stated by Berkhout et al. (2003); Bleischwitz (2003c, 2004); Harrison and Bryner (2004); Jordan et al. (2003).

Rather than praising the efficiency of market-based instruments in environmental policy, one should look at cross-cutting instruments with both legal and economic incentives (Bleischwitz and Hennicke, 2004). The legal system, for instance, can provide tools for change caused by courts' decisions. In particular the Anglo-Saxon countries have a strong tradition of law-making by courts, and to a lesser degree by governments. Such an evolution offers advantages of flexibility and regional diversity: courts can decide according to best available knowledge and regional contexts. In democracies, the rule of law is an essential aid to citizens and SMEs in dealing with markets and governments (Nonet and Selznick, 1978). Relying on such an evolution of law is, however, a double-edged sword. The system demands many lawyers, and requires fees to feed them. Those fees may have negative side-effects on the rich and against poorer people who cannot afford a lawyer. A second disadvantage might be seen in information deficits (that is, high search costs) due to ever-changing laws. Flexibility comes at the expense of high transaction costs for the whole system.

Such risks should not be overlooked in any search for a comprehensive governance system. A putative shift to governance approaches will not make governments superfluous. How such a shift transforms governments, firms and markets will be analysed in more detail in Chapter 5. A desirable direction could be to control both markets and governments and to enable companies as well as citizens to participate in markets. 'Controlling' laws include legal regulation for markets, accounting procedures, liability of producers and individuals, mandatory reporting and measurement, and so on. 'Enabling' laws include different freedom of information acts, prosecuting laws for NGOs, and so on.

Our short summary confirms that bad governments produce bad market outcomes, while good governments can improve market outcomes. Just as market failures are a stimulus to improve markets rather than to give up the whole idea of markets, so government fallibility is no reason to give up regulatory policies. Two central government functions remain crucially important: (1) setting and improving a framework to counteract major market deficits with severe negative impacts on society; and (2) enabling a learning society. Both tasks are immensely complex and call for comprehensive governance structures at each level of society that actively involve corporate and societal actors. Such an involvement is not only necessary in terms of making the voices of interest groups and/or affected groups heard: it is fundamental in terms of learning and the coordination of networks. It is a permanent search for both market and policy improvements. Here, the concept of responsible corporate governance finds its place.

NOTE

1. The 'crowding out' effect has been analysed by Bruno Frey in the areas of social and environmental policies where governmental action may undermine civil or voluntary activities. See Frey (1997), Frey and Osterloh (2002).

5. Outline of governance structures: co-evolution at the meso-level

Raimund Bleischwitz

Our outline of governance structures starts from the conclusion based upon the previous chapters that corporate and political actors alike have a positive role to play in societies' development, not a negative one. These positive roles can be seen where firms provide goods and foster new technologies, and where governments guarantee the conditions for a fruitful and fulfilling life. Both functions are interrelated: markets rely on guidance and rules for which governments are indispensable; governments can only provide for the context of a fruitful life if markets serve their function too. At the same time, both players rely on civil society, whose positive role in development is evident.

Co-evolution refers to these positive roles (v.d. Bergh and Stagl, 2003; Bleischwitz, 2004). A market economy relies on a wide array of both market-based and political institutions that perform stabilizing, regulatory and legitimizing functions. Governance clearly takes place on multiple arenas, partly within and partly outside the scope of the state. The debate on multilevel vertical integration usually refers to governance within the public sector, across local, national and regional (European Union – EU) levels (Scharpf, 2001; Héritier, 2002; Hooge and Marks, 2003). Subsidiarity, which has become prominent as a guiding principle of the EU's Amsterdam Treaty, aims at doing policy at the lowest possible level within such vertical integration. Multilevel horizontal integration refers to the integration of policies such as environmental policy into other sectors (Lafferty and Meadowcroft, 2001; Persson, 2004). The meso-level is especially important here since it links the micro-level of products and markets with the macro-level of economies and states. The meso-level captures: (1) industries, value chains and international business operations; and (2) regions and efforts of regional integration.

Our book takes a view on governance at the meso-level according to which co-evolution and subsidiarity can tap the changing role of business and societal organizations. Such a governance structure needs to ensure that markets coordinate economic action properly within an institutional frame and at the lowest possible transaction cost level. Seen from this angle, the traditional dichotomy between market and state or between laissez-faire and intervention loses importance. Firms, markets and state serve complementary functions that keep the system running. A well-performing market economy is a mixed composition of state and markets. According to Metcalfe (2001, p. 579), 'it is the combination of institutions for selection and development that gives to capitalism its undoubted potential to change itself from within'. Langlois and Robertson (1995) on business institutions, Dixit (2000), March (1999), North (1990), Wegner (1997) and Rodrik (2000) formulate similar views.

According to Harvard researcher Dani Rodrik (2000), there are five basic types of market-supporting institutions that form a regulatory frame: property rights, macroeconomic stabilization, social insurance, regulatory institutions and conflict management:[1]

- Property rights are needed in order to provide incentives for both conservation and investment. Perhaps it is illustrative to compare cows and fish: cows will never become extinct because of existing property rights, fish species have become endangered because property rights are extremely difficult to administer. This example can be applied to houses, land, utilities, investments and so on. In this context, the freedom for contracts should also be mentioned. More recently, De Soto (2002) stresses the overwhelming importance of property rights for developing countries.
- Macroeconomic stabilization basically means anti-inflation policy: the control of money supply in the economy via an independent central bank authority.
- Social insurance is needed in order to protect individuals from unforeseeable risks of becoming ill or handicapped, to provide income for elderly people, and to bridge the income gap in times of unemployment. Despite huge differences among countries and ensuing needs for reforms, there is widespread agreement that governmental regulation should safeguard social insurances.
- Regulatory institutions are designed to balance market failures (see Chapter 4).
- Conflict management refers to the necessity of arriving at a societal consensus when preferences change or unexpected events occur that demand a decision by society as a whole. Conflict management presupposes that no benevolent dictator exists and processes of deliberation, painful redistributions and interaction among interest groups will have to be managed. This task is seemingly important for democracies.

In our context, conflict management relates to the participatory capacities of a society. Concerned citizens participate for example by political referendums on individual issues (as in Switzerland), by being involved in public hearings, by acting collectively as consumers, by taking part in stakeholder consultation, by pooling financial power on the stock markets, and through their ability to control information provided by businesses. An econometric analysis across several countries by Rodrik (2000) reveals that participatory politics does enhance economic stability. It is worth underlining that such stability is defined in terms of resilience, that is, the ability to adapt, and not in terms of sluggishness. Such resilience is an important feature of adaptive systems in order to respond flexibly to surprises, and to turn them into opportunities (Gunderson and Holling, 2002).

One can take the example of sustainability targets to illustrate the governance approach outlined here. The standard approach (for example of welfare economics) assumes a perfectly informed government able to set proper targets for the provision of public goods and for the internalization of negative externalities. It supports attempts to steer societies towards a predetermined outcome. Market enthusiasts, on the contrary, would claim that forces of supply and demand do the job; targets would intervene in allocation efficiency and might not be needed at all. In contradistinction, our governance approach considers target formulation as a learning process rather than a one-off event. Targets are relevant because businesses need to widen their set of choices; they have to readjust their expectations in order to search for new directions of innovations. People also need to reconsider their habits; they rely on communication in order to take other views into account. Hence, targets need to be made consistent among different policy sectors and among different arenas of action in order to improve overall clarity. Scenario methodologies (such as back-casting or constructive technology assessment) can be used for that purpose. In this sense, we propose that eco-efficiency increase by a Factor Four (doubling wealth, halving resource use) can serve as a strategic open target, able to be translated to the individual level of decision-making and, at the same time, serving as a goal for development without being fixed to a narrow schedule (Weizsäcker et al., 1997; Bleischwitz, 2003b). Because such clarity is essentially a learning process, the legally binding character of such target formulation can even evolve over time without hampering ambitions of sustainability. Setting sustainability targets in such a way seems especially relevant for areas where: (1) driving forces in society cannot be connected to specific impacts on the environment; and (2) new technologies need critical mass production in existing markets in order to overcome cumbersome technologies.

Another task can be added that also belongs to any governance architecture for sustainability: shifting taxes from labour to natural

resources. The explanation stems from the notion of externalities as introduced in the previous section. Environmental problems are surely one negative externality. At the same time, unemployment remains a concern in many
countries. It can be proposed to view unemployment as a negative externality, too. In both cases, the overall price level contributes to the problem rather
than solving it. Prices for using natural resources are, by and large, too low,
whereas prices for labour as a factor of production remain high because they
include various taxes and fees. In cases like the global commons, using nature
comes free of charge. It is therefore proposed, for example by the Club of
Rome, that taxes should be shifted from labour (where they are raised traditionally) to natural resources. Such a shift would provide incentives to ratio-
nalize the use of nature, and enhance employment. In doing so, the price
mechanism will facilitate the emergence of new markets and other problem-
solving activities. It will enable markets to discover new technologies and new
production processes (see also Clinch et al., 2006).

A question on eco-taxes relates to knowledge generation. Theoretically,
high prices for labour spur investments in human capital because of its high
return on investment. Would that change under a regime of eco-taxes and
lower taxes on labour, perhaps leading to a society on a rural subsistence
level? No, two reasons speak in favour of further increases in human
capital. Firstly, eco-efficiency and new technological progress heavily
depend upon new knowledge, which can only be gained by human creativity, cooperation and enhanced skills. Technologies and learning co-evolve.
Increasing prices for natural resources will spur investments in human
capital, too. Secondly, lower prices for labour as a factor of production do
not determine lower income. The playing field for income negotiations will
be enlarged, if tax and social security systems are redesigned in parallel. As
the employment situation can be expected to improve, more people are
involved in providing goods and services. They will improve their skills via
learning-by-doing, learning-by-using, learning-by-experimenting, and so
on. The knowledge society will be facilitated if taxation shifts from labour
to natural resources.

Seen from this angle, shifting taxation becomes an important principle
for industrial transformation towards sustainable development. For the
new policy areas of eco-efficiency and resource productivity, it is in the long
run as important as the other principles described in this chapter.
Instruments that are more specific to certain market barriers will add it.
Given that interest groups will fight for privileges and national differences
will remain (Backhaus, 1999), the introduction of eco-taxes will surely take
time. The principle, however, should be as clear as possible.

In order to safeguard stability, it will be wise to change taxes gradually.
The plea is for a moderate change, allowing businesses and administrations

to adapt. Such a gradual change might be in the order of a 3–5 per cent annual shift. It should include revenue neutrality or even a lowering of the overall level of taxation. The tax base should be rather broad. Besides taxing certain pollutants with low elasticity of demand (such as CO_2) or taxing energy sources, a taxation of raw materials should be considered. The rationale is partly based upon the necessity to innovate towards resource productivity, partly based upon recent developments in environmental research, which underline the 'material matters' issue with regard to resource scarcity, solid waste, landscape alteration through resource extraction, and emissions (v.d. Voet et al., 2003, 2005). While eco-taxes have become prominent in recent years, raw material taxes are just emerging. For practical reasons, they are raised on well-defined materials such as crushed rocks or gravel, and not yet on any aggregated resource index. Some examples have been analysed in Wuppertal Institute for Climate, Environment, Energy's (WI) latest study in the Millennium Collaboration Projects (Bleischwitz and Hennicke, 2004).

Our analytical framework stresses the importance of knowledge generation in and among different actor groups. Managing complex governance structures requires decentralized processes of knowledge creation, bringing forward a variety of actions within regions and the means to implement them. However, knowledge generation is not just the result of individual actions but also – and essentially – of organizations (such as research labs and firms). Further striking examples of how organizations shape the state of knowledge include the Millennium Ecosystem Assessment, the Intergovernmental Panel on Climate Change, and the World Business Council for Sustainable Development.

From a policy cycle perspective, topics emerging throughout these bottom-up processes can be picked up later on at a federal or at an international level when the need for coordination or harmonization arises. That becomes visible, for example, in the case of measurement methodologies and performance indicators on eco-efficiency, where a huge variety of approaches have emerged. Harmonizing those approaches now means that policy-makers can already rely on the practical experience of pioneers and early adopters. Their experience allows for selection of the most favourable solution. It also allows for setting either more ambitious and/or legally binding rules for the majority. Stakeholder orientation, thus, is not in contradiction to ambitious policies decided by the state (and/or respectively by the parliament). Our governance proposition is that whatever the teething problems, formulating sustainability targets endorses individual and organizational efforts to achieve clarity, which is a necessary prerequisite for reorientation toward sustainability. Governance of sustainable development can be seen as an on-and-off connection between political and corporate activities, where different stages of progress can emerge over time. Policy integration, as proposed *inter alia* by the EU's Cardiff process, takes place in multiple arenas, including those of firms and markets.

In addition to reforming structural conditions, any governance of sustainability will have to deal with manifold forms of doing business as well as with day-to-day policies of a wide variety of actors. Of course, this may include command-and-control approaches and other policies that restrict businesses in case of permanent non-compliance or high-risk activities. But governance also becomes relevant when long-term tasks like climate protection are to be performed, which require learning, technology development and change. For such tasks, the notion of 'innovation-inducing regulation' (Jänicke and Jacobs, 2002) is of interest. This type of regulation is not only conducive to innovation but also differs along with the specific developments in each case. It is based upon the notion of market failures (see Chapter 4) and the need to develop appropriate policy tools for each specific case.

One may ask, however, whether any regulatory approach towards innovation properly takes into account government failures and the side-effects of any regulation. Our approach proposes that flexibility remains important both for day-to-day operational decision-making and for long-term strategies. Flexible responses cannot completely be determined *ex ante* by any regulation. Even support of lead markets does not safeguard further dissemination later on. Public support for a certain technology always bears the risk of leaving aside other innovative solutions. Regulation should be rather flexible in order to adapt to the momentary phase of technological development while supporting the institutional setting. Any innovation-inducing regulation hence should co-evolve with corporate activities and the development of new markets for sustainability. In contrast to Jänicke and Jacobs (2002) who put great emphasis on political actors, we would argue the strength of governance as a stakeholder-oriented process at different levels of society.

Given the possibility of governmental failures, public support for innovation activities may even bear the risk of doing too much. This is particularly relevant when no immediate threats are perceived. Two examples from environmental policy may illustrate the risk of high transaction costs for such systems:

- In the UK, the environment ministry devoted 17 person years to negotiating 42 climate change voluntary agreements (in addition to the negotiation costs from their counterparts).
- In Germany, the emerging monitoring system for CO_2 tradable permits started with more than 50 staff members in spring 2004.

The general argument of 'high transaction costs with poor results' can, however, be counteracted with evaluation procedures (such as the one developed below) and a few arguments (Munton, 2003, p. 130): (1) that the incertitude associated with many environmental issues demands a wide range of knowledge be brought to bear on their management; (2) that the complexity and breadth of impacts requires integrated approaches, cutting across narrow confines of compartmentalized expert knowledge; and (3) that the concerns of environmental justice speak to the under-represented interests, including those in favour of nature and future generations.

According to our governance approach, any structure should entail more than technology support. It is about institutional change and capacity-building. Governance therefore is related to market failures as well as to the governmental function of absorbing societal problems, bringing together heterogeneous actors and arriving at solutions for certain problems. It should take into account that governments do not necessarily have the knowledge about what exactly can be done. They should draw business' attention to certain problems rather than telling them what they have to do. This is also relevant in the area of developing radical and systemic innovation (Geels, 2005; Weber and Hemmelskamp, 2005). Governments may help to establish win–win coalitions, but they should not (and cannot) specify what action should be taken. In our view, they participate in networks and other forms of multi-actor coalitions without being in a dominant position.[2] The phenomenon of 'entrapment' (Walker, 2000), where institutional commitments at different levels of decision-making lead to technological inertia, also favours co-evolution of regulation along with actual business development. Such an approach certainly entails elements of knowledge-creating competition. Policy-making hence shifts from policy-makers towards a multitude of actors including corporate actors and environmental and/or social non-governmental organizations (NGOs). Here, the concept of responsible corporate governance matches the requirements of co-evolutionary action undertaken by governments and by societal actors at various levels.

Coming back to the issue of adaptive flexibility and efficiency, this suggests using a two-pronged strategy of exploitation and exploration. Exploitation refers to trapping potential and systematic efforts to gain the efficiency benefits occurring through implementation of this potential. Exploration refers to processes of discovery and selection, which require openness and adaptive flexibility within an economy. Innovation, consisting of both technological and institutional innovation, is an element in both strategies. Incremental innovation of products and processes may come closer to the exploitation of potential and ensuing efficiency gains, while radical and systems innovation require exploration and adaptive flexibility. Certainly, any governance of sustainability will have to rely on both dimensions. Our book therefore assesses the ability of networks to innovate in both dimensions, exploitation of potential and exploration towards more radical change.

The promotion of technologies for renewable energy – analysed in the Wuppertal Institute's last study for the Collaboration Projects (Bleischwitz and Hennicke, 2004) – can illustrate the co-evolutionary approach to governance. Most policy documents agree that renewable energy technologies should have a larger market share than they actually do. Market advocates would argue in favour of 'let the market decide', whereas advocates of interventionism would perhaps like to see a public budget financing solar energy. Our approach concludes from both perspectives. It tackles the market deficit of monopolistic electricity markets with large utilities via fixed enumeration prices for producers of renewable energies, thus creating asymmetric competition in favour of new competitors. Those fixed enumeration prices lead to higher electricity prices, which have to be dealt with at the level of the utilities in their function as customer-oriented companies. If some utilities have to bear a higher burden (for example because of climate conditions), a compensation scheme can be agreed upon. What kind of renewable energy technologies will be developed at what location is almost completely up to the market, to local or regional governments, and specific demands. Over time, the enumeration fees will have to be reduced in order to avoid subsidies. The mechanism, however, leads to the emergence of new markets created by market forces and supervised but not determined by governments.

Figure 5.1 illustrates this co-evolutionary view of bringing together heterogeneous actors. It basically shows that sustainability policies and management develop through different stages, moving from immediate environmental problem-solving (stage 1) to institutionalization (stages 2 and 3) to low-cost, innovative and preventive approaches (stage 4). The conclusion for governance analyses is twofold. Firstly, each stage serves a certain function, and any institutional leapfrogging strategy may come at the expense of comprehensiveness and the non-emergence of major actors such as environmental industries. Secondly, any progress depends on co-evolution, not only on success in either policy or management. There is hardly a country in the world where eco-efficient services (stage 4 in environmental management in Figure 5.1) emerge without incentives being set by governments or, vice versa, where horizontal coordination among ministries and institutional adaptation flexibility (stages 3 and 4 in environmental policy) improve without support from vested or newly established interest groups.

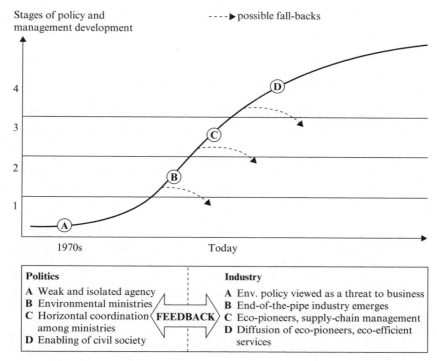

Stages of policy and
management development   ----▶ possible fall-backs

Politics		Industry
A Weak and isolated agency		**A** Env. policy viewed as a threat to business
B Environmental ministries		**B** End-of-the-pipe industry emerges
C Horizontal coordination among ministries	⟨**FEEDBACK**⟩	**C** Eco-pioneers, supply-chain management
D Enabling of civil society		**D** Diffusion of eco-pioneers, eco-efficient services

Source: Bleischwitz (2003a).

Figure 5.1 Co-evolution of corporate and political governance

NOTES

1. This is very similar to the German 'Ordnungspolitik', which can be seen as an essential driving force behind the German economic miracle of the 1950s and 1960s and one basic idea of the European Union; see for an overview Grossekettler (1997).
2. Our approach comes close to what is called 'transition management' as developed in the Netherlands by for example Rip and Kemp (1998) and being used by the Dutch government to 'manage transitions' to sustainable energy, mobility, agriculture, biodiversity and the sustainable use of natural resources. It is a model of goal-oriented modulation which is concerned with processes of variation and selection. Elements of this model include the use of strategic experiments, long-term goals, guiding visions, the creation of capacities for integration across horizontal and vertical levels, iterative and interactive decision-making.

6. Integrated systems analysis

José Acosta Fernandez and Stephan Ramesohl

In order to implement the normative concept of responsible corporate governance together with suitable structures of political governance, a practical concept is needed to make sustainability operational for business processes. Eco-efficiency and resource productivity, in this respect, provide hands-on tools which are compatible with the functions and practices of business and, at the same time, respond to the goals of the policy-makers at the macro-level. Moreover, eco-efficiency is a powerful concept requiring consideration of multilevel aspects and, further, a focus on the most relevant ones in accordance with the regional or local (social, environmental or economic) priorities. In doing that, eco-efficiency would take into account all environmental impacts and concerns of the relevant stakeholders willing to stir business practices towards sustainability.

The underlying idea of resource productivity is de-linking growth and environmental pressure, while eco-efficiency is more directly oriented towards reducing critical impacts on the environment (see the European Union thematic strategy on the sustainable use of natural resources, COM(2005) 670 final). Ensuing strategies assist in implementing and integrating economic and social risk minimization for companies, industries, economic areas and households. Benefits can be achieved by the delivery of competitively priced goods and services that satisfy human needs and bring quality of life, while progressively reducing ecological impacts and energy and resource intensity throughout the life cycle, to a level at least in line with the earth's estimated carrying capacity (Cowe, 2000).

Against this background an integrated systems perspective that focuses on the physical and societal as well as the economic sphere is necessary. While eco-efficiency strategies can be applied to products and processes on the company level, supply chain applications are also common, involving the upstream and downstream parts of the chain in the search for more efficient solutions. In physical terms, all stages of the transformation processes along the production chain, that is, from the very first raw material extraction to the very last treatment of waste disposal, are to be investigated.

In this regard, resource management expands to the existing approaches of systems analysis. The current state of energy system and climate policy modelling, however, hardly takes the material flow dimension into account. Being focused on single policy variables such as greenhouse gas (GHG) emissions or primary energy input, other environmental dimensions are still systematically neglected.

In this context, a broader discussion and more integrated analytical treatment of energy and material flows in needed. As a starting point for this debate, recent systems approach applications are illustrated. The next section deals with material flows as a part of the total resource flows of several nations, whilst the following section focuses on key elements required for constructing a nationwide sustainable energy system.

THE MATERIAL FLOW PERSPECTIVE

The economies of industrialized countries along with the efforts of the private sector have made great improvements over the past 30 years in material efficiency. The United States, Japan, the Netherlands and Germany have all reduced their total material requirement as a measure of gross domestic product (GDP) (that is, overall material intensity) by approximately 20 to 30 per cent between 1980 and 2000, according to a World Resources Institute co-sponsored report; 'Resource Flows' (Adriaanse et al., 1997, p. 14).

However, there are also signs that the change is not happening fast enough. The evidence shows that the total material requirement in Japan, Germany and the United States rose by an average of 27.7 per cent over the past 20 years, even in the face of the efficiency gains described above (Adriaanse et al., 1997, p. 12). This surely implies that the use of natural resource commodities may now be growing in parallel with economic growth. In emerging economies, which have more rapid growth trends, it is most likely that the picture will get even worse.

The even more hideous side of the picture is that hidden material flows[1] accounted for between 55 and 75 per cent of the total material requirement in 1991 (Adriaanse et al., 1997, p. 12). The implication of this finding is that significant dematerialization, in the sense of absolute reduction in natural resources, is not yet happening. Other sources also imply that the economy is now 'rematerializing', that is, the resource efficiency is decreasing per GDP instead of growing (Reijnders, 1998). In this sense, production-level efficiency improvements would not prevent losses from the natural capital unless they are elevated to product-level innovations.

The major contributors to the total material requirement (TMR) in the countries indicate varying areas of resource intensity. For example, in Japan metals and industrial materials contribute heavily to the country's total material requirement, reflecting strong automobile and steel sectors and construction. In the Netherlands, renewable materials are the largest contributor, while in Germany the high level of fossil fuel consumption is the reason for the high TMR level (Adriaanse et al., 1997, pp. 11–12). In this regard, some countries require initiatives for land use practice improvements, whilst some need energy efficiency schemes in order to reverse the trend.

A similar picture can be attained when material outflows from industrial economies, namely Austria, Germany, Japan, the Netherlands and the US, are analysed by a more recent study called 'The Weight of Nations' (Matthews et al., 2000). Even as decoupling between economic growth and resource throughput occurred on a per capita basis, overall waste flows into the environment continued to grow (Matthews et al., 2000, p. xi). Reductions in quantities of solid waste sent to landfills have been stabilized or have declined, in some cases by 30 per cent or more, though greater use of incineration as a disposal option has resulted in waste outputs being diverted from land to air (Matthews et al., 2000, p. vi).

A result derived from such analyses is that advances in a single life-cycle stage are not enough for the de-linking objective (Voet et al., 2005). Hence, product-level eco-efficiency improvements considering all impact categories, and as early as possible in the life cycle, are required. Business-level initiatives involving stakeholders along the product-chain gain importance in that respect.

ENERGY SYSTEM PERSPECTIVE

As well as the dematerialization of resource flows over the whole production chain, the overall energy input to the economy also has to be reduced. Although many links between the two spheres exist, material and energy flows used to be treated separately, both from an analytical perspective and in business practice, for example when accounting for production factors. While neglecting the indirect aspects of energy use in terms of the energy content of materials ('grey energy'), energy analyses tend to focus only on the direct input of energy, that is, on:

- the supply-side transformation of primary energy sources such as coal, oil or renewables to final energy carriers such as electricity, gasoline, and so on; and
- the demand-side transformation of final energy to useful energy and energy services such as space heating, mobility, lighting and so on.

In this tradition, the subject of energy has been discussed in the scientific and political arena for a long time. Due to the specific nature of energy infrastructures such as huge capital requirements, long lifetimes and a natural monopoly (for example in the case of grid structures), energy has always been an area of intense regulation and strong political involvement through state-owned companies. Politics and industry can build on comprehensive experience with methodologies, planning tools and policy concepts, and an extensive data basis. This allows for a systems analysis merging supply-side and demand-side perspectives in order to analyse the opportunities to achieve political goals of environmental protection and climate change abatement. The following example of a recent national scenario analysis for Germany illustrates the key elements of such a possible path towards a sustainable energy system.

A Scenario Analysis of a Sustainable Energy System for Germany

German climate policy is orientated towards the recommendation of the Intergovernmental Panel on Climate Change (IPCC) and aims at a reduction of GHG emissions of 80 per cent by the year 2050 compared to the base year 1990. In order to achieve such substantial contribution to climate change abatement, the coming years will be of strategic importance for triggering the intended long-term investment. From today's perspective, however, current development will most likely not be sufficient to pave the way towards a sustainable energy system. As illustrated by a synopsis of all the most recent major scenario analyses in Germany, little more than a stabilization of GHG emissions can be expected until 2030. When looking at the resulting mismatch between a 'business-as-usual' scenario and a sustainable path of GHG abatement, the question arises as to how to close the gap. What are the strategy options available that can be activated?

In order to grasp the scope of action and the variety of options, scenario analyses can make a valuable contribution to the policy debate. Scenarios provide a plausible and logically consistent set of parameters that are compatible to a predefined framework. Hence, scenarios do not deliver a forecast of how the future in reality will most probably look, but they provide a discussion on how the future could look like if certain assumptions become reality. Developed by Shell in the early 1970s scenario techniques are built on 'if–then' considerations. They are a valuable tool for strategic planning by companies as well as for the political debate on policies and measures.

In Germany, two recent studies are currently driving the energy policy discussion:

- Within the work of the Enquête Commission of the 14th German Bundestag, a comprehensive scenario exercise was undertaken.

Overall, 14 alternatives were calculated, each aiming at realizing the primary goal to achieve 80 per cent GHG emissions reduction in 2050 (base year 1990) (Enquête, 2002). The variety of scenario definitions reflects the wide range of assumptions that can be made concerning the future fuel mix, policy framework, and so on.

- The 'Long Term Scenarios for a Sustainable Energy Future' of the Federal Environment Agency (UBA, 2002) starts from the same analytical foundation and basic assumptions concerning population growth and so on as the Enquête Commission. The scenario analysis distinguishes a reference scenario and a sustainability path that leads to an 80 per cent reduction of GHG emissions by 2050 (compared to 1990).

The recent scenario discussion offers a multitude of different perspectives to develop the energy system and to mitigate GHG emissions, and the underlying policy philosophies might deviate substantially. A comparison of results, however, reveals a convincing set of common key findings that represent 'robust' criteria and options for policy-making. In the following, the two areas of electricity generation and the building sector are taken as examples *pars pro toto* for the strategic framework of a sustainable energy system.

Electricity Supply of the Future: Efficient, Decentralized and Widely Interconnected

Not only is economizing on electricity needed in a changed energy world, but its supply also has to change drastically. The unavoidable increase in electricity generation from renewable energy sources and CHP (combined heat and power) plants leads to a growing relocation of the formerly centralized generation of electricity to a more and more decentralized location near to the end-use applications. Intelligent control systems must ensure that these decentralized electrical power units are coordinated and conveniently fitted into the load management of the consumers (virtual power stations).

While natural gas extends its contribution of electricity supply in the mid-term, renewable energy sources will become the dominant factor not later than 2040 (in 2050 their share in generated electricity will amount to approximately 65 per cent, whereby all available options as well as the electricity import of renewable energies from foreign countries (for example offshore wind energy from the North Sea countries, electricity from solar thermal power stations in Southern Europe or North Africa) will be of importance). Large condensation power stations, which dominate today's generation of electricity, will play only a subordinate role in 2050. After 2030 sufficient scope for electrolytic hydrogen production will arise under these conditions because the generation of clean electricity will continue to grow.

These structural changes represent a historic transformation of the current energy system that can take place under favourable framework conditions. Due to regular ageing processes of the German and European power park up to 70 per cent of today's generation capacities will have to be replaced by the year 2020. This corresponds to a capacity of 30–40 GW; in Europe 200–300 GW are to be replaced by this time. The necessary replacement of German power stations expected by 2020 therefore offers a unique opportunity to minimize transformation costs and to direct investment capital efficiently towards innovative and forward-looking technologies.

Renovation of Old Buildings and District Heat Concepts: Characteristics of an Efficient Fossil-Regenerative Energy Supply

In all scenario discussions, heat demand for space heating and warm water supply represents a major variable for emissions reduction. Apart from the improvement in insulation standards of buildings, the sustainability scenario primarily requires a drastic increase in the renovation rate. Although 2.5 per cent of all existing buildings are being renovated on a yearly basis (for example façade renewal), only in every fifth case is an energy saving measure renovation completed at the same time. The specific reduction possibilities of 50 to 70 per cent can only be attained when there is a constant increase in the number of buildings, which are also optimized in terms of energy demand.

Comparable to the interconnection of smaller and medium-sized generators of electricity to virtual power stations, the sustainability scenario requires the expansion of intelligently linked local and district heating systems. This permits a number of efficient techniques and their individual advantages being combined in the best possible way. In the first step, efficient co-generation systems with fossil fuels can be the foundation for introducing renewable energy sources to a larger extent later on.

For the structural changes assumed in the sustainability scenario, it is necessary to distribute about two-thirds of the heat requirement reduced by 45 per cent over district and central heating systems by 2050. The restructuring of the heat sector causes the number of individual heating systems supplied on the basis of crude oil to disappear completely, and a strong decrease in those supplied with natural gas can also be expected. In the sustainability scenario the increasing share of district and central heating supply systems are based on fossil fuels, biomass, and solar-thermal and geothermal energy, with the remaining energy demand being covered by conventional solutions. The German settlement structure, with closed communities and relatively small properties, represents in principle a good starting point for the development of district heating systems. Nevertheless, the necessary measures will take decades to be implemented and will have to be introduced as fast as possible.

The Energy and Material Link: a Forgotten Dimension

Both examples from the electricity sector and the building sector point to close links between the energy system and the area of material flows. However, the energy and material link remains a rather under-represented dimension of systems analysis:

- The building sector is very material-intensive due to its raw material consumption. Both concerning new building concepts that increasingly incorporate renewable materials such as wood and straw, and with regard to the refurbishment of the existing building stock, energy-saving strategies will affect the material flow balance.
- In the electricity sector, too, a climate-friendly path will induce severe structural changes in the power sector. Type, number, location and primary resources of power plants are likely to change significantly.

From the overarching perspective of governance for sustainable development this leads to the important question as to whether the trends in the energy sector can be reconciled with the demand for dematerialization. Will energy-saving strategies lead to a win–win situation with less resource input? Is a power sector with high shares of renewable energy sources less material-intensive than the traditional utility business with a resource chain in the coal, oil and gas businesses? To what extent are advances in climate change abatement counteracted through environmental losses in terms of resource use?

THE NEED FOR AN APPROACH FOR INTEGRATED SYSTEMS ANALYSIS

Due to the fact that the various policy arenas currently tend to be developed rather independently from each other, an integrated approach is needed that offers the possibility to investigate the interlinkage and possible side-effects between energy and material flows and related policies. First, it should provide data sources and methodologies to analyse current trends and future perspectives of energy and resource use in order to specify upcoming problems and tomorrow's requirements for policy action. Second, integrated systems analysis and related modelling frameworks should allow for an evaluation and *ex ante* assessment of policy strategies and instruments. In this regard, systems analysis delivers the techno-physical foundation for (quantitative) analysis of institutions and policy settings. Tools for integrated systems analysis could be helpful in designing integrated resource policy approaches.

As one possible first step in this direction it appears to be useful to explore the material impacts of present energy and climate policy, that is, estimating the 'physical footprint' of climate policy scenarios, such as the recent work in Germany described above. In order to advance in this field a heuristic is needed that allows us to map the direct and indirect physical effects of the transformation processes on which our economy and society are built. Two aspects are of importance:

- An adequate representation of the socio-economic metabolism that covers both the real exchange of the anthropogenic sphere with the physical environment, and the network of interactions between the manifold components such as economic sectors, households, and so on.
- A proper estimation and analysis of the impact of changes in transformation processes that result from technical progress, growth processes, political interventions, and so on.

Physical Input–Output Tables as a Tool for Integrated Systems Analysis

In both terms, the concept of the physical input–output tables (PIOT) promises to make a useful contribution. Building on the rich work concerning monetary I–O tables, the concept of the PIOT has received increasing attention worldwide. Basically, a PIOT represents a conceptual enlargement of an I–O table by adding a sector of primary inputs (resources) and a sector for physical waste (outputs) emitted back to the environment. It is the specific feature of I–O tables that the various sectors of the socio-economic system are mutually linked through transformation coefficients. This allows the study of both direct and indirect impacts of changes in the structure of production.

For example, when decreasing the relative share of electricity production from coal-fired power plants, the impacts comprise reduced direct GHG emissions of the electricity sector, less intermediate input of coal from the coal mining sector, less demand for equipment and machinery in the mining industry and, thus, less demand for steel in mechanical engineering, less energy and resource inputs to the iron and steel industry, and so on.

Against this background it appears to be an interesting point of departure to take the electricity sector as an example. In order to describe the significant structural changes that result from the climate policy scenarios, it would be necessary to divide the sector of energy production and distribution into a feasible number of key processes, such as coal power, nuclear power, gas power, wind power, solar power and others. Correspondingly, the resource input, for example from the mining sector, needs to be differentiated. Moreover, for all these prototypical power technologies the mix of physical inputs from the other sectors has to be determined, that is, the 'recipe' of transformation or production. In this regard, a broad stock of data from life-cycle and process-chain analyses such as the GEMIS database could be used that provide interesting information on the material mix of a certain type of power plants.

Modelling Energy and Material Flows in Industry

Although quite some advances could be made in the field of analysing industrial energy use, here the important aspect of the interrelations between energy and material flows has received less attention (de Beer, 1998; Worrel, 1994). Regarding both the aspect of GHG emissions (Patel, 1999) and the energy content of material flows in industry (Enquête, 2002) a more holistic approach is needed.

With regard to the industrial sector, energy policy traditionally focuses on energy-intensive sectors such as the iron and steel industry. Considerable improvements in production technology could have been achieved and even further efficiency gains can be realized in line with coming investment cycles. On the contrary, steel processing sectors such as mechanical engineering are considered to be less energy-intensive due to their low share of energy cost in total costs. However, due to their position near the end of the production chain, these sectors can have a major impact on the domestic demand for energy-intensive materials like steel. Innovations in design and material use, therefore, can have a remarkable impact on industrial energy use and should be taken into account. In this regard, eco-efficiency represents a promising enlargement of the traditional focus of energy policy. With its emphasis on companies from investment and consumer good sectors it can provide an additional impetus for economizing on precious resources and materials with a high content of so-called 'grey energy'.

IMPLICATIONS FOR POLICY-MAKING

The further integration of energy systems analyses and material flow analyses, for example with the help of PIOT, promises to supply new instruments for assessing the macro-level. Research could give indications as to whether current trends in energy and climate policy develop in line with the requirements for a dematerialization of our economy. Moreover, insights can be gained about which sectors and supply chains are of relevance and, thereby, are most suited as dedicated target areas for action. When using the forward-looking results from scenario analyses for feeding tools such as the PIOT, it appears to be possible to:

- assess energy and climate policy strategies from an *ex ante* perspective; and
- simulate the effects of eco-efficiency strategies in the sectors that deliver energy technologies, for example when designing material-efficient wind turbines.

Progress has to be made in terms of a broader discussion of environmentally relevant policy issues from a holistic point of view in order to become aware of the interlinkages, synergies and conflicts between the various policy areas. This is one precondition to balance better the possible trade-offs between energy, climate and resource policies. So integrated systems analysis can contribute to enhance the consistency of the policy framework with regard to targets, priorities and regulations – a triggering factor for stimulating activities at the company level.

NOTE

1. This is the portion of the total material requirement which is associated with making those commodities available for economic use, but do not enter the economy themselves. Examples of hidden flows are rock and earth moved during construction, soil erosion from cultivated fields and infrastructure development.

7. Conclusions to Part 1

Raimund Bleischwitz

In contradistinction to many other approaches, our analytical framework welcomes the self-interest of business as a beneficent force. Business self-interest is not content with the exploitation of 'low-hanging fruit' but promotes the creation of new knowledge as businesses recognize changing market expectations and the resulting needs for market evolution. This is captured by the notions of 'responsible corporate governance' and 'knowledge-creating competition'. A cloud on this horizon is, however, that if profits fall short of expectations, business can always opt out of governance processes. The function of governance, thus, is to support processes of mutual learning, with governments in a strong but not dominant position. This function goes well beyond the usual compliance procedures.

Governance systems ought to level the playing field for corporate actors in their daily operations, leaving it up to society and markets to determine which solutions are discovered and how they are implemented. The provision of common goods and the internalization of externalities, usually thought of as core competences of states, may at least partly shift to co-evolutionary processes managed by corporate, societal and governmental action. Monitoring remains a public task, as does the provision and maintenance of a legal order that is able to deal with free-riders and serious non-compliance. But the general indication is that actors learn from their mistakes, and that further involvement of corporate and other societal actors is likely to improve governance processes.

States remain important not only for monitoring or coordination efforts, though. They also have a role to play in internalizing externalities, be it in the form of constraints on overusing the environment or be it in the form of support for research and development (R&D) and learning processes. In both regards it can be stated that the traditional dichotomy between 'either legal or market-based' instruments loses importance. Our approach calls for a next generation of analytical tools, cross-cutting policy instruments spurring innovation, creating new knowledge and adaptation flexibility of actors towards sustainable development. In that regard, Chapters 8, 9 and 10 will introduce networks as a possible meso-element of such governance systems. It will also seek to translate our governance approach into an assessment methodology, which will be used for analysing case-studies later on.

PART 2

Network analysis and evaluation

8. Overall approach and research premises

Thomas Langrock and Raimund Bleischwitz

In the preceding chapters responsible corporate governance was introduced as a new concept to analyse behavioural patterns of companies. It is the purpose of the following two chapters (9 and 10) to derive a methodology for the evaluation of the case-studies that are presented in Part 3. This methodology shall help to understand the new steering mechanisms that may emerge due to the adoption of the responsible corporate governance concept by companies and by policy-relevant networks.

In order to approach the subject the following chapters will analyse two research fields in the political sciences: evaluation research and policy network analysis. Evaluation research on the one hand has contributed much to understanding the impacts of policy interventions on many different policy levels (local, national, international). Policy network analysis on the other hand has been one attempt to conceptualize the empirically observed changes in the policy-making process since the mid 1980s.

It is important to bear in mind that our book puts companies in the centre of the analysis; more particularly, companies that adopt responsible corporate governance. The evaluation methodology will transfer the analytical techniques from the public policy level to the corporate level. In order to undertake this transfer the emphasis will be on analytical techniques and much less on theories that are related to policy network analysis and evaluation research. The evaluation methodology therefore rests on two very important premises:

- For the purposes of our book, the relationship between a company and its various stakeholders is assumed to be comparable to the relationship between public policy and various interest groups, corporate actors and so on (notwithstanding the unique possibilities of policy-makers in setting property rights and so on). This first premise makes the application of policy network analysis possible.
- The actions that companies undertake can be interpreted as policy-relevant processes or as policy-relevant outcomes. That is: (1) the

interactions within networks (including organizational features, contracts and so on) analysed here are assumed to be comparable to policy-relevant processes; and (2) the action plans, voluntary commitments and indicators are assumed to be comparable to the policy-relevant outcomes (policy interventions) on the various public policy-making levels. This second premise makes the application of techniques from evaluation research possible.

In the two subsequent chapters the terminology as well as the techniques of evaluation research and policy network analysis will be introduced. It is important to bear in mind that a complete review of all the techniques that exist in these two branches of the social sciences is beyond the scope of this volume and has therefore not been attempted. The presented approach has been chosen after a survey of the literature. The selection has been done with a view to the feasibility of application.

9. Networks, decision-making of companies and evaluation: concepts and terminology

Thomas Langrock and Raimund Bleischwitz

Analysis on policy networks is often used when it comes to conceptualizing new patterns of governance. Most often these new governance structures are subsumed under the heading 'governance without governments'. Unfortunately, the multitude of policy network studies has not brought forward one single approach but many different concepts. Various political scientists concede that as of yet the scholars cannot decide whether the policy network approach merely is a good tool for understanding the (fragmented) policy-making process, or whether the policy network approach has the potential to become a theory of the policy-making process (see van Kersbergen and van Waarden, 2001; Carlsson, 2000; Börzel, 1997). In fact it seems as if the least common denominator of all the studies on policy networks is the network metaphor itself: there are always *actors*, which represent the knots, and *links* between them, which represent the ropes.

VARIOUS DEFINITIONS OF POLICY NETWORKS

Definition 1. 'Governmental orientation':

> Policy Networks are new forms of government, which reflect a changed relationship between state and society. Their emergence is a result of the dominance of organized actors in policy-making, the fragmentation of the state, the blurring of boundaries between the public and the private, etc. Policy networks typically deal with policy problems which involve complex political, economic and technical task and resource interdependencies, and therefore presuppose a significant amount of expertise and other specialized and dispersed resources. (Kenis and Schneider, 1991, p. 41)

Definition 2. 'Informal interaction':

> Policy Networks are best understood as webs of relatively stable and ongoing relationships which mobilize and pool dispersed resources so that collective

(or parallel) action can be orchestrated toward the solution of a common policy. A policy network includes all actors involved in the formulation and implementation of a policy in a policy sector. They are characterized by predominantly informal interactions between public and private actors with distinctive, but interdependent interests, who strive to solve problems of collective action on a central, non hierarchical level. (Börzel, 1997, p. 5)

Definition 3. 'Resource dependency':

The term 'Policy Network' can be understood as a broad generic category with a great number of subcategories. Policy networks are clusters or complexes of organizations connected to each other by resource dependencies and distinguished from other clusters or complexes by breaks in the structure of resource dependencies. The term presupposes the existence of two main features, links and actors, viewed from a horizontal rather than a vertical perspective. (Carlsson, 2000, p. 504)

Based upon such weak grounds, our survey of various studies (Bressers et al., 1995; Weidner, 1996; Reinicke and Deng, 2000; Adrian, 2003; Smith, 1997; Marsh and Smith, 2000), which employed policy networks reveals a set of striking similarities concerning the understanding of actors as well as the links between them.

Actors in policy networks are always single entities; in many cases they are legal entities or sub-units of legal entities. There are usually public actors, non-state actors and private actors in the policy network. Some of the non-state actors act on behalf of members and most importantly these actors can have substantial steering and control capacity with regard to their members. The prototype of such so-called corporate actors are the German industry associations and the trade unions, which negotiate on behalf of their members the wages and salaries of the employees. It can be concluded from the research that our type of networks can be characterized as networks driven by heterogeneous actors with strong corporate involvement acting towards responsibility and public policy interests.

With respect to links there are also striking similarities between the different policy network approaches. Most importantly, all the links are characterized by the fact that they are non-hierarchical. That is to say, resources are distributed between the various actors so that one actor always has an interest in the resources of the other actors (resource dependency theory). These resources can be very different objects, as Table 9.1 shows. The distribution of resources and the mutual interest in these resources by different actors is labelled 'resource-dependency relations'. This labelling is in line with other scholars active in the field of policy network analysis (van Kersbergen and van Waarden, 2001, p. 38; Smith,

Table 9.1   *Examples of resources and different types of actors*

	Public actors	Non-state actors	Private actors
Examples	Ministries, local authorities, European Commission, German Bundestag, Committee on the Environment within the German Bundestag	Association of European Car Manufacturers, BDI, Greenpeace, International Organization for Standardization (ISO)	Private companies, foundations, individuals
Resources (examples)	Financial Resources (subsidies, financial support, tax breaks) General steering and control capacity (mainly legal authority)	Steering and control capacity (mainly with respect to members) Capacity to establish standards authoritatively Knowledge (particularly tacit knowledge)	Material ways of contributing to sustainable development through other means of production or consumption Financial resources Steering and control capacity (mainly with respect to clients) Knowledge (particularly tacit knowledge)

1997, pp. 41–7) and is well in line with recent economic analysis (Osterloh and Frey, 2000; Hart, 2003).

Resource-dependency relations can be very difficult to observe and in most cases they will certainly not be obvious. In contrast to that, the actual interactions between the actors can be observed relatively easily. Here the objects under scrutiny are the ways of proceeding, formal negotiations, informal meetings, legal procedures (for example veto power, voting, rights of access to information) and so on. These actual interactions can assume wide-ranging forms. On the one hand, they can be completely informal; on the other hand, they can be regulated through formalized rules of procedure. Of course, the new institutional economics literature is also of relevance here since it focuses on rules of interaction and on their transaction costs in relation to outcomes.

In line with the usual distinction between politics, polity and policy, the results of the interactions between the actors are labelled 'the policy' throughout this book. Usually this policy is laid down in a set of policy-relevant outcomes. From an economic perspective, these policy-relevant outcomes can be labelled as formal institutions (North, 1990, p. 4), that is, decisions, treaties, reports, standards or other written documents. Especially for networks, those outcomes often influence the decision-making of the actors involved. Other forms of network performance, be they learning processes, or be they more indirect or informal forms of coop-eration, will also be taken into account – our approach captures those processes by drawing upon recent findings on dynamic efficiency (see below) which is translated into a questionnaire.

One last distinction with regard to the prevailing typology of policy net-works should be mentioned. Sometimes policy networks are categorized according to their function in the policy-making process. Some authors exclusively use policy networks in order to analyse or conceptualize the process of policy formulation. Other scholars also employ the concept of policy networks for the implementation of policy. In contradistinction to those approaches, we emphasize the role of private actors in the formula-tion and implementation of policies. Therefore, our book looks at their function for networks and at the regional scale where – by their nature – the function of national governments is less important.

Evaluation research is the branch of the social sciences that develops techniques for the systematic assessment (evaluation) of all sorts of policy interventions or even broader governance activities. Research institutions, development projects and policy instruments can all be assessed using eval-uation techniques (compare Stockmann, 2000 for an overview).

Our book leaves aside all those evaluation techniques that focus on the causal chains that underlie the policy interventions – the so-called theory-based evaluation. This branch of evaluation research is theoretically and empirically much more demanding than those evaluation techniques that focus on outcomes and impacts of governance activities. Therefore it has been decided not to attempt its transfer on the company level. For the purpose of our book, the analytical framework for responsible corporate governance (Chapter 3) is a necessary device.

Our assessment approach will combine qualitative and quantitative methods and will focus on the concrete shape of the (policy) outcomes and the measurement of the impacts. The assessment approach presented here will include the standard categories 'effectiveness' and 'efficiency' of imple-mentation. These two evaluation categories are widely accepted by social scientists, economists and political scientists. It will further include the cat-egory 'relevance'. This category is very often included in the 'effectiveness' category; however, it was decided to separate the two because some reflection on the tasks is worth pursuing, thereby accepting the possibility of overloading agendas and administrations. Additional sections on the side-effects and on adaptation flexibility[1] will also be included, this increasingly being an accepted way of proceeding within the evaluation community.

RELEVANCE OF NETWORKS

Testing legitimacy to ascertain the relevance of any specific network is an approach that can be traced back epistemologically to Immanuel Kant's principle of universalization and to John Rawls's idea of action taken behind a 'veil of ignorance'. A legitimacy test for state measures is needed in order to assess the ability of self-regulation to correct deficits and to evaluate corresponding proposals. These require careful evaluation, because regulatory failures might be worse than market failures. Factors included in the scope of this test include (see Table 9.2) which specific problem is being addressed, which potential damage costs may be expected, and how

Table 9.2   List of criteria and questions for the assessment of cross-cutting governance approaches (I)

	Criteria	Questions
Relevance	(C1) Process of problem identification; Pressure to act	How and by whom is a relevant problem addressed? To what extent does a consensus about causes, effects, and the need to act exist? How urgent is the need for action seen from the actor's perspective? Does the approach address main actors? Is the process stakeholder-driven? Is the process used for priority area identification in line with other stakeholders' agenda? Is it in line with global or regional trends?
	(C2) Decentral solutions; Possibilities for compensation	Is there an obvious link with other policy issues, to whom the approach might add negotiated solutions? Does the approach include relevant groups of society? Does it lead to an exchange of (financial or other) resources, which is considered fair and does not lead to additional externalities?

great is the political pressure to take action. In this context it also makes sense to pre-assess self-regulation, that is, to determine whether social groups are able to negotiate solutions, and which mediating function the law or the state should assume in the process. Alternatively, referring to Ronald Coase (1960), assessment can address regulations to strengthen the legal position of particular groups if their articulation would promote decentralized learning processes, and if no immediate risks have to be averted. The legitimacy test usually privileges institutional reform over and above the establishment of new institutions, and thus may favour networks over regulatory interventions.

EFFECTIVENESS OF NETWORKS

If the results of the legitimacy test are positive, the next step is to assess the effectiveness of networks. Is there a clearly stated target with a clear analytical relationship to the specific problem calling for regulation? A verifiable goal is desirable in empirical assessment. Clear criteria for measuring success allow for observing how goals are reached over time, making it possible to downsize a network or any intervention as the problems in its remit are solved, and thus to prevent governance structures from growing ossified and obsolete. Where the target is not clearly defined, effectiveness can nevertheless be assessed by relating a baseline year to a business-as-usual scenario and a scenario of changes effected by the network. If several targets exist, the relationships among them have to be taken into account – including targets set earlier that entail activities with an impact on the achievement (or not) of new targets. Our assessment approach – as we see it – does not stipulate complete consistency in balancing conflicting goals, though fundamental inconsistencies are to be avoided.

While welfare economics certainly favours targets, evolutionary economics takes a sceptical but not hostile view of policy targets. Although Wegner (1996, p. 39) suspects that targets 'collide with all evolutionary ideas of economic order', it can be argued that evolution, however dynamic, has a direction. Eggertson (1997, p. 1197) similarly supports a process of economic policy development that includes the setting of targets. Meier and Slembeck (1998, pp. 84, 246) also subscribe to this view. The kind of open development that evolutionary economics calls for thus depends on a general orientation for which targets are useful.

To combat sceptical views, the assessment of targets also extends to possible measures and potential for reaching them. Does a given measure propel developments towards the target? Does it at least achieve a quantitative deviation from the norm or from a minimum target? Technically

Table 9.3   *List of criteria and questions for the assessment of cross-cutting governance approaches (II)*

	Criteria	Questions
Effectiveness	(C3) Targets and strategies	Are there clear and verifiable targets?
		How consistent are sets of targets in the relevant area beyond the case-study?
		Is the structure suitable for policy-relevant deliberations?
		Does the structure allow for stakeholder participation and interaction on targets and strategies?
		How consistent is time horizon of targets with appropriate policy-relevant action?
		Is there a defined norm or a baseline year?
	(C4) Target implementation	Is there a specific action plan with concrete measures?
		How can the targets and/or the action plan be related to individual action?
		Are there performance indicator systems?
		Are these approaches supported by written and continuously reviewed routines? Do these approaches entail a monitoring of costs (see C5)?

speaking, that involves bottom-up analyses that establish which solutions are close to market maturity. Grossekettler (1996, p. 548) describes these steps in assessment as the 'condition of impulse direction' and the 'condition of impulse strength'.

The assessment of effectiveness (see Table 9.3) involves two steps for weeding out inappropriate governance arrangements. The first step excludes obviously ineffective forms from further consideration. In a second step, the potential for self-regulation is reassessed. Following the Kaldor-Hicks criterion (Zerbe, 2001, p. 4.), which says that it is better for social groups to compensate each other than for a central authority to intervene, the possibilities of decentralized control are compared to the risks of any more central regulation. Does the new governance approach fundamentally limit market processes, and does it interfere more strongly with the decision-making power of organizations (for example associations) and individuals than is necessary for eliminating market deficits? This second step serves to smooth out obvious snags. The remaining approaches can then be ranked in a provisional order.

EFFICIENCY OF NETWORKS

Defining a normative criterion is the main problem in efficiency assessment. New institutional economics is just as sceptical as evolutionary economics when it comes to a static concept of allocation efficiency. In our view, however, this scepticism does not rule out efficiency assessments. Efficiency assessments should address transaction costs, learning processes and externalities. In our understanding of policy as a collective learning process, the dynamic efficiency of coordinated learning processes is more important than static allocation efficiency. In addition to static allocation efficiency, dynamic coordination efficiency also involves: (1) long-term effects of successive, incremental reforms; (2) radical reform (changes in the system); (3) generation of new knowledge about solutions that go beyond alleviating situations of asymmetric information; and (4) appropriate incentives from policy. The concept includes both actor initiatives and reactions from the social environment. Instructive background is to be found in Ahrens (2002, p. 98), Pelikan and Wegner (2003, p. 29) and Metcalfe (2001). The assessment category of adaptive flexibility (see below) also reflects this concept of efficiency.

An important criterion for assessing the efficiency of new institutions results from the standard function of reducing transaction costs (North, 1998; Nelson and Sampat, 2001). According to Dixit (2000, p. 148), policy should take care at least to prevent new or additional transaction costs when introducing new regulations, its goal being a stable system that reduces the insecurity often attached to interactions. Reducing information asymmetries between social groups is therefore a priority in this context. Measures ensuring that suppliers and consumers have equal access to information, and correcting the traditional asymmetry that is so detrimental to small and medium-sized enterprises, have the overall effect of reducing transaction costs in the economy. Admittedly, simply providing access to information is not enough; actors also need support in acquiring knowledge.

A further assessment criterion, the reduction of negative external costs, derives from the general function of institutions as constraints. A new regulation (in whatsoever form) that causes additional external costs is to be rejected unless a higher net benefit can be demonstrated. This criterion can also be applied when reducing external costs was the explicit purpose of testing an existing regulation. In this case analysis will determine which other external costs would be affected by a change in regulations, and which negative side-effects such a change would have. Methodologically the reduction of negative external costs can be assessed through economic analyses as well as empirical studies of the articulation of interest groups.

Since the psychology of perceived ownership and loss aversion leads to a disproportional articulation of potential losers, flanking analyses are essential.

External costs can be made to 'disappear' by shifting them geographically. National policy-makers and lobbying groups share an interest in shifting burdens, which then occasion costs in other parts of the world – an effect that needs to be borne in mind when researching economic systems and effects. To support longer-term improvements (Dixit, 2000, p. 148), analyses of the effects of any policy must identify where costs are being shifted, and estimate the extent of these costs. On this basis alternative arrangements can be devised that reduce burden-shifting through collaborative and compensatory solutions.

Part of the test should address the 'Delaware effect', a term that describes how a reduction of institutional constraints in one area or state puts pressure on others to follow suit.[2] The phenomenon is also described in terms of a 'race to the bottom', or alternatively 'race to the top', where positive effects on regions at the forefront of development are discernible (Vogel, 2000). Weak and stagnant systems in developing countries are characterized as 'stuck at the bottom' (Porter, 1999) in contrast to the strong and dynamic systems of industrialized countries. The potential pressure to reduce constraints is subsumed in the criterion of external costs, as this yields a logical evaluation. Relaxing regulations, we would like to argue, is legitimate where this does not cause new external costs or burden-shifting, and where it is the result of democratic processes. In such a context, lowering standards can be seen as a sensible way of exploiting a region's comparative cost advantages. However, if the reduction of certain standards causes new external costs or shifts them elsewhere, our assessment will arrive at a critical evaluation. Sykes (2000, p. 262) distinguishes social and environmental standards, saying that lower social standards generally do not cause higher external costs,[3] while lower environmental standards always do.

ASSESSMENT OF SIDE-EFFECTS (POSITIVE AND NEGATIVE)

The goal attainment evaluation has very often been criticized for its narrow focus on the achievement of the specified policy objectives. It has been argued that very often the interventions lead to side-effects that can positively or negatively contribute to the mission. Such negative side-effects are quite often called leakage effects. In addition to that there can be various side-effects, both positive and negative, that contribute to policy objectives that are not on the agenda of the intervention under scrutiny.

A further assessment criterion based on this principle is the stimulation of innovation, learning effects and competition. New regulations should be oriented to the medium rather than the short term, and aim for improvements that go beyond the technologies available in the market. Short periods of transition preclude the necessary processes of adaptation and distort competition in favour of a small number of suppliers. The 'knowledge-creating competition' model, in contrast, stipulates medium-term periods of transition that enable companies to test a series of hypotheses and develop specific capacities. Whether a new regulation stimulates competition is therefore an important sub-criterion.

A further assessment criterion deriving from studies on institutional change evaluates the desired scale and network effects of new regulations. These effects occur where a potentially high number of users are inter-linked; telephony is an obvious example. Centralized regulation is more likely to meet this criterion than decentralized regulation, so it should be carefully weighed against the advantages of decentralization. According to Sykes (2000, p. 259), harmonization generally proves advantageous where preferences are homogeneous, and where external effects need to be taken

Table 9.4   List of criteria and questions for the assessment of cross-cutting governance approaches (III)

	Criteria	Questions
Efficiency	(C5) Cost reduction	Is there a visible striving for minimizing overall costs? In what ways are transaction costs included? In what ways is there a reduction of external costs? Which damage costs does the approach try to address?
	(C6) Positive side-effects	In what ways does the approach spur incremental or radical innovation? In what ways are processes of diffusion enhanced? Are there tendencies for inertia in the network or is there a systematic effort towards openness for new ideas? What kind of benefits emerge (tangible and non-tangible assets)? To what extent can the approach exploit economies of scale and/or network externalities?
	(C7) Negative side-effects	Are there systemic leakages, which may lead to problem shifting? Are there incentives for free-riding? Are there new and additional negative externalities?

into account; Trachtman (2000, p. 337) and Berg (2000, p. 461) support this view. Conversely, decentralized solutions are to be preferred where preferences are heterogeneous and externalities can be internalized.

ADAPTATION FLEXIBILITY

Further assessment criteria on adaptation flexibility primarily address learning processes in organizations. Derived from findings on interactions between organizations and institutions (North, 1998), the category also takes up Metcalfe's ideas on adaptive learning in politics (2001). They help evaluate the institutional risks of 'capture of the regulator' by the regulated interest groups and similar processes. The assessment criteria described in the following address issues related to organizations. They are based on the assumption that networks, if they are to evolve successfully, have to understand the interplay between rules of the game and players of the game, and should react less to changes in relative prices. Following ideas developed in the context of responsive regulation (Ayres and Braithwaite, 1992; Nonet and Selznick, 1978), they focus on the activation of third parties that may be expected to have a strong orientation on the common weal (for example non-governmental organizations).

One important assessment criteria may be derived from theories according to which institutions have the function of facilitating action (Nelson and Sampat, 2001; Mantzavinos, 2001; Metcalfe, 2001; Rodrik, 2000). The principle of free implementation and choice of instruments should therefore guide the design of networks, with the diverse processes of market implementation always left to decide which technical solutions and associated services are developed. A 'blacklist' of banned instruments is to be preferred to a positive list of desired options, as it leaves more possibilities open. The principle of free implementation and choice of instruments should also govern certain markets. For example, although standards of supply may be defined for a regional economy or other economic area, their technical implementation will take different forms and shapes in different regions, taking account of regionally heterogeneous preferences and patterns of demand. In this respect, our approach goes beyond the traditional regulatory principle of allocating an instrument and an agent to each target (Grossekettler, 1996, p. 544). The reason for this departure lies in our understanding of decentralized learning processes as sources of new strategies for reaching any given target. Specifying the use of even one instrument would pose unnecessary constraints.

An essential criterion for assessing networks concerns the monitoring of any mechanism. This criterion however only applies to regulatory bodies that are, as Karl Popper (1987) put it, 'properly manned', that is, have the status of an organization. Examples are authorities supervising capital markets, regulatory commissions and authorities overseeing natural monopolies, as well as international regimes regulating global collective (or even public) goods.[4] Effective monitoring is vital where principal–agent problems arise, budgets are involved and regulation is needed to negotiate interests. Monitoring can operate through supervisory boards or similar bodies, budgetary controlling, auditing and accounting, and regulations on reporting. Generally speaking, *ex post* monitoring is less problematic than *ex ante* regulation.

Assuming that any network has to preserve sufficient leeway for flexible adaptation, we would like to discuss evaluation and review mechanisms as a further assessment criterion. Though the ideal is a framework that obviates the need to introduce process regulations in retrospect, it is only realistic to postulate a certain adaptive flexibility. Recent research on technical institutional change supports this view (Nelson, 2002; Nelson and Sampat, 2001; Mantzavinos, 2001; North, 1998). Adaptive flexibility allows for allaying teething troubles, tackling new obstacles and repairing defective framework regulations. Such a mechanism is essential for resolving conflicts of interest where a basic consensus on general principles needs to be reconciled with specific targets or regulations. Networks for managing conflicting interests, moreover, have to set up formal procedures for resolving conflict. An agent that is given powers and a budget to carry out the network's tasks can use a general mandate to establish appropriate mechanisms gradually, as Posen (1998) has shown in the development of money supply and monetary policy. Héritier (2002) discusses this in the context of the European Union. Assessment will have to pay particular attention to the periods of time, procedures and decision-making processes involved in evaluation and review.

A final assessment criterion refers to ideas on deliberation (Ahrens, 2002, p. 134), that is, rule development on the basis of articulation and the deliberation of proposals. Participation and transparency are assessed in networks, with the assessment of participation concerning individuals, organizations and new organizational structures. Formal participation of regulated interest groups harbours risks of ossification and collusion. Appropriate mechanisms of participation anchor a network in informal rules, and deliberative development takes account of clients' wishes – the mechanism is familiar from stakeholder consultations in companies. Internal participation reduces the risk of individuals being dominated by regulated interest groups. Transparency describes the accessibility of reports and information on individual decisions to outsiders. High transparency exists where the media and representatives of civil society are invited to voice their opinions. This increases the possibilities of

Table 9.5   List of criteria and questions for the assessment of cross-cutting governance approaches (IV)

	Criteria	Questions
Adaptation flexibility	(C8) Freedom and flexibility	Can relevant actors (network members) freely choose among a set of instruments? Is there sufficient flexibility to make investment decisions consistent with network aims?
	(C9) Evaluation and review	Is there a formal mechanism for evaluation and/or review? Does it include reviewers outside the network? Are there clear performance criteria that help to readjust the network?
	(C10) Participation and transparency	What mechanisms for participation and transparency exist? Are all relevant groups (affected parties) members of the network? Do public interest actors hold specific competences? Is the process open for new participants?
	(C11) Control	Which formal and informal control mechanisms exist? Is there a sufficient division of competences between controlling and controlled actors? What processes ensure independence and power of control over time? What sanctions are foreseen in case of non-compliance?

articulating the dissent and external knowledge that make up an institution's selection environment.

NOTES

1. For the purpose of the book, we will define 'adaptation' as the maintenance of functional processes in systems. Adaptation results from cognitive and institutional influences and is not limited to adaptation to the social environment. Flexibility refers to the depth and speed of adaptive processes. A high adaptive flexibility can therefore be characterized as the ability of a system to change quickly and thoroughly so as to maintain the functionality of its processes.

2. The effects of lax corporate law emerged clearly in the American state of Delaware. Neighbouring states adapted their regulations in a bid to prevent enterprises from moving away. State regulations on company reporting were tightened at a later date.
3. Exceptions are, for example, health and safety at work, where lower standards have a negative external effect on health.
4. Standard features of organizations include a secretariat, a conference of parties endowed with decision-making powers, and a number of standing committees on which the parties are represented.

10. Application to case-studies: approach and appraisal of results

Thomas Langrock, Raimund Bleischwitz and Bettina Bahn-Walkowiak

The case-studies will be approached in five steps that are derived from the concepts introduced in the preceding chapters. Obviously, the case-studies are different in character and therefore the authors of the case-studies were encouraged to be flexible in using the approach. The case-studies themselves are structured along the characteristics of informational and formal networks, that is, those networks whose focus is on information exchange come first, and the more intensive networks as regards formal relations follow.

Assessments are usually confronted by a lack of reliable and homogeneous data, which can be characterized as general (the availability of coherent data being the exception). Particularly if private and societal actors are involved, the question of data availability becomes crucial. For developing countries data gaps affect almost every field (from economic to social and environmental). Even in the economic field when some data are available, they are often not reliable because of the importance of informal sectors. Even for developed countries data gaps exist or data are not reliable (Bleischwitz and Hennicke, 2004, Chapter 5). Questions to be addressed in empirical studies are:

- Are the data sufficiently available?
- How can the data be compared in order to validate them?
- Can data availability significantly influence the content and validity of the assessment?

FIRST STEP: IDENTIFICATION OF THE MISSION

The identification of the mission is a necessary preparation for the identification of the actors involved as well as the evaluation. Obviously, the authors have to define the mission that they wish to focus on in their case-study. Therefore the first step helps to frame the issue under scrutiny in the individual case-study.

SECOND STEP: IDENTIFICATION OF ALL THE ACTORS INVOLVED, OF THE ACTUAL INTERACTIONS AMONG ACTORS AND OF RESOURCE-DEPENDENCY RELATIONS

Using qualitative policy network analysis the authors identify the actors (stakeholders) involved and the actual interactions between them. Usually, the starting point will be the interactions between the company adopting responsible corporate governance and its stakeholders. However, the policy network analysis can also be used to study interactions between the different stakeholders.

As mentioned previously, resource-dependency relationships are analytical constructs and therefore they cannot be observed empirically. The authors of the case-studies are encouraged to derive these relationships indirectly from their analysis of the actual interactions.

THIRD STEP: IDENTIFICATION OF THE POLICY-RELEVANT OUTCOMES

In the third step the policy-relevant outcomes that are results of the actual interactions in the network are enumerated. Policy-relevant outcomes can have very different forms: they can be contracts, voluntary commitments, decisions and so on.

FOURTH STEP: ASSESSMENT AND EVALUATION

Table 10.1 summarizes our assessment approach as introduced above and provides a list of questions that guide and structure the evaluation of networks.

FIFTH STEP: CONCLUSIONS AND SCORING CHART

To reach an overall assessment and to draw conclusions, however, the criteria need to be specified in more detail. A monetary evaluation of effects is highly difficult to model as there is hardly a sufficient basis of information

Table 10.1   *Indicative list of questions for the evaluation of policy-relevant outcomes*

	Criteria	Questions for Review
Relevance	(C1) Process of problem identification; Pressure to act	How and by whom is a relevant problem addressed? To what extent does a consensus about causes, effects, and the need to act exist? How urgent is the need for action seen from the actor's perspective? Does the network address main actors? Is the process stakeholder-driven? Is the process used for priority area identification in line with other stakeholders' agenda? Is it in line with global or regional trends?
	(C2) Decentral solutions; Possibilities for compensation*	Is there an obvious link with other policy issues, to whom the network might add negotiated solutions? Does the network include relevant groups of society? Does it lead to an exchange of (financial or other) resources, which is considered fair and does not lead to additional externalities?
Effective-ness	(C3) Targets and strategies	Are there clear and verifiable targets? How consistent are sets of targets in the policy-relevant area beyond the case-study? Is the structure suitable for deliberations? Does the structure allow for stakeholder participation and interaction on targets and strategies? How consistent is time horizon of targets with appropriate policy-relevant action? Is there a defined norm or a baseline year?
	(C4) Implementation	Is there a specific action plan with concrete measures? How can the targets and/or the action plan be related to individual action? Are there performance indicator systems? Are these mechanisms supported by written and continuously reviewed routines? Do these mechanisms entail a monitoring of costs (see C5)?
Efficiency	(C5) Cost reduction	Is there a visible strive for minimizing overall costs? In what ways are transaction costs included? In what ways is there a reduction of external costs? Which damage costs does the network try to address?

Table 10.1   (continued)

	Criteria	Questions for Review
Side-effects	(C6) Positive side-effects	In what ways does the network spur incremental or radical innovation? In what ways are processes of diffusion enhanced? Are there tendencies for inertia in the network or is there a systematic effort towards openness for new ideas? What kind of benefits emerge (tangible and non-tangible assets)? To what extent can the network exploit economies of scale and/or network externalities?
	(C7) Negative side-effects	Are there systemic leakages, which may lead to problem shifting? Are there incentives for free-riding? Are there new and additional negative externalities?
Adaptation flexibility	(C8) Freedom and flexibility	Can relevant actors (network members) freely choose among a set of instruments? Is there sufficient flexibility to make investment decisions consistent with network aims?
	(C9) Evaluation and review	Is there a formal mechanism for evaluation and/or review? Does it include reviewers outside the network? Are there clear performance criteria that help to readjust the network?
	(C10) Participation and transparency	What mechanisms for participation and transparency exist? Are all relevant groups (affected parties) members of the network? Do public interest actors hold specific competences? Is the process open for new participants?
	(C11) Control	Which formal and informal control mechanisms exist? Is there a sufficient division of competences between controlling and controlled actors? What processes ensure independence and power of control over time? What sanctions are foreseen in case of non-compliance?

Note: * This refers to Coase-type negotiation among actors, a possibility which can be seen separately from C1 (referring to a broader set of relevance criteria).

Source: Own compilation, based upon Bleischwitz (2005).

for calculating probabilities, yielding only approximations that are at best rough estimates. This is especially relevant for cross-cutting approaches. With organizations, on the other hand, some monetary evaluation is possible as certain relevant types of cost arise (fixed and variable costs, labour and material costs, investments).

Also, a lack of reliable data should be taken into account. The questionnaire entails ambitious criteria which may hardly be met with availability of data within networks where at least some processes tend to be informal. However, there should be an attempt to address data needs, to assess them and to express remaining gaps.

In an overall assessment, a scoring system (as shown in Box 10.1) that is visualized in a spiderweb graph can be used to compare different networks, with questionnaires to break down and specify the assessment criteria (see above). In our study, each criterion will be awarded four points determined through ordinal scaling, with a table to illustrate results such that a transparent evaluation of the pros and cons of a specific approach is possible.

BOX 10.1   SCORING FOR PERFORMANCE ASSESSMENTS

0 = no action / result
1 = low action / result
2 = moderate action / result
3 = above-average action / result
4 = high action / result

Fine-tuning and review methods as used in scientific policy consulting have proved helpful in this context. In the mid-term and beyond the scope of our book, a standardized matrix for performance analysis is definitely a possibility.

The following case-studies (Part 3) have been selected from our database on various policy-relevant networks with strong involvement of corporate actors. The meso-level is chosen for the reasons outlined in Part 1; it is also a follow-up to our previous study, which tackled selected regulatory tools from EU member states (Bleischwitz and Hennicke, 2004).[1] The sustainability dimension focuses on the environmental issues of climate change, energy and eco-efficiency, and resource management, while taking into account social and economic concerns. It should be emphasized that the focus is on facilitating innovation and learning, that is, not on restricting prevailing patterns of production. Following our approach it means that those networks have translated challenges of providing for common goods into missions for private actors. The case-studies are assessed with the methodology presented in Chapters 9 and 10. Each of the case-studies illustrates a typical network with certain characteristics, which can be summarized as follows:

1. ProKlima: a network of local actors on funding for local climate protection based in Hanover (Germany).
2. Ecoprofit: a decentralized network of various cities acting on local learning for integrated environmental technologies.
3. PIUS: well known as production integrated environmental protection, our case-study illustrates how small and medium-sized companies can cooperate in their efforts and how an agency can facilitate corporate action.
4. Eco-industrial parks: our case-study features those parks as networks for a horizontal integration among industries.
5. Energy+: a network designed to develop markets for energy-efficient appliances in Europe.
6. Responsible Care: a well-established network of the chemical industry tackling transboundary cooperation and change over time.
7. BP plc: the oil company has been innovative in introducing tradeable emissions permits among its various production sites and in shaping the policy agenda later on.
8. Dow Jones Sustainability Index: a rating agency runs a network and demonstrates how financial markets might shape the behaviour of large corporations.

NOTE

1. Udo Ernst Simonis has written a critical remark on that book, stating that bottom-up approaches ought to be taken into account. The two books now capture what he claims research should do: develop an assessment methodology and deal with policies from a micro- and meso-perspective.

PART 3

Case-studies on sustainability at the meso-level

11. ProKlima: funding for local climate protection

Stephan Ramesohl

MISSION

The proKlima fund is a climate protection fund that was established as a model of cooperative climate protection (global thinking) by combining management interests, consumer needs and local activities (local acting) in the region of Hanover. The scheme covers an area of about 20 636 km² with about 677 000 residents.

The proKlima fund addresses energy efficiency and greenhouse gas (GHG) reduction potential on the local level with special focus on private end users and public administrations. It aims at enhancing the implementation of measures that are usually hindered through a series of market barriers. Hereby, the scheme makes a contribution to implementing the national obligations under the Kyoto Protocol as a keystone of sustainable development. Its particular contribution can be seen in linking the global perspective of climate change to the scope of local activities, which is a prerequisite for success in this field.

ACTORS INVOLVED AND RESOURCE-DEPENDENCY RELATIONS

The proKlima climate protection fund is a public–private partnership formed by different local organizations in the Hanover region. Building on extensive activities in the field of integrated resource planning (LCP/IRP) during the mid-1990s, the fund was founded in June 1998 when the proKlima partnership contract was signed three years after the first outlines were drawn up (proKlima, 1999). The proKlima office also started operating in 1998. The term of contract of the proKlima partnership is effective until June 2006; the agreement will automatically renew for one year unless terminated.

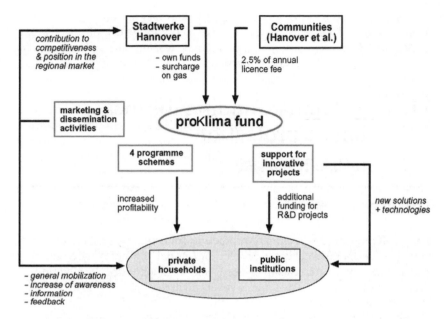

Figure 11.1   Organization and impact mechanism of the proKlima fund scheme

The fund members provide up to 4.5 million euro annually to support climate protection measures undertaken by their customers and citizens. The capital of Lower Saxony, Hanover, the surrounding towns of Langenhagen, Seelze, Laatzen, Ronnenberg, Hemmingen and the local energy supply company Stadtwerke Hannover AG/enercity are financing the fund (Figure 11.1). The corporate share amounts to 76.7 per cent of the total budget whereas the public share covers 23.3 per cent. Thereby, the majority of the fund comes from the Stadtwerke Hannover AG's previous year's profit and from a newly introduced surcharge for gas paid by all customers. The contribution of the municipal partners such as the City of Hanover, which ranks first among all municipal fund partners, is linked to the annual revenues from the license fee paid by the utility and is defined as 2.5 per cent of these payments.

In signing this nationwide unique partnership contract the Stadtwerke Hannover AG, the City of Hanover and the additional partners agreed on the goal for the proKlima climate protection fund: 'to support and progress monitoring of measures and third party projects . . . for climate protection . . . which otherwise would not have been realized or only in scaled-down extent due to a lack of (given) economic efficiency' (proKlima, 2001).

From an organizational perspective, three actors are of relevance. The proKlima board of trustees consists of representatives of Stadtwerke Hannover AG/enercity and of all municipal fund members. The advisory council is composed of representatives of all partners. Both committees decide together on individual projects and the setting-up of support programmes.

The proKlima office decides on plans within the framework of the public support programme. It is responsible for management and monitors progress of this climate protection fund. In addition, it cooperates with well-known organizations in conducting studies, so-called 'impulse programmes' and innovative projects. The office also participates in local climate protection activities via networking with the City of Hanover or the Greater Hanover Regional Association.

POLICY-RELEVANT OUTCOMES

According to its strategic goals, proKlima supports local climate protection measures that could not have been implemented without financial aid and for which the applicants are not obliged to pay. Furthermore, the fund aims at mitigating economically unacceptable costs of innovative projects that are not paid off by reduced energy costs.

Four public support programmes have been established:

- Energy-efficient modernization of existing residential buildings (for example better insulation, optimized windows, efficient ventilation systems, the use of co-generation, quality control).
- Heating energy conservation in new apartment complexes (for example ambitious low-energy houses, meeting the 'passive house standard' – 15 kWh/m^{2}a, quality control).
- Solar water heating.
- Solar energy and climate protection in schools, organizations and public administrations (for example solar panels for demonstration, educational material, measures to popularize the use of solar energy).

In addition, individual projects and promotion measures are funded each year, for example:

- Investment measures (for example hydroelectric power station, various photovoltaic projects).
- Development and research (for example scientific research to meet the 'passive house standard', development of the Energie Pass (low energy consumption certificate).

- Educational measures (for example qualification in the field of solar marketing, energy coaching in social institutions).
- Promotional and advisory measures (for example support of campaigns dealing with solar energy and insulation for existing houses).

An additional 200 000 euro p.a. is spent for promotion and the support of campaigns with other partners, for example: the 'Haus-Partner-Hannover' older buildings campaign is canvassing for optimized insulation on buildings and the 'Solarenergie Kommt!' campaign furthers the demand for the use of solar energy.

An additional programme for solar generation of electricity is on standby since the German Renewable Energy Act (Erneuerbare Energien Gesetz) was enacted in March 2000 and provides special support for electricity from renewable energies on the national level.

ASSESSMENT AND EVALUATION

Relevance

For the City of Hanover the commitment to climate protection plays an important role in order to meet their obligations within the framework of the Local Agenda 21 process. For the Stadtwerke Hannover AG the objectives are the following:

- Promotion of energy efficiency and back-up of its voluntary commitment to environmental protection.
- Better positioning ahead of other competitors in a deregulated energy market through promotion of regional responsibility and innovation leadership.
- Implementation of the 1996 declaration of the German corporate sector on global warming prevention imposing a voluntary commitment of industry to reduce GHG emissions.

The proKlima scheme enlarges the already ongoing activities of the utility in the field of market-orientated services and environmental actions. Since October 1999, for example, the Stadtwerke Hannover offers customers the electricity tariff 'enercity Strom & More' which includes electricity from cogeneration plants and a set of energy services, several of which are designed to enhance energy efficiency. There are some included in the tariff offered for free, and some for which rebates are given (for example a detailed individual on-site energy audit for domestic customers).

The fund is supported non-materially and with know-how by the Trade Corporation of Hanover, National Association of Energy Consumers, Consumer Advice Centre Lower Saxony, Citizens Action Group for Environmental Protection, Ruhrgas PLC and Thüga PLC (non-public shareholder of Stadtwerke Hannover AG). All partners signed the proKlima partnership contract.

The proKlima approach is characterized by the cooperation of various local stakeholders. This very fact caused some problems in the beginning and it took three years to find a cooperative model to combine the interests of all shareholders of the Stadtwerke Hannover AG, the license-granting municipalities and the lobbies for clients' interests. During the years to come, however, the common commitment stabilized the initiative under changing framework conditions. After its successful introduction proKlima was put to a severe test in 2000. Due to the deregulation of the German energy market the Stadtwerke Hannover faced difficult economic conditions. The company was forced to reduce expenses drastically. A consultant outlined a potential for savings of 45 million euro and advised the Stadtwerke to terminate the contract. In addition, the budget of the City of Hanover showed a deficit that jeopardized the financial support of proKlima. The fund came out of this conflict with a somewhat reduced budget but also with new strength and support by its stakeholders. To cut a long story short: the fund was created before the deregulated energy market, put into action in spite of the (beginning) deregulated energy market and, finally, continued because of the chance to achieve comparative advantages within a deregulated energy market. The concept has proven its efficacy even under the difficult circumstances of the deregulated energy market. It is able to prevail as all participants realize advantages:

- The Stadtwerke Hannover AG can give interesting offers to its clients and gain a credible and convincing profile concerning environmental issues.
- The City of Hanover fulfils a part of its commitment in the Agenda 21 process.
- The clients of the Stadtwerke Hannover AG/enercity and the people in the region gain on several levels, for example reduced costs, improved standard of living and value of buildings.

Effectiveness

Within the funding structure all project proposals are assessed with regard to the following criteria for supporting individual projects or establishing programmes:

- CO_2 efficiency (US\$/tonne of avoided CO_2);
- overall reduction of CO_2;
- multiplier effects;
- introduction of new technologies for climate protection to the market.

These criteria provide a flexible and sufficient framework for evaluating the project proposals without prescribing quantitative threshold values. In some aspects such as the eligibility of certain heating technologies, however, the practical application of rules for funding surpass the current standards in Germany, hereby contributing to advancements in the field.

In terms of internal monitoring and control, the fund is subject to a comprehensive financial audit as is common for any organization of comparable size and budget. Actual achievements and results are monitored and evaluated on an annual basis and published in annual progress reports. The financial structure of the fund is controlled and certified every year through independent certification bodies.

The proKlima fund generates a significant response among the target groups, triggering an increasing number of applications (2025 proposals in 2002, 1804 in 2001, 1015 in 2000). Table 11.1 provides an overview of supported projects from 1998 to 2002. Summing up, the following result of the activities of the climate protection fund can be derived:

- Overall reduction of CO_2: in the period 1998–2002 the granted measures led to a direct GHG reduction by about 38 944 t CO_2 p.a.
- CO_2 efficiency: putting the direct effects of CO_2 reduction in relation to an average duration of effects for a period of at least 10 to 20 years the efficiency amounts to about US\$20 per t of avoided CO_2 emission.

On account of the long duration of investment measures (at least for a period of 15 to 20 years, in some cases for more than 50 years) the annual reduction is increasing year by year on condition that the support by proKlima is continuing. After ten years this will be annually 80 000 tonnes and an accumulated 440 000 tonnes of avoided CO_2 emissions. To give an impression of the possible dimensions: the proKlima numbers projected on to the Federal Republic of Germany would give a budget of 550 million euros p.a. and 1 million tonnes of avoided CO_2 p.a.

Efficiency

The efficiency of the proKlima scheme can be judged with regard to the specific costs of GHG abatement induced by the funds. As mentioned

Table 11.1 Balance sheet of support 1998–2002 of the climate protection fund proKlima

Programmes	What will be supported?	Grants provided (euro)	Reduction of CO_2* (in t per year)	Approved applications
Renewal of existing residential buildings	Investments in insulation and efficient heating systems, 'Gebäude-Energie-Pass', quality control	7 050 000	13 900	4833
New buildings	'5-litre' and '1.5-litre' houses (passive house), quality control	884 000	410	825
Solar water heating	Solar panels for water heating	496 000	265	621
Photovoltaics	Solar panels for generation of electricity (until 2000)	147 000	40	22
Solar energy & climate protection at schools, organizations and public institutions	Solar panels, models, materials for teaching, further education and dissemination at schools, public institutions and organizations	685 000	Not quantifiable	136
Sub-total of public support programmes	Applications that were approved directly by the office	9 262 000	14 617	6437
Individual projects	Larger or smaller projects that were approved individually by the board of trustees and the advisory council	7 253 000	14 639	122
Water power	Hydroelectric power plants	1 779 000	8746	2
Completion of the long-distance heating system	Connection of 47 objects with overall power of 7.2 MW	546 000	942	47
Total		18 840 000	38 944	6566

Note: * Only as far as quantifiable; including the multiplier effects the general effect will be higher.

Source: proKlima (2003).

above, this aspect is one key assessment criteria in selecting project proposals. Referring to the – still limited – quantitative database of the first year's results it can be estimated that specific abatement costs are about 20 euro per tonne of avoided CO_2 emission when related to the lifetime of investments. In terms of investment impacts it can be estimated that each euro of programme funding induces an additional investment of a factor of 8–10 higher (proKlima, 2003). Especially with regard to the numerous other ecological, economic and non-monetary benefits of the measures, this can be considered a positive result.

From an administrative perspective the scheme is characterized by a lean structure. The proKlima office is headquartered in the Stadtwerke Hannover AG building and the part-time working staff of nine persons are recruited from the Stadtwerke personnel. Costs for personnel are less than 10 per cent of the overall budget.

Moreover, the majority of funds stem from the Stadtwerke budget and the surcharge on gas. This way, not only do the shareholders of the energy supply company contribute to the fund, but also the Stadtwerke's customers participate as consumers. The resulting additional costs per household amount to merely a few euros a month. According to recent surveys, the population in the development area accepts the surcharge because the money flows back to the region, and because they are able to take part in a considerable and recognized climate protection programme through 'their' energy provider and 'their' city.

Side-Effects

Besides reduced energy consumption and GHG emissions the measures undertaken induce manifold other environmental effects such as water savings, reduction of local air pollution, and the greening of urban housing areas. Furthermore, the initiative fosters qualification and innovation of industry and trade within the region, for example in the case of building constructors and installers.

Additional impacts can be expected in terms of:

- Introduction of new technologies: obviously the concept of funding by proKlima assists the introduction of innovations in the regional market as well as with the qualification of different enterprises. On the one hand this is caused by the standards required for funding, on the other hand by innovations and educational measures provided by proKlima itself.
- New investments and effects on the labour market: due to methodological difficulties we cannot provide exact figures concerning new

investments. In terms of effects on the labour market an economical survey dealing with the public support programme for 'existing buildings' 1998 and 1999 shows a total effect of 700 person-years (proKlima, 2002).

Adaptation Flexibility

The proKlima scheme is an offer to actors from the region. As long as the general principles of the scheme are followed, the funding rules provide sufficient flexibility to the investors concerning the choice and detailed outline of projects. In cooperation with the various stakeholders and market players in the field of clean energy, a continuous search for new activities, campaigns or modes of collaboration takes place. Whereas the formal and financial frame of the proKlima is contractually fixed, the content of work is a result of an ongoing process. However, in order to establish trust and acceptance among the target groups, reliability is a key. This means that programmes and procedures need to be valid for a sufficient time so that potential users and clients are given the possibility to accommodate to the scheme. Frequent changes in strategy or implementation practice would be counterproductive.

In terms of internal control, the mandatory requirements of good accounting have to be met, including an annual financial audit and revision through independent certification organizations. Moreover, the double supervision by the board of trustees and the advisory council provides a regular assessment of the technical content of work, for example when evaluating and choosing the project proposals for specific funding.

CONCLUSIONS AND SCORING CHART

Note: Numbers in relation to questionnaire, see Table 10.1.

(4) Strong Link to the Local and Regional Level

The proKlima fund is unique and exemplary in Germany and Europe due to the involvement of all essential local stakeholders (including the local energy supply company). All partners are bound to the partnership contract on a cooperative basis but show a strong commitment to secure the funding even in times of tight budgets.

With regard to the Stadtwerke Hannover AG the case illustrates the opportunity for a local utility to take up responsibility for an efficient use of its product, energy, and to investigate new business models in the area of energy services while supporting sustainable development within the region.

The initiative starts from a strong commitment of public actors to advance towards more energy efficiency and climate protection in the Hanover region. This impulse was the necessary precondition for the establishment of the public–private partnership that builds on voluntary commitment and involvement of stakeholders from the region.

(5–8) A Forum for Learning

The impact mechanism relies on two core elements. On the one hand, proKlima provides economic incentives to private consumers and public bodies to engage in climate protection measures. Hereby it affects the objective pros and cons of the alternative, and, in addition, triggers the subjective perception of pros and cons of the participants.

On the other hand, proKlima initiated widespread marketing campaigns in order to promote the scheme and its key message of local climate protection. It contributed to increasing knowledge about already available, market-proof options as well as about innovative approaches to reduce energy consumption and GHG emissions.

Moreover, proKlima supports innovative ideas and has provided the ground for testing new concepts and innovations. At least in the long run, therefore, the scheme has contributed to enlarge the set of options. It has to be taken into account, however, that the scheme does not focus on the classic production chain and its network of suppliers. With emphasis on the building sector it is rather directed to the end users and the professionals providing services to them such as installers, electricians, and so on. The major impact of proKlima can be characterized as the creation of a supportive milieu for motivated consumers to choose the best available technologies and to help them to perform their projects in a satisfying manner, for example through quality checks for building contractors.

(9) Applicability and Transferability

Due to its uniqueness proKlima has gained recognition in Germany as well as in neighbouring countries. A transfer of the approach, however, has not yet taken place although the model is replicable. The proKlima partnership contract demonstrates how – under the conditions of a deregulated market – the economic interests of the local energy providers, the public interest and consumers' interests are united in order to support climate protection effectively. Given comparable motivation and political commitment, therefore, a successful application in other countries appears to be feasible.

(10) Regulatory Context

When discussing the proKlima case it has to be taken into account that the fund is embedded within a multitude of energy-related regulations. In the building sector, for instance, the existing building codes and standards and resulting requirements for minimum energy performance in Germany clearly prescribe a need for action. The implementation of the European Directive on the energy performance of buildings will add to this momentum. In the field of electricity generation, several policy instruments aim at supporting generation from renewable energy sources of combined heat and power (CHP) plants. All these factors contribute to the motivation of market players, especially concerning the economic feasibility of investments.

Without the existing framework of regulation and policy incentives it can be doubted whether proKlima would have achieved the impact it has today. In this regard, the fund offers an opportunity for proactive and well-equipped actors to benefit from a policy environment. This holds for both the municipal utility as well as the project partners. All participants involved can be characterized as rather progressive and being placed at the innovative edge of the market. In other words: proKlima provides seed funding for best practice and it makes a contribution to the diffusion of innovation to early adopters. Large-scale dissemination impacts within the

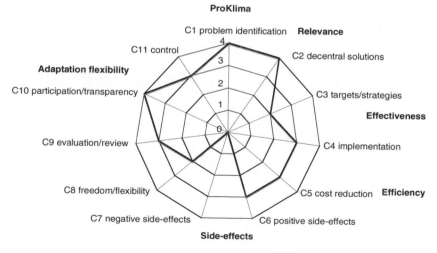

Note: 0 = no, 1 = low, 2 = moderate, 3 = above average, 4 = high action/result.

Figure 11.2   Scoring chart of proKlima

group of average consumers, however, cannot be realized with proKlima alone; the same holds for the ill-performing segments of the market.

ProKlima makes a contribution to enable market actors and consumers to respond to the intention of energy and climate policy. It enhances the readiness to act and increases the capability to act. Activities of this type can be seen as a necessary supplement to the policy mix.

The results of the proKlima case-study are assessed and summarized in the scoring chart in Figure 11.2.

12. Ecoprofit: local learning for integrated environmental technologies

Holger Wallbaum

MISSION

Various concepts for implementation of sustainable development are suggested such as, for example, corporate social responsibility, social accountability, Cleaner Production, Factor 4/10, Eco-Efficiency, management of resource flows, environmental management systems (for example the ISO-14000 series and EMAS), or Ecoprofit, which is presented briefly in this chapter. Ecoprofit is an excellent example of a stakeholder dialogue and it is earning an outstanding reputation across Europe. Ecoprofit is a simple yet highly effective methodology for cooperation between municipalities and enterprises, aiming at additional company profits and increased competitiveness through improvement of companies' environmental performance.

Ecoprofit stands for 'ECOlogical PROject For Integrated Environmental Technologies' and is an ongoing project initiated by the city of Graz, Austria, which attempts to offer small and medium-sized enterprises (SMEs) consultative and financial support in order to help them apply preventative environmental strategies regarding processes, products and services. Based on a cooperative approach between municipalities, companies and experts, Ecoprofit's core objective is to strengthen companies economically by the reduction of costs through the minimization of waste and emissions, in other words increased eco-efficiency. The project is an outstanding good-practice initiative and has been given awards by many European institutions for several reasons, for example:

- triangle cooperation between SMEs, environmental authorities and expert consultants;
- help for self-help for SMEs;
- setting up of an educational programme for SMEs;

- paving the SMEs' way to the ECO-audit;
- dissemination to other cities.

ACTORS INVOLVED AND RESOURCE-DEPENDENCY RELATIONS

The Ecoprofit methodology is based on a graduated plan, which consists of the Ecoprofit Academy, the Basic Ecoprofit Program, follow-up programmes and the Ecoprofit Club (Cleaner Production Center Austria), as illustrated in Figure 12.1. In a first step, consultants and representatives of local authorities are trained in the Ecoprofit methods – a variety of aspects in sustainable and eco-efficient management – via a Train-the-Trainer Program at the Ecoprofit Academy. The lecturers and trainers are selected from a pool of participants of ongoing Ecoprofit Projects (companies, consultants, local authority representatives, universities) – international experts complete the team. The graduates of the Ecoprofit Academy receive the necessary qualifications and authorization to manage Ecoprofit projects according to official guidelines; they become certificated Ecoprofit Project Managers or Ecoprofit Consultants.

After that, a Basic Ecoprofit Program is launched, in which the trained Ecoprofit Project Managers from the authorities will organize and manage the whole project, whilst the Ecoprofit Consultants hold workshops. To reach the targets of this first step, one year is the minimum required time. Experience shows that the shorter the Basic Program, the more difficult becomes the implementation in companies. Employees

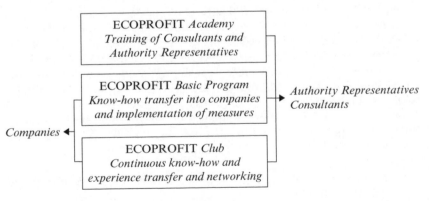

Source: Cleaner Production Center Austria (2006).

Figure 12.1   Ecoprofit's three steps

from companies of different sectors and size come together in monthly workshops. Candidates for the Ecoprofit Certification undergo a Basic Program of at least ten workshops. A single workshop programme covers a maximum of 15 enterprises. Each company sends a number of employees to participate in the workshop programme, which covers at least the following subjects:

- waste and emissions and how to avoid them;
- development of a company environmental programme;
- creation of a company environmental team;
- logistics of waste and environmental cost identification and evaluation;
- material and commercial aspects of waste reduction (analyses of material flow, energy flow, and so on);
- treatment of hazardous material;
- development of creative and innovative ideas and measures;
- environmental regulations;
- ecological purchasing methods;
- ecological controlling, best practices.

POLICY-RELEVANT OUTCOMES

The workshops are programmed to teach basic knowledge on cleaner technologies and production processes as well as additional organizational and management skills. The participants will be able to transfer the knowledge they acquire in the workshops into their company and its environmental team. The programme is fully based on a 'learning by doing' approach, making use of training material that has been developed.

After successfully having attended the workshops, the company is awarded with the Ecoprofit Label. In Austria, this is based on the criteria of the municipality of Graz: companies have to define their ecological performance, and write an internal ecological programme as well as an internal ecological policy. Additionally, the environmental authority of Graz performs a legal check.

Many successful implementations can be recognized during the Basic Program, but not everything can be optimized in this period. Thus, participation in follow-up programmes that concentrate on special and relevant issues is essential.

Companies that have attended at least the Basic Program can join the Ecoprofit Club that supports networking of experience and knowledge between the members. The Ecoprofit Club Program was developed to ensure the continuous development and implementation of new measures in participating companies and promote cooperation between companies, consultants and authorities.

The Ecoprofit native city is Graz, Austria. Meanwhile Ecoprofit programmes exist in many Austrian, German and other European cities and regions. There are some differences between the various programmes, but basic intentions and procedures are the same.

ASSESSMENT AND EVALUATION

Relevance

Although many municipalities gave their commitment to foster sustainable development on a local or regional level, not all can present verifiable results today. Despite this observation, the need for action is more urgent than ever especially under the current demanding economic conditions. The reduction of waste is – apart from the ecological point of view – an important economic issue, in particular in smaller countries with a high population density like Germany. The prices for land are quite high in urban areas, and perpetually rising costs for waste disposal in landfills can be observed. Incineration processes with the best available technologies as an alternative do not exist and/or are not profitable in all places.[1] This economic effect naturally stimulates the enterprises' interest in waste reduction through more efficient production processes. The need to find significant optimization potentials is more urgent in cases of highly competitive markets or products and in difficult economic situations. Under the recent demanding economic conditions, Ecoprofit consequently offers an opportunity for both municipalities and enterprises.

The objectives of Ecoprofit address the official and more or less quantified positions of the European Commission and especially some of its member states to minimize waste and emissions with a primarily output-oriented approach. Apart from the European and national positions, many municipalities signed the Aalborg-Charta and frequently set more ambitious goals to contribute to the challenges of sustainable development. Much too often the municipality goals are the result of a dialogical process with actors on this level instead of being based on EU or national objectives.

Small and medium-sized enterprises (SMEs) are increasingly regarded as an important target group of urban environmental policies as policy makers no longer underestimate their cumulative contribution to pollution. Although these companies generate relatively small amounts of waste, one has to pay special attention to these undertakings as they use many different hazardous and/or toxic substances in their production processes.

However, from the municipal authority point of view there is only a limited scope of action to influence SMEs in order to change their production patterns. With regard to the low degree of regulation or the lack of statutory instruments, and in view of the great number and variety of SMEs, local governments are adopting a cooperative policy style to a greater extent.

Ecoprofit helps the responsible environmental authority to put itself into a position from which it can facilitate preventative environmental strategies by mobilizing the technical expertise and entrepreneurial skills of the academic, business and industrial sectors. The close cooperation between public bodies such as municipalities or regional development organizations, private companies and external experts on a voluntary basis is characteristic for the implementation of Ecoprofit. Its success formula is based on its particular partnership approach between municipalities and companies, and networking between small and large enterprises of different business sectors. Partnership and networking produces synergies, which turn Ecoprofit into a public–private win–win methodology.

Effectiveness

The Ecoprofit's core objective, which is to strengthen companies economically by the reduction of costs through the minimization of waste and emissions, is clear, verifiable and consistent to political objectives. To achieve the objective the main impetus of the workshops is on increasing the knowledge of the participants. Nevertheless, the methodology is not based on a defined norm and apart from the core objective the implementation performance depends on the quality and the willingness of the participating enterprises and experts.

The implementation of necessary measures discovered during the single workshops can address all areas in the enterprise: management of resources, material flows, process optimization, energy, water, waste, mobility, and so on. Measures are accomplished regarding ecological and economical aspects, corresponding to usefulness and company priorities. Measurement plans for implementation exist in the form of worksheets that consist of checking lists and examples. They are not clearly structured but do serve formally as a foundation for projects. Concrete measures are always built up and transferred in cooperation with the company.

However, since the beginning of the 1990s, the methodology has spread mainly over Germany, Austria and Switzerland. Since its inception in Graz, Austria, in 1991, numerous leading businesses have successfully implemented Ecoprofit. Graz counts about 20 new participants every year. Companies having earned the Ecoprofit Certificate often join the Ecoprofit Club and continue to strive for increased eco-efficiency. So far, Ecoprofit is disseminated by municipalities who learn about this best-practice methodology at international conferences, study facts and then start its implementation. A number of European cities such as Vienna, Munich and Heidelberg have already opted for Ecoprofit as their environment protection scheme. In recent years, the Ecoprofit Academy has helped to spread Ecoprofit at an international level. Its goal is to advise and train future Ecoprofit Consultants from all over the world and to serve as a platform and competence centre for public–private regional eco-efficiency programmes to follow the Graz example.

The Ecoprofit Certificate improves the public image of the individual company as well as that of the region as a whole. Companies that achieve the environmental standards of the programme (significant reduction of pollution and implementation of environmental management) are awarded the Ecoprofit Certificate. They are allowed to use the certificate for marketing purposes for one year. The certificate is granted to the company and not to its products, that is, it is a certificate giving information on how the business is run, not on what it produces. After one year, companies will have to continue to participate in the ongoing activities of the programme and will have to implement further waste minimization and pollution prevention measures in order to gain re-authorization to continue to use the certificate. The criteria for earning the certificate are derived from the EU environmental auditing scheme (1863/1993) and they are modified for SMEs. The standards that must be achieved are as follows:

- 30 per cent reduction of solid waste;
- 50 per cent reduction of hazardous waste and air emissions;
- environmental capability in production and handling;
- transparency of internal and external information;
- compliance with all legal regulations.

Efficiency

The level of cost-efficiency of Ecoprofit certainly depends on the quality of workshops and on the experience of participating experts as well as on the competences of the business actors. Based on multiple workshops performed in the past it can be assumed that the instrument achieves its objective relatively cost-efficiently. The more the expert is aware of so-called 'best practices' closely related to the production process of the business case, the more he is able to support specific efforts. Nevertheless, the Ecoprofit results illustrate the economic range of different activities.

Ecoprofit addresses internal and external costs: the external costs result from measures taken by companies, for example regarding resources, waste, energy, water, and so on. The internal costs can be reduced for example by

Table 12.1   *Annual savings and one-time investments of the 123 measures assessable of the 24 participating companies upon project conclusion*

Amortisation category	Savings in €/a	Investments in €
Measures without investment	250 000	0
< 1 year	282 000	135 000
1–3 years	101 000	141 000
> 3 years	44 000	322 000
Economically not assessable	0	142 000
Total	677 000	740 000

Breakdown of measures by environmental fields

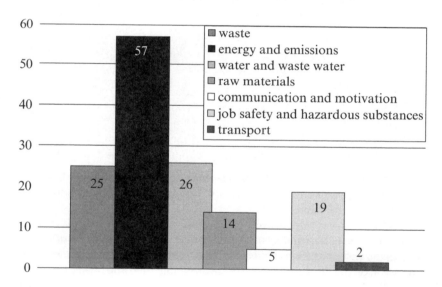

legend:
- waste
- energy and emissions
- water and waste water
- raw materials
- communication and motivation
- job safety and hazardous substances
- transport

Source: Ökoprofit Bergisches Dreieck, Auszeichnung 2001/2002, S.6 and 7

Figure 12.2   *Results of Ecoprofit in Wuppertal, Remscheid and Solingen (Bergisches Städtedreieck)*

increasing the social components: increased safety and motivation leads to fewer accidents and a decline in sick notes. Next to cost reduction, the results of Ecoprofit projects are mostly given as a reduction in the use of energy and materials and of waste, as these can be measured in absolute numbers. Table 12.1 and Figure 12.2 show the benefits for the 'Bergisches Dreieck' (the region covering Wuppertal, Remscheid and Solingen).

Examples for annual reductions based on Ecoprofit measures in other German regions can be described as follows:

- In Hamburg in 2004, 16 enterprises, reductions of 2 043 555 euros, 13 483 207 kWh, 3769.58 tonnes CO_2, 634.1 tonnes waste/raw material, 178 839 m^3 water/waste water (http://ffhhamburg.de/stadt/Aktuell/behoerden/stadtentwicklung-umwelt/umwelt/betriebe/oekoprofit/service.start.html).
- In Berlin in 2002, 20 enterprises reached reductions of costs by 275 000 euros, of 277 000 kWh energy supply, 120 tonnes of material, 16 000 m^3 water (www.oekoprofit-berlin.de).
- In Augsburg in 2003, 12 enterprises, reductions of 382 000 euros, 60 million kWh, 60 000 tonnes CO_2, 27 100 kg raw material, 21 313 250 tonnes waste, 60 million m^3 water (http://www2.augsburg.de/fileadmin/www/dat/04um/umanag/umweltvereinb_augsburg/pdf/Broschuere_2003.pdf).
- In Wiesbaden in 2005, 27 enterprises, reductions of 2.3 million kWh electricity, 4.2 million kWh heat energy, 31 000 litre fuel, 1630 tonnes CO_2, 384 tonnes of waste/raw material, 6668m^3 water, 677 241 euros in total (http://www.wiesbaden.de/loader.php?menue=die_stadt/umwelt/menue.php&content=die_stadt/umwelt/oekoprofit/erfolgsbilanz.php).

Many more cities and regions give similar summaries of their Ecoprofit programmes. There are also tables of enterprises with their respective reductions and invested money.

These figures are impressive but not easy to interpret: not all of these reductions can be attributed to the Ecoprofit programme, as several measures taken by the enterprises would have been taken anyway.

Most likely a few reasons are responsible for the success of the Ecoprofit methodology, expressed through the increasing number of participating enterprises. Ecoprofit provides a framework where business actors can broaden their knowledge while receiving financial support. Possible management deficits are set off through offered workshops with practical information materials. In general, the management should be aware of the opportunities for production cost reduction through the minimization of materials used and waste produced but the experiences of the 1990s tell another story. The management deficits on the emissions side depend more on the fact of lack of internalization of external cost effects. The new emissions trading rules will probably counterbalance these market deficits. This step is not observable for the input side. A shortage of the different ecological rucksacks of certain materials are often not reflected in market prices. As a result, prices do not give a sufficient incentive to take the necessary steps by business actors.

Side-Effects

As discussed in the second Wuppertal Report (Dalkmann et al., 2005), the implementation of taxes for certain resources could probably foster a more resource-efficient economy. Nevertheless, it has to be discussed further as to whether such implementation on a national level is good policy and feasible. Implementation is certainly more effective on the European level in an increasingly globalizing economy. However, the higher the institutional level, the more difficulties will appear while trying to form a political majority.

The Ecoprofit programme does not have an obvious effect on issues like individual freedom, free markets, employment, social security and social capital. A negligible effect can be assumed for the question of employment. The cost-reduction effects through resource-saving activities theoretically give the enterprise the opportunity to hire new employees or to save jobs in danger. Protagonists of the true theory of free markets will possibly make out a market intervention through the financial support by the state. This could be neglected because the Ecoprofit programme is a voluntary approach that is open to all enterprises.

The idea behind Ecoprofit is to create a methodology that helps to identify and realize classic win–win solutions. Companies benefit economically from implementing environmentally sound processes and technologies and at the same time improve the environmental conditions in the respective city or region. Both the companies and the municipalities share the profit, each of them in the area of particular interest. The main benefits Ecoprofit offers can be summarized as shown in Table 12.2.

The international network of Ecoprofit participants counts more than 1000 companies so far with a worldwide increasing number of cities and regions. It offers knowledge transfer to the participants as well as international market opportunities.

Whether the Ecoprofit programme spurs innovation within an enterprise also depends on the framework mentioned. Regarding organizational innovations, separate workshops specializing in this issue are offered. An enterprise can certainly support an innovation process through establishing a specific innovation team. Unfortunately, the available reports on finished Ecoprofit activities do not explain the success of launched

Table 12.2   Benefits of Ecoprofit for enterprises and municipalities

Ecoprofit benefits for enterprises	Ecoprofit benefits for municipalities
• Reduces employment of working capital, raw material, auxiliary material and energy • Enhances transparency of cost structures and processes • Prepares the implementation of environment management systems such as EMAS or ISO-14001 • Fosters motivation and teamwork • Supports accomplishment of legal requirements • Honours companies with the 'Ecoprofit' award and integrates them into the project-related PR activities • Creates partnerships between enterprises and public bodies • Offers joint training programmes	• Improves the environmental conditions for inhabitants of the region • Provides competitive advantages to bring in international investment • Saves expenses for ecological recovery • Improves the image of the region • Attracts visitors and tourists • Prevents environmental pollution • Improves the municipal infrastructure • Helps successful businesses to create local employment

organizational or implemented technological innovations. One may argue that a more input-oriented approach probably stimulates an innovation process more than this primarily output-oriented approach. In the case of Ecoprofit it is more likely that best available technologies and organization models, at least at the beginning, have been transferred from company to company rather than innovations having been implemented. However, at the time an input-oriented view is also part of the Ecoprofit programme so that innovation can be stimulated easier.

By analysing internal production processes, inefficiencies are discovered and thus necessary measurements can be developed. These measurements are very different in the various participating companies and so are the resulting innovations, ranging from small technological or organizational to big technological or organizational innovations. In the first years of Ecoprofit technological innovations prevailed. Now enterprises with low-technological equipment take part and therefore in that area organizational innovations outweigh. Mr Holzner, responsible for Ecoprofit at the Cleaner Production Center Austria, estimates that in total about one-quarter to one-third are organizational innovations.[2]

Whether tendencies of inertia during the programmes exist strongly depends on the personalities of consultants and participants. The fundamental content and structure of Ecoprofit, especially in the Basic Program, is fixed. The Basic Program consists of workshops in cooperation with the participating companies, homework (data capture, practicable changes in companies, collecting employees' opinions and suggestions for improvement, publicizing the project internally), regular meetings and social events. Due to the great amount of new information and of new tasks, there is not enough time in the Basic Program for extensive innovative ideas.

In order to satisfy efforts towards innovation, companies can and should participate in follow-up programmes. The system of these programmes is quite similar to the Basic Program: they consist of workshops (4–6), but the content is flexible and builds up in agreement with consultants and participants. Working groups on special subjects are formed.

Another possibility is to join the Ecoprofit Club, a union of companies that have participated at least in the Basic Program. At present, the Ecoprofit Club Graz counts about 50 active members and about 85 per cent of Ecoprofit companies take part in it. As Mr Holzner says, the club is a 'productive field of new ideas'. It results in increased communication between the companies: they meet at the workshops, get to know each other through consultants or communicate via telephone or e-mail without interconnection by any project leader.[3]

Besides innovations gained by companies, there are also other benefits of an ecological and economic nature for companies as well as for municipalities. Ecoprofit starts a learning process in which companies change their behaviour regarding eco-efficiency and municipalities change their role and become more practically oriented. Thus, the cooperation between these two main actors improves and a better mutual understanding evolves. Another additional benefit for municipalities is Ecoprofit's support for accelerating the Local Agenda 21 processes.

Adaptation Flexibility

The Ecoprofit programme could very easily be adapted to new conditions by changing the workshop contents or adding specific issues dealing with emerging problems. The workshop materials have to be revised under new conditions and the expert has to train himself, for example for modified limiting values. However, the programme does not yet provide an explicit formal adaptation process.

In some cases, the Ecoprofit activities of an individual business actor are involved in overall business strategies. This depends more or less on the business objectives, which are set up by the top management. In harsh times the top management tends to adjourn the so-called 'green activities' in order to concentrate on the company's main business. Unfortunately, they often forget that saving resources is profitable business in itself. This is even truer in harsh times when new customers do not invest in articles apart from real basics.

The Ecoprofit Commission, consisting of cooperation partners (city/region) and other related experts, evaluates all measures that are successfully implemented by the participating companies. In Graz, these experts are for example representatives from the Chamber of Economics, Chamber of Commerce, University of Graz, Chamber of Labor, consultants of STENUM (a consulting company based in Graz) and the Cleaner Production Center (CPC) Austria. In total, the commission counts about 10–11 members, but mostly 6–7 members take an active part. The members change frequently, though most institutions are fixed.

In addition to the evaluation, no specific control mechanisms exist. There is always feedback from the companies in the workshops, but it is regarded as informal and not really as a control mechanism. Nevertheless, steady contact and flow of information exists between the participating consultants, companies, project leaders and the CPC.

In principle, the CPC would do a separate evaluation if there were concrete demand, but usually this does not happen. Due to the close relationship to consultants and the possession of all resulting reports, the CPC has a good overview of the projects. This is necessary because in Austria Ecoprofit is a trademark and therefore special quality control has to take place. Additionally, the City of Graz once ordered an external evaluation about customer satisfaction. According to Ms Engelhardt from STENUM, the results were excellent.[4]

The number of companies partaking in the workshops is limited to about 15. The canvassing of new participants in Graz is done by STENUM and the Department of Environment. They address companies with problems regarding environmental issues as well as the 'Leading Companies of Graz', which are regarded as very innovative. Also, companies consider the selection process as transparent. However, direct inquiries by companies are rare. Therefore, it is difficult to reach the minimum number of participants which lies between eight and ten.

In the beginning of Ecoprofit, predominantly manufacturing companies were addressed. Meanwhile services enterprises, banks, schools, tourism companies and so on also participate. Thus the company size also varies extremely: the smallest company in the Ecoprofit programme of Graz, a pizzeria, counts five employees; the biggest, a car manufacturer, about 5000.

Ecoprofit is most suitable for medium-sized companies with a number of employees between 100 and 500. Therefore, only specific fields from major companies are taking part in the workshops. In order to cope with the special requirements of small enterprises (different legal regulation, production plan, and so on), a 'Micro-Program' is in progress now.

CONCLUSIONS AND SCORING CHART

The main interest of enterprises is the reduction of costs that may arise from changes in the production process. In order to support these business efforts new models of cost controlling are probably necessary, implementing cost and material flows within the production process. A successful approach in this direction has been started with the CARE project, a joint cooperation between several SMEs and the Wuppertal Institute (www.oekoeffizienz.de). This general motive has its variations in different firms. The interest in programmes like Ecoprofit and PIUS is especially great when problems are established or ideas for improvements have already been formed. These programmes help enterprises to develop a broader basis or in other words an enhanced knowledge for decisions that have to be taken. This leads to a higher capacity to act, which could simultaneously be an advantage for the economic interests of the enterprises as well as for other stakeholders, as in the Ecoprofit case.

The most pressing problems are seen in the fields of waste production and treatment, hazardous substances and energy (Evaluation Report Munich, www.sustainability.at/oekoprofit/; Umweltbehörde Hamburg). Concerning energy, however, there seems to be no potential of cost reduction especially for high-energy-using enterprises as they (or some) have very good contracts with energy suppliers.

Important for enterprises is the consulting (the view of a neutral consultant from outside) and the gaining of information. Furthermore, good contact with authorities is of use; firms are interested in non-bureaucratic treatment.

So-called multiplicators have great influence on the decision for participating in Ecoprofit, such as talks between business people, chambers of commerce (IHKs), RKWs and other associations that make information available and organize meetings.

Mr Holzner and Ms Engelhardt consider Ecoprofit as an additional measure of companies; they suppose only about 5 per cent of projects would have taken place anyway or are seen as image gain.[5] Many companies might think about realizing theoretic approaches, but without Ecoprofit those measures probably would never be carried out. This is Ecoprofit's problem: the acquisition of newly interested companies.

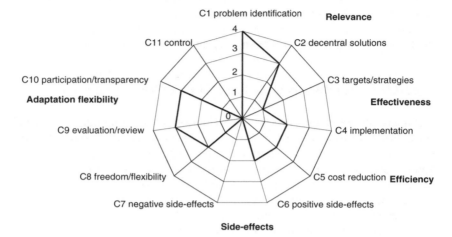

Note: 0 = no, 1 = low, 2 = moderate, 3 = above average, 4 = high action/result

Figure 12.3   Scoring chart of Ecoprofit

It is considered difficult to convince companies of the benefits of Ecoprofit.

Both experts saw some other optimization potentials regarding the overall organization as well as workshop contents. For example it was stated that it is necessary to build up one coordination centre that handles all inquiries from interested persons, municipalities, regions and so on from different countries. So far, no international contact coordination exists; the Cleaner Production Center Austria will take this role in future.

Furthermore, an entire data bank for the German-speaking region is planned. Data banks of measurements of single Ecoprofit programmes already exist and the CPC Austria is presently planning the set-up of a complete data bank.

Also desirable is an enhanced exchange of international experiences through the Ecoprofit network.

The content of the workshops is considered appropriate, but improvements are always possible. Considered examples are:

- update of the contents within the workshop topics;
- use of latest didactic methods;
- intensified employment of experts for certain topics;
- use of EPD-supported technology;
- better marketing strategies.

There are plenty of suggestions, but they can be seen as an optimization of an almost optimal programme. The main benefit of Ecoprofit must be regarded as the improved communication between municipalities and companies.

The scoring chart in Figure 12.3 summarizes the results of the Ecoprofit case-study in a spiderweb graph. This evaluation method gives a visual overview of the specific values of the 11 criteria alongside the five categories as introduced in Chapter 10 and thus facilitates the comparison between the different networks. It should be noted that the ordinal assessment of qualitative results involves some uncertainties that will be discussed in detail in Chapter 19.

NOTES

1. For ecological reasons an input-oriented approach to minimize the waste production is more favourable.
2. Interview with Mag. C. Holzner, Project Manager, Cleaner Production Center, Austria.
3. Interview with Mag. C. Holzner, Project Manager, Cleaner Production Center, Austria.
4. Interview with Mag. G. Engelhardt, STENUM, Austria.
5. Interview with Mag. C. Holzner, Project Manager, Cleaner Production Center, Austria; interview with Mag. G. Engelhardt, STENUM, Austria.

13.   PIUS: production integrated environmental protection

Holger Wallbaum

MISSION

PIUS is the abbreviation for 'production integrated environmental protection' or, in German, 'ProduktionsIntegrierter UmweltSchutz'. While most people use the term in this sense, it is simultaneously used for 'product integrated environmental protection'. This is a slightly different approach by focusing not only on the production process but also on the qualities of the product (environmental performance, durability, recycling ability, degradation ability) and primary products.

PIUS has been discussed at least since the early 1990s as a desirable alternative to end-of-pipe-technologies in industrial production. These measures had a great effect on environmental standards in the 1980s and led to a substantial reduction of air, water and soil pollution but produced high expenses at the same time. The integrated approach on the other hand (clean technologies) has the entire production process in view, aiming at the optimization of each step in a complex system. It is at the same time able to lower costs by the reduction of resource use (energy, water, raw materials), decrease of waste production and the use of new technologies. Thus, the use of PIUS gives the chance of an increase in competition capacity.

Magazines, professional associations, unions and public authorities have been treating this subject since the 1990s. For example, PIUS was made a major topic for prevention of environmental pollution from industrial production in the support framework of the German Federal Ministry of Education and Research (BMBF) in 1994. Many projects were conducted by producing enterprises and/or research institutions, and PIUS is now part of the economic studies of several universities as well as of international research projects (BMBF protocol with Romania; German–Japanese PIUS Conference 2001).

ACTORS INVOLVED AND RESOURCE-DEPENDENCY RELATIONS

Today, PIUS projects are being promoted by several of the federal states of Germany (for example Bremen, North Rhine-Westphalia). In North Rhine-Westphalia (NRW), the most prominent PIUS project has its office in the Efficiency Agency (EfA) of NRW. Originally, it was an initiative of the Ministry of Environment in Schleswig-Holstein and waste management agencies (privatized public agencies), especially of hazardous waste, of five federal states and was subsidized for two years (1999–2001) by the German Federal Foundation for the Environment (Deutsche Bundesstiftung Umwelt). It is now supported by the EfA NRW, the Environmental Agency (LANU) Schleswig-Holstein (SH) and the Hazardous Waste Management Association (SAM) Rhineland-Palatinate (RLP). More than a dozen further cooperation partners also support this initiative in various ways.

POLICY-RELEVANT OUTCOMES

The central part of PIUS is the Internet Forum, an information pool of PIUS material (www.pius-info.de). It provides free access to project reports, industry sector manuals, fact sheets, seminar proceedings and literature and is continually being extended. There are also interactive services for information exchange and expert discussion. The PIUS Internet Forum is a good complement to the website 'Cleaner Production Germany' (CPG) of the German Federal Environmental Agency (www.cleaner-production.de), an information service for innovative environmental technology and federal projects in Germany. The Efficiency Agency of NRW is offering further support for small and medium-sized enterprises (SMEs) by finding consultants and sponsors and by integrating single initiatives in aggregated projects. The main tool for SMEs is the 'PIUS Check', an initial check of an enterprise to make a status quo analysis and find potential for improvements by PIUS measures. EfA finances 70 per cent of the consulting costs.

The target group for PIUS are small and medium-sized enterprises (SMEs) but the information material is also valuable to authorities, associations, innovation centres, universities and other research institutions.

ASSESSMENT AND EVALUATION

Relevance

For the development of sustainability, especially ecological sustainability in this case, efficiency is an important factor. Production integrated environmental protection is aiming at the increase of resource efficiency in production processes, that is, reduction of use of water, energy and materials. This objective is consistent with policies of all levels proclaiming resource preservation (raw materials, energy, soil, and so on) and thereby also with worldwide climate protection.

Damage as result of a wider distribution of production integrated environmental protection are possible but not probable; ecological charges may not be reduced, but shifted. The elimination of toxic parts of a production process may lead to higher use of water or energy and vice versa. First evaluations, however, show mainly ecological improvement for most environmental issues (Gege, 1997; WBCSD, 2000a).

An economic evaluation showing reduction of costs for ecological repair is still not possible due to the well-known difficulties of internalizing external costs for common goods like nature. The available figures in the literature vary about a factor of ten. However, the contribution of PIUS to minimizing the material input will reduce all outputs (not only emissions) and simultaneously the external costs. Following the estimations of Arthur D. Little (ADL, 2002), an ambitious eco-efficiency programme could lead to a cost reduction of over 60 billion euros per year for energy savings in enterprises in Germany without including only the external costs. The respective national and international reports for the Johannesburg Conference have emphasized the need for action. Besides the reduction of the worldwide human mortality rate, the protection of the ecosphere is the essential condition for sustainable development. All actors are called upon to cope with this challenge. Meanwhile the economy actors have also realized their responsibility or have been forced to by customers and capital markets (see European Commission, 2001), and have started acting proactively. The more enterprises go this way, the more pressure will be exerted on those who refuse to change.

On a national level the picture is complex. Ecologically sensible behaviour often leads to higher (economic) expenses but not necessarily to more customers and better competitive strength. Several 'eco-firms' have closed and were bought by 'normal' competitors. However, the reasons for their failures are many. It many cases, a simple lack of economic know-how led to false estimations of market and economic capacity. Today, most enterprises have learned their lessons and there are many examples of economy and ecology going hand in hand. Not only customers, but also capital markets, the insurance industry and municipalities honour more responsible entrepreneurial action today. Resource-efficient business is therefore profitable in many cases.

Incentives for companies to participate in the PIUS Check are rarely based on ecological aspects but predominantly consist in the possibility of reducing operating costs. Another conceivable reason is public pressure. In most cases, the PIUS Check has to be conveyed to the enterprises through personal conversation and by visualizing the advantages. External consultants who carry out the consulting part of PIUS acquire about 80 per cent of the participating companies.

However, despite starting problems, the PIUS Check is successful and this mainly results from the partial takeover of costs by EfA NRW. The concrete amount depends on the consultants' fee. Average consulting costs are quoted as about 6500 euros. EfA NRW takes over max 70 per cent or max 4500 euros. The remaining costs for companies range between 1000 and 1500 euros. Due to this moderate amount, the incentives for the PIUS Check can be called adequate. Dr Jahns, Director of EfA NRW, estimates that in retrospect about 50 per cent of the partaking enterprises would perform the PIUS Check even without any financial support.[1] By reason of the current difficult economical situation and low investments, the demand of financial support declines.

As PIUS only deals with internal processes, societal stakeholders are not involved; possible exceptions are the users of products. Dr Jahns claims that it can be called a success, when a majority of employees are involved.[2]

The benefits of communities from PIUS are:

- improvement of environmental conditions of the region, prevention of environmental pollution;
- close contacts to enterprises;
- improvement of the image of the region;
- competitive advantages (economy support, job maintenance);
- saving of expenses for ecological recovery;
- 'control' of enterprises (more information about environmental 'behaviour', data survey);
- support in realization of environmental laws.

Effectiveness

There are no definite objectives in terms of numbers and amounts. The reduction of negative environmental impacts is the aim of the described measures, but there is no set norm. A before- and-after comparison can show improvements in eco-efficiency. It is desirable that supporting authorities keep a record so that the development of a region is shown. Objectives do naturally vary from enterprise to enterprise. It might be a possibility to define overall objectives for a region, which would then give a framework to all cooperating actors.

Like the Cleaner Production programme launched by UNEP, PIUS is contributing to ecological sustainability. In comparison to the Cleaner Production programme, PIUS focuses more on the optimization of single processes for one product than the life-cycle-wide production chain. Another related issue worth mentioning is EMAS. Opinions about the difference between PIUS and EMAS diverge. One argument is that PIUS and EMAS are the same; the only variation of PIUS is that external consultants for moderate prices are called in. Another view is that the PIUS Check is worthwhile, even if EMAS is already realized. The advantage of PIUS is the technical analysis that leads to necessary measures. After the PIUS Check the companies also took other related measures, so that a greater sensitizing towards eco-efficiency can be achieved.

In order to ensure better and present support for interested companies, EfA NRW established four regional PIUS offices in Aachen, Bielefeld, Münster and Siegen. Their aim is the collection of results and the transfer of good examples into other regions.

However, PIUS does not concentrate on the development of regions but on different lines of business. Therefore various catalogues of measures for industry sectors like automotive, chemicals, glass or textiles are available. Furthermore, industry textbooks for selected sectors also give an overview (http://www.pius-info.de/en/pius_info_pool/branchenleitf aeden/index.php?tag102=br_leitfaden). These textbooks are optimized once a year.

As another practical guidance, the results of the PIUS Check can be made visible, and by partaking, measures in diverse parts of the company can be realized. The results from the PIUS Check are collected and presented to the public.

Questions about the suitability of PIUS for being integrated into political programmes were not answered concretely. The obligation was rather handed over to politics itself: because of the still small attention to eco-efficiency in politics, the use of PIUS for political programmes is problematic. Dr Jahns even stated: 'The establishment of EfA itself can be seen as a political achievement'.[3]

Support schemes of public authorities are based on Agenda 21. Financial support comes from different programmes of federal states, of the Federal Republic or the EU (http://www.efanrw.de/downloads/ publikationen/Tab.pdf). Generally, the extent depends on the number of enterprises taking part in the programme and on the kind of business and measures taken in the course of the programme. To give an example: in NRW 150 PIUS Checks were carried out in 2005–2006; another 100 are expected in 2007. The quantity and quality of changes caused by these checks are not recorded.

Thus, the question arises how enterprises can be reached. According to the RKW Bremen and EfA NRW a mix of enterprises are taking part in PIUS programmes, depending on individual interests, problems and contacts (for motives of enterprises see the section on 'Relevance'). There are also objections to partaking in PIUS that may lessen the success of the programme:

- One problem in partaking in the programme is the amount of time needed.
- The period of amortization of investments is important: it should not exceed two years. Small firms are more sensitive to these factors than bigger ones; the amount of time needed by employees as well as the amount of money for investments has more weight in a smaller business.
- Apart from that, a businessman has mainly his product and marketing in view. It takes an impulse to make him look at the whole production process.
- It is often necessary to break with long-lasting contacts, for example between enterprise and facility constructor (for example installation constructor or machine constructor).
- Generally, there is restraint in enterprises especially while no problems arise ('never touch a working system').

It seems to be difficult to reach enterprises, even through Internet information; technology transfer projects of universities claim it challenging to find interested firms (Schleswig-Holstein). Political actors support the instrument in different ways. Examples are the awards of a competition of the MUNLV NRW (Ministry of Environment and Nature Conservation, Agriculture and Consumer Protection in North Rhine-Westphalia), that generated a lot of media attention. There is also always some financial support by public authorities. The PIUS Internet Forum (www.pius-info.de) gives free access to relevant information for all interested firms and other actors.

Apart from that, the instrument supports the economic interest of the enterprises in reducing expenses; it directs the attention to resource efficiency and production processes and shows them how to use reasonable measures for public relations. These described support structures and public relations do help to make the concept of the ecologically sustainable economy better known. For the customer there is the chance to gain more information about products and sustainable production.

Efficiency

Partaking enterprises are interested in reducing costs, so they will rarely choose measures of which the amortization is not clear. The focus is on financial expense so that the 'lowest cost' may not be the optimal ecological solution. From a political point of view, the PIUS concept does not seem to be cost-intensive. PIUS is trying to spread and broaden knowledge on eco-efficient management within and between enterprises. The need for other probably more expensive political instruments like taxes seems to be low, at least in case of the partaking enterprises. However, the small number of partaking enterprises in total leads to the assumption that PIUS should be promoted in another way or (at the same time) other instruments may have to be chosen to stimulate more enterprises to behave as ecological responsible actors.

Public authorities do not have much means to provide either, but there may be organizational synergies not yet used. Theoretically, the optimization of a production process as a whole can initiate innovation (see MIPS in Ritthoff et al., 2002); practically it probably mostly spurs the achievement of the latest technical and/or legal standard.

As mentioned above, the main incentive of partaking companies is the reduction of costs. Drawn from the interviewees' experiences, PIUS has the potential of reducing especially the following internal and external costs. Internal costs: operational costs – costs for use of:

- water;
- energy;
- organizational costs (for example expenditure of time with officials).

External costs: reducing costs by:

- saving of resources;
- waste reduction.

In the period from 2000 to 2006, more than 360 PIUS Checks were initiated in NRW, and 152 companies have already adopted new and sustainable production processes. The total amounts of investments amount to 23.6 million euros, while the annual reductions in the production process are about 7.1 million euros. For all initiated PIUS Checks, total investments

Table 13.1   Facts of PIUS Check in North Rhine-Westphalia

	Already implemented projects	Long-term potential of all projects (estimated)
Number	152	338
Investments	23.6 million EUR	52.6 million EUR
Annual resource savings in production process	7.1 million EUR	15.9 million EUR
Annual resource savings in water	804 281 m³	1 788 467 m³
Annual resource savings in waste	11 329 t	17 928 t
Annual resource savings in energy	44.7 GWh	99.4 GWh

Source: EfA NRW (2006), p. 10.

of 52.6 million euros are expected. These will result in about 15.9 million euros annual reductions in production processes (http://www.efanrw.de/?id=90, 2006-09-28).

Side-Effects

Politically PIUS and similar projects are connected with the Local or Regional Agenda 21. It could be useful to organize programmes on a federal level. Nationwide consistency would allow comparability and transparent support structures for enterprises with several sites. The financial support for PIUS programmes mostly depends on the policy of the federal states, Federal Republic or EU; that is, it works on a given setting of policies and programmes. Legal regulations have to be favourable.

The partaking of an enterprise in a PIUS programme makes information available about the 'ecological acting' both for the enterprise itself and for public authorities. On this basis, cooperation such as in environment alliances of some federal states is facilitated.

PIUS does not interfere with individual freedom, free markets, employment, social security and social capital. Generally, resource efficiency can enhance employment, although there are no validated data. For an evident effect, however, it needs intensified activity in this field.

PIUS includes the assessment of best available technology (BAT). To optimize processes, in 70 per cent of cases, new production equipment has to be installed; the remaining 30 per cent can be described as organizational measures. Therefore, these improvements can predominantly be characterized as the diffusion of already existing innovations, especially regarding technology. One way that PIUS can exploit economies of scale is through its online portal where experts can communicate and exchange experiences. A negative side-effect of implementing modern technology is the additional costs for the necessary investment, though.

Adaptation Flexibility

PIUS is a very flexible, voluntary instrument for two reasons. As stated above, it has no defined objectives but works with the general directive that production processes should be optimized from an ecological point of view. Thus, it is open to any changes of law, of limit values, of knowledge. Secondly, it works with individual enterprises, giving them every freedom to find the optimal way for themselves. Two or three priorities are set and worked through. An external consultant forms necessary measurements regarding chosen topics for the individual company.

After 9–12 PIUS Checks have been completed, EfA NRW appoints an engineering office for evaluation. Their expert opinion deals with the successful implementation at the corporation level as well as with consumer satisfaction. The PIUS Check is most suitable for small and medium-sized companies with 30–40 and a maximum 1500 employees and one product line.

As mentioned above, each participant is free to find their individual solution. It is up to the respective enterprise to spot the possible improvements, choose measures and define the extent. It is merely necessary to reach improvements in environmental protection. Generally, all kinds of enterprises are free to use PIUS at any time. Financial support, however, is limited and is restricted to SMEs. As far as is known, enterprises are not forced to make anything public, but a commission of the sponsor validates them. External consultants in cooperation with the enterprise perform the initial 'checks' of the enterprises. Thus, PIUS is a voluntary instrument and consequently the initiators provide for no formal process for sanctions.

The objective of PIUS is the reduction of resources used for the production process without sanctions. In some sectors production integrated environmental protection is part of an overall strategy. Examples are 'Responsible Care' of the chemical industry and sustainable development programmes of the European aluminium industry (www.oekoeffizienz.de). It is then not officially a PIUS programme. The benefits actors are hoping for in working with PIUS are described above (motives of enterprises, interest of public authorities, see the section on 'Relevance').

CONCLUSIONS AND SCORING CHART

PIUS is a good flexible instrument for aiming at ecological improvement in production processes and is a good example of a responsible management system. It is easy to handle for improving production processes. Companies are able to focus on self-estimated relevant parts and reaching individual solutions.

It is not used by enough enterprises, though. However, enterprises are, as well as all other institutions, 'learning organizations'. Therefore, it is reasonable that not all enterprises realize eco-efficiency promptly, but it ought to be ensured that political regulations encourage more enterprises to become learning organizations. Results of the PIUS approach are hard to ascertain. In North Rhine-Westphalia more than 360 PIUS Checks were carried out in the period from 2000 to 2006.

It is necessary to reach more business actors with this programme. This could be tried by improvement of information and communication; communication between public authorities and business actors seems to be especially problematic. More incentives should be created (like profit-sharing financing, tax reductions and so on). If a verified publication would be a goal, the programme needs an obligatory manual and possibly an independent validation or inspection. Ecologically sensible behaviour over all areas must be secured. However, what is problematic is the initial acceptance of PIUS. Even though afterwards most companies are satisfied with the results, there is still a need to reach more companies.

A life-cycle optimization should be the overall objective. A shifting of problems (for example to other environment areas, other dimensions or other locations within a life cycle) should be precluded. A programme like PIUS is easily applicable in other countries. For practical use it seems to be important to instal a legitimate agency, which is accepted as being neutral by both public authorities and economy. The federal state NRW did this in establishing the EfA, which is widely accepted by enterprises.

Also for municipalities PIUS is a practicable key for improving eco-efficiency. They provide the necessary platform, especially by coordination and financial support.

Other potentials to optimize PIUS are not seen in the PIUS Check itself. However, present efforts are leading to contacting first businessmen and secondly engineers. This should secure financial backing of possible strategies. The possibility to focus on only a few thematic fields was regarded as a disadvantage of PIUS. Dr Herzog as a PIUS participant states that working through all relevant issues would be more suitable.[4]

Programmes in other federal states do not necessarily use the name of PIUS. In Hamburg, for example, it is called 'Enterprises for Protection of

Resources'. Furthermore there are other 'programmes' aiming at innovation processes in SMEs, like Ecoprofit and EMAS. The question arises whether these different measures (or systems) complement or rather supplant each other, or if this can be ignored because they lead to the same results.

Comparing Ecoprofit and PIUS, both programmes are implemented successfully in various European cities and regions. Though both are unique, many similarities can be seen. PIUS as well as Ecoprofit has the overall aim to improve eco-efficiency in companies.

Similarities can be discovered not only regarding goals and contents but also by looking at the problems they have to deal with. PIUS as well as Ecoprofit has difficulties in reaching enough interested companies to take part in the programmes. Most canvassing of new participants is done through personal contact. Another common statement is that in retrospect participants of both programmes are convinced of its usefulness.

Despite the similarities there are different advantages and disadvantages of the programmes. PIUS is very easy to adopt because it is very flexible and compared to Ecoprofit the initiation does not require a large amount of effort for coordination, training, and so on. During the process the work of the central authority consists in coordination of projects and financial support. The inclusion into specific individual project concerns is limited;

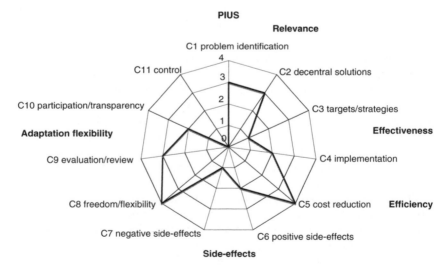

Note: 0 = no, 1 = low, 2 = moderate, 3 = above average, 4 = high action/result.

Figure 13.1   Scoring chart of PIUS

the consulting is done by external consultants and the evaluation by an engineering office.

In the case of Ecoprofit the involvement of municipalities is much stronger. On the one hand this goes in hand with much more coordination and personal efforts, but on the other hand it results in better communication and understanding.

The scoring chart in Figure 13.1 summarizes the results of the PIUS case-study.

NOTES

1. Interview with Dr P. Jahns, Director of the Efficiency Agency North Rhine-Westphalia.
2. Interview with Dr P. Jahns, Director of the Efficiency Agency North Rhine-Westphalia.
3. Interview with Dr P. Jahns, Director of the Efficiency Agency North Rhine-Westphalia.
4. Interview with Dr H. Herzog, CWS Lackfabrik GmbH & Co. KG, Düren, Germany, as PIUS participant.

14. Eco-industrial parks: Burnside and Kalundborg

Ulf-Manuel Schubert

MISSION

The increase of environmental pollution and the growing scarcity of natural resources have led to intensified research in the fields of sustainable technologies and industrial development in recent years. As a system-oriented approach industrial ecology views industrial systems in concert with their environment, linking them with natural ecosystems as a model of highly efficient use of resources, energy and waste. One of industrial ecology's core aims is to find strategies and methods which would minimize the negative impact of industrial systems on their respective environments by studying their material and energy flows. Combining economic and ecological aspects, industrial ecology can be viewed as an approach to the application of environmentally sustainable economic development (Coté and Cohen-Rosenthal, 1998).

Among industrial ecology strategies, eco-industrial parks have been widely applied as a form of local and regional sustainable development (Lowe, 2001b). First formalized in the early 1990s by Indigo Development, a number of eco-industrial parks initiatives have been emerging in several countries. Unlike traditional approaches of industrial economic development, eco-industrial parks try to increase business performance while focusing on environmental and societal improvement within a corporate network (Schlarb, 2001). Lowe et al. define an eco-industrial park as 'a community of manufacturing and service businesses seeking enhanced environmental and economic performance through collaboration in managing environmental and resource issues including energy, water, and materials' (Lowe et al., 1998). Thus, eco-industrial parks can be characterized as a regional corporate network, providing a framework for sustainable industrial development.

The following sections analyse two case-studies on eco-industrial parks. Kalundborg[1] in Denmark is the most established eco-industrial park in the world, while the majority of the projects operated elsewhere are still in their development and testing stages. Thus, the selection of this case is a 'must'. While Kalundborg is the prototype of an evolving eco-industrial park, Burnside[2] in Canada represents the efforts to transform already existing industrial parks into industrial ecosystems. Information on actors is included in different sections below.

ASSESSMENT AND EVALUATION

Relevance

The core idea of eco-industrial parks is to move away from a linear throughput to closed-looped materials and energy use (Ehrenfeld and Gertler, 1997).[3] In an industrial ecosystem, participants gain ecological and economic benefits by mutually optimizing the consumption of energy and materials (Dunn and Steinemann, 1998). Via corporate networks, by-products and waste of one firm are inserted into the production process of another. The exchange of materials lowers the costs for disposal and factor utilization for all businesses (Bleischwitz and Schubert, 2000). Since they increase resource efficiency, such processes have significant economic and environmental benefits. Through cooperation, the collective gain of all businesses involved is greater than the sum of all individual benefits each company would be able to realize by optimizing their individual performance only (Lowe et al., 1998). Thus, the success of an eco-industrial park will be a function not only of its environmental record but also of its ability to compete in the marketplace (Coté and Cohen-Rosenthal, 1998).

Components of different designs of eco-industrial parks include green design of park infrastructure, cleaner production, pollution prevention, energy efficiency and intercompany partnering (Lowe, 2001a). Besides substance or product-related exchanges, corporate networks also obtain economic and ecological advantages through an exchange of information with interactions among the park's member businesses as critical elements (Lowe, 2001b). Analytical criteria for differentiation can be seen rather in the intensity of the cooperation in such parks. According to Chertow some parks are restricted to the exchange of specific materials, whereas others develop fixed ties and joint types of use for infrastructures, logistics and marketing between the located companies (Chertow, 1999, p. 9).

Two different approaches in the establishment of eco-industrial parks can be identified: first, self-organized system approaches which facilitate organic growth of connections between participating companies, evolving from pioneering industrial locations; and, second, engineered system approaches, usually initiated by academic and/or regional governments, which follow previously designed plans (Bleischwitz and Schubert, 2000; Coté and Cohen-Rosenthal, 1998; Fleig, 2000).[4] Additionally, one has to distinguish between newly established eco-industrial parks and already existing industrial parks that have been transformed into industrial ecosystems. The majority of the eco-industrial parks have involved governmental or scientific accompaniment and support. This can be explained by the inflow of know-how, which all participants anticipate from the alliance.

Kalundborg
Research on eco-industrial parks is decisively affected by Kalundborg as the pre-eminent case of successful by-product exchange within a corporate network. Kalundborg is a city of approximately 20 000 inhabitants, located about 100 km west of Copenhagen in Denmark. The formation of the local eco-industrial network is mainly driven by the business interests of resident companies with the aspect of profitability as the original incentive for establishing local business cooperation. The network was established as an economic solution to growing costs for waste disposal due to stricter environmental regulation, as well as high costs for input-related raw material. The motivation behind the material exchanges is therefore the reduction of costs by searching for income-producing use for residual products.

Since the early 1970s, the emphasis in Kalundborg has lain in exchanging co-products, which are then utilized by other companies. The eco-industrial park is characterized as a resource-dependency collaboration between five primary independent industries, which are the main actors of the network: a coal-fired power plant (Asnæs), a pharmaceuticals and enzymes maker (Novo Nordisk), a refinery (Statoil), a soil remediation company (A/S Bioteknisk Jordrens/Soilrem) and a plasterboard manufacturer (Gyproc). Additionally, the municipal government as well as a few smaller businesses such as a fish farm also participate as recipients of by-product and raw material exchanges. The local synergy began in 1962 with a project to use surface water from Lake Tissø for a new oil refinery in order to save limited supplies of ground water (Christensen, 1999). In 1972, an industrial eco-network in Kalundborg came into existence, evolving until its present state with business cooperation in 19 projects (see Table 14.1). In its present form, the eco-industrial park represents an attempt to create a highly integrated industrial system that simultaneously optimizes the use of by-products and minimizes waste that leaves the system.

In ecological terms, the eco-industrial network at Kalundborg exhibits the characteristics of an ecological food web, where organisms consume each other's waste materials and energy. Agreements about trade with relevant goods facilitate a closed substance cycle on the micro-level.

Table 14.1   The historical sequence of industrial symbiosis at Kalundborg eco-industrial park

Year	Symbiosis development
1962	Surface water from Lake Tissø to Statoil
1972	Excess gas from Statoil to Gyproc
1973	Surface water from Lake Tissø to Asnæs power plant
1976	Biomass from Novo Nordisk/Novozymes to local farmers
1979	Fly ash from Asnæs power plant to cement industry
1980	Cooling water from Asnæs power plant to fish farm
1981	Excess heat from Asnæs power plant to district heating system
1982	Steam from Asnæs power plant to Statoil and Novo Nordisk/Novozymes
1987	Surface water from Lake Tissø to Novo Nordisk/Novozymes
1987	Cooling water from Statoil to Asnæs power plant
1989	Yeast slurry from Novo Nordisk to local farmers
1990	Liquid sulphur from Statoil to fertilizer industry
1991	Wastewater from Statoil to Asnæs power plant
1992	Excess gas from Statoil to Asnæs power plant
1993	Gypsum from Asnæs power plant to Gyproc
1995	Subsequent treatment of Novo wastewater at the public waste water plant
1995	Reuse basin to wastewater from Asnæs power plant and Statoil
1998	Sludge from public water treatment plant to Bio technical Soil Cleaning/Soilrem

Source: Jacobsen (2003), p. 271.

For example, the power plant receives gas from the refinery that formally was flared as waste, and burns it to generate electricity as well as steam. The power plant supplies residual steam to the refinery, the fish farm, the pharmaceutical plant and to a district heating system. It also collects fly ash from coal combustion with an electrostatic filter system and sends it to a cement company where it is reused. Additionally, gypsum from its desulphurization processes is supplied to Gyproc.[5] Figure 14.1 outlines the major materials and energy flows that drive the industrial ecosystem at Kalundborg.

Burnside
Burnside Industrial Park at Dartmouth, Nova Scotia was established in the early 1970s and is one of the largest industrial parks in Canada. It is approximately 1400 hectares in area with 1300 businesses and 17 000 people employed. Ninety per cent of the located businesses are small and

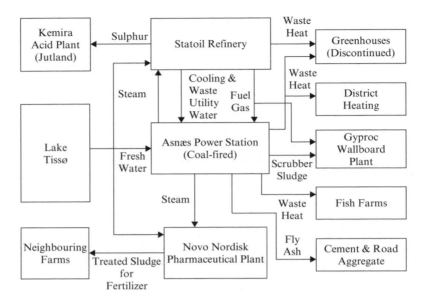

Source: Ehrenfeld and Gertler (1997), p. 70.

Figure 14.1   The industrial ecosystem at Kalundborg

medium-sized enterprises employing between two and 50 people. Burnside Industrial Park is characterized by the existence of several dozen sectors including a large number of companies in the same or similar business categories. The park is composed of different areas such as old sections that have been redeveloped, sections that are relatively new and other fields yet to be developed. Thus, materials, energy and information flows are very complex at Burnside Industrial Park.

In the early 1990s, a multidisciplinary team of researchers at the School of Resources and Environment Studies of Dalhousie University in Halifax brought a project into being which seized the opportunity of restructuring the Burnside Industrial Park, integrating ecological components. The focus of the eco-industrial park project is to create a harmonious relationship between business interests intertwined with natural interests. The eco-industrial network at Burnside therefore addresses interested companies within the industrial park. The project represents several efforts worldwide to redesign existing industrial parks to be more environmentally sound and to become engaged in reuse, repair, remanufacture and recycling functions. Contrary to the evolving eco-industrial park model at Kalundborg, the development of Burnside Industrial Park follows public planning with Dalhousie University and the municipal government as initiators. For this reason, the Burnside eco-industrial network shows a high public influence on the private resident companies.

Effectiveness

Kalundborg

The Kalundborg eco-industrial network was established as an economic solution to growing costs for waste disposal due to stricter environmental regulation as well as high costs for input-related raw material. The motivation behind the material exchanges is therefore the reduction of costs by searching for income-producing uses for residual products. By-products utilized in the production process of another company save costs for waste disposal as well as for the purchase of raw material. The outcome is reduced resource consumption and a significant reduction in environmental strain. All exchange projects were negotiated between the respective partners and are based on commercial principles whereby all collaborating partners gain financial benefits from the cooperation. Thus, the Kalundborg eco-industrial network has entirely developed through market forces and depends on the economic interests of the businesses involved.

As described, the eco-industrial network at Kalundborg is based on voluntarily commercial cooperation between the on-site companies. With separate corporate negotiations, no consistent set of key targets exists in the whole eco-industrial park. Rather, there are several bilateral treaties with specific targets and mechanisms. Since these business contracts are not public, statements about verifiable environmental or economic key targets cannot be given here. That applies as well to descriptions of specific action plans, formal control mechanisms or mechanisms for evaluation and review within the eco-industrial network. Additionally, due to the non-public bilateral business agreements, nothing can be said here about sanctions in case of non-compliance, mechanisms for transparency and performance criteria.

Since the eco-industrial network at Kalundborg mainly consists of private business companies, it is characterized by a loose connection between private and public actors. Beside the municipality government's participation in the network, there is only the Kalundborg Center for Industrial Symbiosis (KCIS) as a resident public institution. It collects and promotes information on the eco-industrial park as well as making a contribution to forming new network connections. The KCIS is a project under the auspices of the Industrial Development Council, Kalundborg Region, and obtains its basic financing from the participants of the network.

Burnside

In 1995, due to negative experiences with landfills and difficulties in siting new ones, the Halifax Regional Municipality was under pressure from its citizens and regulators to manage solid waste in a more environmentally friendly way. Through a process of community consultation, the municipality adopted cutting-edge waste strategies that emphasize the tools of separation and diversion. Additionally, the municipality joined a national initiative to reduce greenhouse gas emissions. Thus, businesses came under an increasing pressure to apply source control of materials. The municipality's Solid Waste Resource Management Strategy, which came into force in 1995, pursues the following targets:

- achieve 50 per cent diversion of solid waste from disposal sites by the year 2000;
- improve environmental standards across the province;
- establish and support regional cooperative programmes to reduce implementation costs;
- encourage development of economic opportunities around solid waste resources.

Additionally, the municipal government, as a responsible actor for Burnside Industrial Park, increased its interest in improving the park's environmental management through enhanced cooperation and networking between located stakeholders.

In September 1998, the Eco Efficiency Center (EEC) in Burnside Industrial Park was founded by Dalhousie University and Nova Scotia Power Inc., the province's electricity utility, with the support of the governments of Canada and Novia Scotia. In the first three years, it obtained financial support from local and regional environmental and economic development agencies. The centre is an important connection between government, business and industry associations, local industries, development agencies and small and medium-sized businesses. Thus, the Burnside network is characterized by a very close connection between public and private actors. Since the EEC points out guidelines and stipulations for the coexistence of business practices with natural obligations of the community, it can be regarded as the heart of the eco-industrial network at Burnside: it improves the efficiency of individual companies while supporting an ecosystemic perspective in the whole park.

The EEC is a non-profit organization that addresses primarily small and medium-sized businesses as primary stakeholders. As a new support mechanism, its responsibilities are both consulting individual companies for efficiency improvements and encouraging an ecosystemic perspective by promoting cooperation between the companies within the park. Information is promoted through personal contact and columns in the monthly park newspaper. Materials exchanges within the network are supplementary organized through a Web-based database. This way, markets in material flow management and production integrated environmental protection are promoted within and between companies. Additionally, strategies for reducing the substance cycle, a joint use of infrastructure and a joint knowledge management for continual innovations are promoted. Since 1999, the centre's Eco-Business Program has become the principal tool to encourage environmental improvement. It adopts an eco-efficiency code and sets reduction and conservation targets for participating businesses. Regarding input-oriented factors, the EEC recommends goals in solid waste diversion, toxic chemical reduction, energy and water conservation, and greenhouse gas reduction. As a basic element of the Eco-Business Program, the centre offers an environmental review. Visiting the participating companies, the EEC provides them with a report including specific recommendations to improve operating efficiency as well as assisting them in committing reduction and conservation targets within the bounds of the Eco-Business Program.

Efficiency

Kalundborg
Since the early 1970s the emphasis in Kalundborg has lain in exchanging co-products, which are then utilized by other companies. By-products utilized in the production process of another company save costs both for waste disposal as well as for the purchase of raw materials. The outcome is reduced resource consumption and a significant reduction in environmental strain. The ecological advantages of the eco-industrial network are based on the decreased use of raw materials and extensive exchange of substances leading to a significant reduction in environmental impact. Annual reductions are estimated in the range of 45 000 tonnes oil/p.a., 15 000 tonnes coal/p.a., 175 000 tonnes carbon dioxide/p.a., 10 200 tonnes sulphur dioxide/p.a. and 600 000 m^3 water/p.a. Annual savings achieved more than US$15 million. While the total investments in the entire 19 projects amount to around US$75 million, the total accumulated savings achieved since the creation of the park amount to US$160 million. The average repayment time of the single collaborations is about five years.

Burnside
The eco-industrial park at Burnside shows two different efforts to reduce environmental impact while enhancing economic performance. On the one hand companies are encouraged in efficient resource use. On the other

hand, corporate network cooperation is promoted that goes beyond the production integrated environmental protection within a single company. Since 1998, more than 130 reviews of Burnside companies have been conducted while more than 100 businesses with more than 2000 employees have been enrolled in the Eco-Business Program. Annual reductions are estimated in the range of 1569 tonnes of solid waste diversion, 99 413 litres of liquid waste diversion and over 11 million litres of water use reduction. Although the EEC's work is largely focused on Burnside, the scope has recently been extended to the broader business community of the Halifax regional municipality and throughout Novia Scotia. However, material flows occur entirely within the boundaries of Burnside Industrial Park.

Side-Effects

The corporate interconnectedness at the Kalundborg eco-industrial network as well as the EEC as a model for eco-efficiency and network promotion at Burnside Industrial Park lead not only to higher resource efficiency but also to positive side-effects in the form of operation benefits. Since allocation at Kalundborg takes place via agreements, the participated companies gain secure conditions for the acceptance or supply of economic services. There are value-adding partnerships as well as corporate alliances that exhibit fixed contractual obligations. The economical advantages lie, firstly, in the price difference between residual products and raw materials, and secondly, in the price difference between the network activities and the least-expensive alternative (Jacobsen, 2003). At Burnside, horizontal corporate cooperation lowers the costs for disposal and factor utilization for all participants. At the same time, the gradual process of the network development also leads to the reduction of transaction costs due to the resulting demonstration effects and information on corporate cooperation. This process is at Kalundborg also supported by the KCIS. The EEC at Burnside addresses factor utilization and waste disposal as the businesses' main internal and external costs. It offers a variety of strategies and tools to encourage environmental improvement within Burnside Industrial Park. Guiding businesses towards practices which can avoid waste as well as save energy and materials input, the centre demonstrates that environmental improvements can lead to cost reduction. The level of cost savings is equivalent to the competitive advantages for participating companies.

Over the course of time, higher resource efficiency and operation benefits must be weighed up against the risks of path-dependencies. Eco-industrial networks can stabilize the industrial metabolism on a high level and, with new investments, give end-of-pipe cleaning or recycling technologies priority over further changes towards eco-efficiency. If partners from traditional industries dominate, this tendency might turn out to be strong because of asset specifics. Furthermore, network members have made specific investments in the production or use of certain by-products (for example gypsum dust at the Kalundborg network); their incentive to continue with eco-efficiency improvement will be low. If only a stabilization of the material flows is achieved, the environmental relief would be limited. Additionally, the risk of path-dependencies points to the latent hazard of networks to enable learning effects and economies of scale initially, and later to tend towards fossilization (Bleischwitz and Schubert, 2000, p. 462).

Adaptation Flexibility

Kalundborg
At the beginning, external consultants did not design the eco-industrial network in Kalundborg, nor did it receive financial support from municipality or governmental offices. Therefore, the eco-industrial park did not develop as a public-planned network. Rather, it resulted from several separate bilateral deals between on-site companies that developed initially spontaneously and quite independently from each other (Garner and Keoleian, 1995). Based on a complex of alliances and contracts that arose without institutional intervention, the eco-industrial network development is a gradual process driven by the private stakeholders' initiative. The interconnections are not under the pressure of superordinate levels. To this day, there is no higher level of a private or public administrative management form to organize the business interactions within the eco-industrial park (Desroches, 2001). Thus, the network has a non-hierarchical character.

All exchange projects at Kalundborg were negotiated between the respective partners and are based on commercial principles whereby all collaborating partners gain financial benefits from the cooperation. The Kalundborg eco-industrial network developed entirely through market forces and depends on economic interests of the involved businesses. Thus, the eco-industrial park is generally open for new members and the development of new tools that have an influence on the network. Otherwise, materials and energy exchanges over long distances are costly. The geographically close network is therefore one of the most important elements of the success of Kalundborg eco-industrial park. Due to this, the network is not generally open for new participants.

Additionally, due to the non-public bilateral business agreements, nothing can be said here about sanctions in case of non-compliance, mechanisms for transparency and performance criteria. That applies as well for descriptions of specific action plans, formal control mechanisms or mechanisms for evaluation and review within the eco-industrial network.

Burnside

Due to the voluntary nature of participation at Burnside Industrial Park there are no formal or informal control mechanisms or sanctions in case of non-compliance. Rather, companies are asked to complete evaluations of the EEC's review and report. Regarding transparency mechanisms, the EEC offers an internal award programme for businesses that have improved their environmental performance and adopted innovative improvements in environmental management; on an annual meeting of all members of the industrial ecosystem, outstanding environmental and economic perform-ances are honoured. The centre does not define clear or verifiable environ-mental and economical key targets for participating business companies however. Furthermore, after three, six and 12 months, the centre follows up with the companies, measuring cost and materials savings. Resulting cost reduction and environmental relief are published by the EEC as publicity support for the businesses.

Since the participation in the Eco-Business Program is voluntary and the companies have committed themselves to achieving specific reduction and conservation targets, the network is characterized by a high flexibility. Businesses possess a sufficient flexibility to make investment decisions that are either consistent with the network aims or have an influence on it. There is no fee to join the Eco-Business Program, thus the eco-industrial network in Burnside is principally open for new participants.

CONCLUSIONS AND SCORING CHART

Kalundborg's two-decades experience show a number of preconditions that must be fulfilled to establish an eco-industrial network. First, deliberate insti-tutional mechanisms were not needed to establish the cooperation between the on-site companies. Thus, the industrial network is mainly based on open-ness and mutual inter-firm trust between the partners. Second, the compa-nies should have a close relation regarding their products, by-products and size. Elements of competition that might prevent corporate networks should be absent. Rather, the by-products of the involved companies should be different. As a third precondition, network participants should be located geographically close to each other, because materials and energy exchanges over long distances are costly. In brief, short distances have been a core element in the development of the Kalundborg eco-industrial park. The strength of the Kalundborg approach lies in the fact that a reduction of envi-ronmental strains has been achieved in the pursuit of rational business inter-ests. Regarding these experiences, the Kalundborg eco-industrial network can be seen as a global pioneer for the eco-industrial park concept.

Burnside Industrial Park can be seen as an experiment in adaptation flexibility since an already existing industrial park has been transformed. It is used as a 'living laboratory', focusing on education and information transfer. The EEC is, additionally, a model for an integrated set of approaches that assists businesses to achieve better environmental and economic performance through resource conservation, reuse, recycling, eco-efficiency and pollution prevention as well as general good environmental practices through individual and collective action. It serves as a catalyst to work with small companies to create network partnerships and to disseminate consulting and information. The centre has been successful in promoting a horizontal eco-industrial business network in waste exchange.

In general, eco-industrial parks have a first-mover advantage in industrial networking which, under favourable conditions, may lead to permanent profits and growing incomes. The minimum reward is knowledge transfer for complexity reduction. Joint environmental management in corporate industrial networks appears to offer good development potential for business and the environment. Hence, the opportunities for continuous further development must continue to be weighed against the risk of path-dependencies and institutional fossilization.

The regulatory functions of government are, in spite of its involvement in some of the eco-industrial parks worldwide, not too large. Entrepreneurial spirit and the design of business institutions by the participating companies are more relevant. Bringing together the actors, supporting a master plan and some area management, public relations and academic support appear to be beneficial as propellants. Also the active maintenance of improvement procedures can be demanded and supported by local governments. Active local and state politicians are, therefore, important as facilitators, while federal governments do not play a visible role.

Scepticism is advisable if the environmental relief of the eco-industrial parks is to be assessed in coming years. Under the current conditions, methodological and statistical deficiencies are ascertainable. Indicators, measuring methods and evaluation methods for environmental life-cycle analysis of eco-industrial parks are not yet sufficiently transparent. It would be desirable if the parks paid systematic attention to this aspect over time. Here, a regulatory need for supporting guidelines and open access to these data still remains. The scoring charts in Figure 14.2 and Figure 14.3 summarize and score the results of this case-study and show how the two eco-industrial parks are differently assessed concerning the 11 criteria.

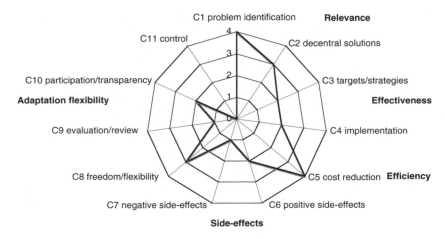

Note: 0 = no, 1 = low, 2 = moderate, 3 = above average, 4 = high action/result.

Figure 14.2   Scoring chart of eco-industrial park Kalundborg

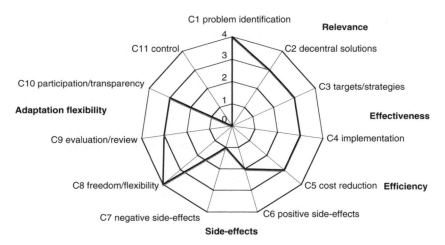

Note: 0 = no, 1 = low, 2 = moderate, 3 = above average, 4 = high action/result.

Figure 14.3   Scoring chart of eco-industrial park Burnside

NOTES

1. Besides the Internet addresses and the cited literature, information on the Kalundborg eco-industrial park refers to e-mail interviews with N. Jacobsen on 4 September 2000 and 23 November 2001, whom I would like to thank here.
2. Information on Burnside Industrial Park refers, besides the cited literature and the Internet addresses, to e-mail interviews with R. Coté on 4 September 2000 and 23 November 2001, whom I would like to thank here.
3. Or in other words, as Wang et al. stress: 'In eco-industrial parks, enterprises simulate nature ecosystem to establish the symbiosis relationship, maximise the resource efficiency and minimise the environmental impact' (Wang et al., 2002, p. 6).
4. For a typology of different models of eco-industrial parks according to their starting points see Fleig (2000).
5. The eco-industrial network, however, is not self-sufficient and limited to the park since the involved companies sell by-products as well as import raw materials from outside businesses (Desroches, 2001).

15. Energy+: a public–private market transformation for household appliances

Stephan Ramesohl

MISSION

The Energy+ project is an initiative of the European Commission and ten national energy and environment agencies and institutes to promote the development and use of highly energy-efficient refrigerators and freezers throughout the European Union.[1] In September 1999 the European Union implemented a Directive banning sales of most E-, F- and G-rated refrigerators and freezers. At the same time, many products have now reached and exceeded the minimum requirements for receiving an A rating. The labelling scheme is currently under review but it is likely to be three to five years before any new requirements come into effect. In order to give visibility to the most efficient products available on the market, the goal of the Energy+ project is to promote appliances that are far more efficient (−25 per cent) than those just meeting the minimum criteria for an A-label rating.

The project builds on the concept of cooperative technology procurement (EM, 1998; Ostertag and Dreher, 2002; Europäische Gemeinschaft/ Wuppertal Institut, 1998; Westling, 1996), and, initially, should serve as a first test for exploring the scope for coordinating purchase power on the European level. Placed as a pilot project, already in its test phase Energy+ has rapidly succeeded in creating genuine market opportunities for Energy+ appliances.

ACTORS INVOLVED AND RESOURCE-DEPENDENCY RELATIONS

The principal idea of Energy+ builds on a public–private partnership aiming at providing an information platform that contributes to increased market transparency in the national white goods markets in Europe

(Ademe, 2001). The national efforts are coordinated through a European platform and coordination team in order to enhance information flow and learning between the member states (Figure 15.1). The project design is simple and follows a three-step approach:

- On the one hand, participating retailers and institutional buyers sign a document where they declare their intention to promote and/or purchase appliances according to the Energy+ specifications. The participating organizations are shown under retailers, supporters and institutional buyers respectively, but the lists are also promoted through a number of channels by the organizations behind the project. Hereby, market power in favour of energy-efficient products is enforced.
- On the other hand, manufacturers who submit products that meet the specifications are compiled on another list promoted in parallel (see Energy+ products). For each model or prototype submitted to the project a test report stating the levels of criteria fulfilment should be submitted with the entry data. Random testing of the appliances is performed at an internationally recognized testing laboratory.

  All models that meet the mandatory specifications will be included in the Energy+ appliance list. Should the random testing show that the model performance does not comply with the reported values in the test reports, the Energy+ project steering group will communicate this to all participants and may decide to withdraw the model from the list.
- Moreover, Energy+ organized the European Energy+ Award competition. This competition was based on the Energy+ specifications with additional optional requirements of importance to buyers. The European March 2001 Energy+ Award competition singled out the best two-door Energy+ appliance and the best one-door Energy+ appliance that met the goal of high-energy efficiency as well as further optional requirements of importance to buyers, such as low overall environmental impact, reduction of noise emissions, and price in line with current markets. A second award round ended in spring 2004.

When discussing the resource interdependencies between the various actors involved in the Energy+ initiative it has to be borne in mind that the initiative was initially designed as a pilot research project aiming at testing the idea of technology procurement in the market for white goods. Triggered by the ongoing legislation work of the EU Commission the project team received funding under the DG Energy's SAVE programme

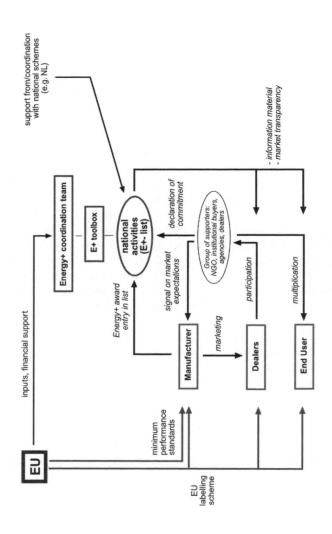

Figure 15.1   The organization of the Energy+ programme

for setting up the conceptual framework and for running the activities such as websites and national awards. Moreover, in some countries comparable policy initiatives could be found (for example in the Netherlands) that provided further support and, even more importantly, allowed benefits from synergies with existing policy schemes.

With regard to the sphere of market actors, existing relations between the manufacturers, the dealers and other institutions such as energy agencies, consumer rights advocates and so on could be addressed. It is a distinctive feature of the Energy+ concept to merge the vital interests of various actors within a marketing campaign based on environmental performance as an indicator for premium quality. The distribution of market power appeared to be fairly balanced, having a situation where frontrunners on all sides depend on cooperation with partners from the other stakeholders. An explicit exchange of resources or funds, however, did not take place.

POLICY-RELEVANT OUTCOMES

From a practical perspective, the so-called Energy+ lists are important tools of the project, where all participating organizations as well as all qualifying Energy+ cooling appliances were listed. The lists were updated during the course of the project. Hence, at the core of the project were technical and functional specifications that defined the criteria of the product type targeted by the project. Manufacturers were invited to present products that would qualify to enter the Energy+ lists by meeting a set of strict specifications. The mandatory specifications set up by the project required that products had to be available on the European market, and to have an energy efficiency index (EEI) of not more than 42 per cent compared to a defined base line to qualify for participation in the project. In practice, Energy+ appliances use three-quarters or less of the energy used by an appliance that just meets the A criteria of the European energy label (55 per cent related to the base line).

Although being active for more than five years, Energy+ has achieved quite substantial results (Wijshoff and Attali, 2003; Ostertag, 2003). The first rounds of Energy+ and the European Energy+ Award competition successfully sped the production and demand for super-efficient appliances on the European market. The winter 2003 lists comprise more than 100 participating organizations and some 600 Energy+ cooling appliances from all leading manufacturers that are available on the European market. Furthermore, Energy+ contributed to a market shift within the frame of the existing labels so that more A-class rated appliances have been sold than before.

The project has clearly succeeded in speeding up market introduction of highly energy-efficient fridge-freezers on the European market that only use less than 35 per cent of the energy consumed by a defined base line that relates to an average European cooling appliance of comparable size and type of the early 1990s. The second Energy+ award was published in spring 2004 and the winning appliance achieved another substantial progress against first results, that is, the EEI will be far less than 30 per cent. Compared to the A-label threshold value of 55 per cent, this corresponds to an improvement of more than 46 per cent. Hereby, Energy+ has helped move the whole market to higher efficiency over time. The project results also indicate that supply and market availability of energy-efficient refrigerators throughout Europe has been enlarged, but it is too early to quantify these effects.

Building on these positive experiences, the impact on energy consumption in the EU can be substantial. Figure 15.2 shows a forecast that up to 50 per cent less electricity in this sector in the European Union (40TWh) would be consumed were all new refrigerators and freezers bought in the EU from the year 2000 onwards to meet the Energy+ efficiency specifications. Also shown is a forecast of the expected electricity consumption trend for refrigerators and freezers resulting from the European Union's current energy efficiency policy initiatives including energy labelling and mandatory minimum efficiency standards.

Forecast refrigerator and freezer electricity consumption in the EU

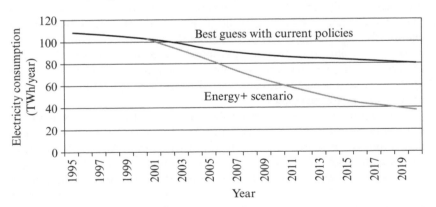

Source: Energy+ (2004).

Figure 15.2   Estimation of quantitative impacts of Energy+ on the European level

ASSESSMENT AND EVALUATION

Relevance

The Energy+ initiative is directed to an important area of household energy end use in Europe. Almost 6 per cent (109 TWh per year) of the whole European Union's electricity consumption is used by domestic refrigerators and freezers. Overall they are estimated to need some 20 large base-load power stations (20 GW_{el}) to satisfy their power demand.

A typical European household will have more than one refrigerator or freezer. On average refrigerators and freezers account for about 25 per cent of the household electricity bill but this share will be higher if the space and water heating is non-electric. At the beginning of the 1990s a typical average-sized European fridge-freezer (one with ~257 litres of net storage capacity) used about 590 kWh of electricity per year and this level is taken as the base line (100 per cent). The same sized fridge-freezer having a European Energy Label class A rating will use less than 325 kWh per year (55 per cent) but if it were an Energy+ appliance it would use less than 248 kWh per year, which is 42 per cent or less of the energy of an average appliance.

The electricity consumed by domestic refrigerators and freezers in the European Union accounts for some 62 million tonnes of carbon dioxide emissions per year, which is the most well-known greenhouse gas. Many refrigerators also use refrigerants and foaming agents in the insulation that are powerful greenhouse gases and which can increase their life-cycle global warming impact by ~10 per cent. Overall, domestic refrigerators and freezers alone account for about 2 per cent of the EU's total greenhouse gas emissions.

In this context, the Energy+ initiative intended to bridge the gap to the upcoming new version of the labelling directive. These efforts were mainly pushed by stakeholders from the research and non-governmental organization (NGO) arena together with the EU Commission. Although a common understanding concerning the general importance and the quantitative dimension of the problem did exist, the majority of industrial actors followed a rather reluctant wait-and-see stance *vis-à-vis* the upcoming regulation.

As a decisive breakthrough for the idea of Energy+, however, two leading European manufacturers considered the initiative to be a chance for positioning their brand at the innovative edge. During the course of the project it could be observed that support for the concept has been growing gradually among the manufacturers until a critical mass of suppliers could be integrated into the scheme. Meanwhile, the total number of 19 manufacturers comprises all major brands in Europe, including foreign importers such as the fast-growing Chinese player Haier.

Effectiveness

On the conceptual level, Energy+ started as a pilot project aimed at testing aggregated purchasing of energy-efficient (consumer) products on a pan-European scale. The project sought to build an international buyer group where, in particular, retailers, kitchen specialists, energy agencies and NGOs were involved as intermediaries between the suppliers and the end users in the process. Institutional buyers, traditionally associated with technology procurement, also had an important role in the buyer group. Although a few business actors on the national and the European level are still missing, the project could achieve its goal (Ademe, 2001).

In order to expand the positive impact of Energy+, to broaden consumers' choice and to allow market actors to market a complete Energy+ range of products, the project is continued and enlarged to all ten categories of cooling appliances defined in the European energy labelling Directive 94/2/EC. Moreover, the concept of cooperative technology procurement gained acceptance as one policy option within the field of market transformation policies, that is, within the new EU programme 'Energy Intelligent Europe'.

On a practical level, the effectiveness is closely tied to the transparent and well-defined quantitative framework. Due to the fact that the Energy+ scheme builds upon the target values and methodology of the EU labelling scheme, a consistent and workable framework was available from the beginning. Moreover, the process of updating and tightening of standards followed a clear and transparent procedure, another contribution to the acceptability of the whole approach among the practitioners.

Efficiency

Due to the innovative character of the pilot project, benchmarks for cost-efficiency are not available. In terms of programme costs, however, Energy+ can be considered as a rather lean activity that has achieved its results at very reasonable cost. The demand for administration and personnel is limited to small coordination teams in the participating countries (1–2 persons each) and a European steering group. The practical realization of the Internet platform does not require large budgets either. In order to expand the scheme and to provide a fast update of information tools, more capacity will be needed.

Due to the fact that the methodological framework strictly corresponds to the EU labelling scheme, the transaction costs could be minimized among the participants. Basically, the participants could be motivated to undertake actions that would have been done anyway at a later stage.

From a macroeconomic view, the Energy+ scheme makes a contribution to mitigate impacts of information-related market failures that still deter consumers from taking economically and ecologically sound purchase decisions. Through provision of specific information and decision support, Energy+ overcomes information deficits and reduces transaction costs. Moreover, it fosters an integrated approach considering the long-term running costs of cooling equipment, which are usually neglected in the average consumer's biased cost calculation.

Side-Effects

The primary focus of Energy+ is on reducing the electricity demand of households in Europe. The instrument thus contributes to all major goals of European energy and climate policy. However, the award competition triggered innovation among manufacturers and pushed new cooling technologies in an evolutionary manner. Radical innovations could not be observed, but there was a continuous improvement of design features, components and materials.

Besides energy efficiency, the strict rules pushed alternative natural gases as foaming agents and as coolants of the appliances. Hereby, additional positive impacts on climate change abatement and the mitigation of ozone layer depletion could be achieved. In economic terms, Energy+ contributes to mitigating the negative externalities associated with cooling equipment.

Furthermore, the instrument induced changes in market structure through a promotion of certain manufacturers and retailers offering high-efficiency appliances. Their competitiveness could be strengthened. Market distortions, however, cannot be expected due to the fact that all major players in Europe are participating in the scheme.

Adaptation Flexibility

Due to the open and cooperative character of the initiative, Energy+ offers comprehensive flexibility to all participants. New participants are able and explicitly encouraged to enter the scheme – at the same time, anyone can leave the scheme at any moment.

In technical terms, from the very beginning Energy+ has been designed as a supporting element of the European labelling system. The energy label itself is organized as a dynamic system and the mandatory requirements for meeting the efficiency classes will be tightened in line with the next revision. Most likely, the current Energy+ standard will be considered as an input.

Thereby it was a guiding principle for the programme design to allow for adaptation to technical progress. Due to the regular update of the appliance list technology advances can easily be integrated. The same holds for modifications of the relevant policy framework, for example in terms of standards and labels. As a result of the dynamic nature of the standard, the instrument can be seen as an innovation-friendly tool that imposes a permanent incentive for improvements as one aspect of market differentiation and positioning.

Typically for an outcome-orientated policy instrument, the practical details of implementation of Energy+ are determined by each participating company. Products have to meet the standard, but by what means the supplier will achieve the target set remains the responsibility of the individual company.

Taking the general process of a continuous shift of the average market efficiency into account, it can be concluded that manufacturers will not fall back behind the Energy+ level. On the contrary, the limited range of available Energy+ appliances so far will most likely become the usual standard (see above for a quantitative estimation).

Due to the initial character of a pilot project for testing the approach of technology procurement, the whole initiative was subject to a research analysis. A formal monitoring and control system was not installed.

CONCLUSIONS AND SCORING CHART

With regard to the research hypotheses on governance approaches, the following lessons can be drawn (note: numbers in relation to questionnaire, see Table 10.1):

(1) Flow of Information Along the Product Chain

The impact mechanisms of Energy+ build on various new communication channels that could have been established in addition to existing policy instruments and market relations. By its nature, Energy+ increased the available knowledge about the set of available alternatives. Through a systematic listing and comparison of available appliances, market transparency could be increased. New knowledge has been generated among both dealers and consumers. Manufacturers used the Energy+ label to market explicitly their high-end appliances to the dealers.

Designed as an information and promotion tool, the Energy+ instrument contributed to change the importance that actors attach to the pros and cons of alternatives. Within the marketing and dissemination campaigns special emphasis has been given to underline the advantages of buying more efficient cooling appliances. Promotion of high-efficiency products gained importance for dealers and especially for manufacturers.

However, attention has not only been given to the advantages for the environment but primarily to the economic benefits for the private energy bill. Especially with regard to the private consumer, the instrument could contribute to a better understanding of the life-cycle cost–benefits of a high-efficiency purchase and, thus, increase the awareness for sustainable investment decisions. In addition to these information effects, the instrument influenced the pros and cons of alternatives to a certain extent. As a result of the Energy+ marketing campaigns and promotion activities, the price of high-efficiency cooling appliances has been reduced. This lowers the typical obstacle to consumers to pay high up-front costs for equipment with low lifetime running costs.

(2) Interdependencies of Actors

The manufacturers of the products have indicated that this project has been very helpful in their efforts to commercialize and promote new energy-efficient products. For the winning companies of the European Energy+ Award, the project appears to have been instrumental in securing internal support within the companies for extra efforts in launching super-efficient products.

Several retailers have explained that the Energy+ project has given them an ability to influence the type of goods offered by the suppliers, especially retailers in countries without domestic producers of cooling appliances (for example, the Netherlands and Norway).

(4) Regional Level of Networks

Already mentioned, it is planned to initiate more pan-European actions of this kind and to expand the scheme to other appliances. The conceptual framework, marketing tools and graphical image created around the Energy+ project could be used to transform other markets as well. Using the work carried out would substantially ease future actions with other product categories. However, lessons that have been learned need to be taken into account. The Energy+ concept depends on a specific market setting, characterized by a limited number of European manufacturers, a strong position of dealers and retailers and a rather homogeneous product profile. Experience from the feasibility studies and the project implementation suggest that Energy+ benefits from the transnational effects in the common market in Europe. Comparable effects can be expected for lead markets of a critical size such as the USA or Japan. Undertaken on a purely national level of minor size, however, more difficulties could be expected because a coordinated market transformation activity needs to cover the whole of the relevant market, that is, in this case the European internal market for white goods. Without major changes, therefore, it appears hardly transferable to completely different technologies such as industrial production equipment.

(5–7) The Role of Policy in Providing a Platform for Learning

Energy+ can be seen as a promising feasibility test of a new type of market transformation programmes on the European level. Taking up the political impetus in the European Commission to foster energy efficiency, it adds to existing national and European initiatives and establishes new information channels that increase market transparency and trigger competition among suppliers of high-efficiency appliances. The scheme serves as a framework to reward these companies striving to improve the energy efficiency of their products and it provides incentives to others to engage in the field. Energy+, therefore, can be seen as a helpful contribution to enhance eco-efficiency among manufacturers and dealers of household appliances in Europe. Companies that take responsibility for the ecological performance of their products and want to position themselves as leaders of innovation benefit from the marketing impact of the Energy+ scheme.

All these impacts are grounded on the platform for information exchange and learning that was financed by the EU (see Figure 15.1). In this regard, the case of Energy+ clearly demonstrates the value of this kind of politically supported activity for market transformation. Policy can play a major role in establishing and implementing effective networks.

(10) Role of Existing Regulation

Energy+ works on the basis of voluntary commitments of the participating actors. It has to be taken into account, therefore, that the working principle is directed to the innovative edge of the market, that is, frontrunners are stimulated to improve even further, whereas less-performing manufacturers are not addressed (Figure 15.3). For this reason, Energy+ represents a promising enlargement but by no means a substitution of the existing regulatory European framework of minimum performance standards and the labelling Directive. It has to be stated very clearly that the whole concept depends on the existence of the EU Directive and the expected

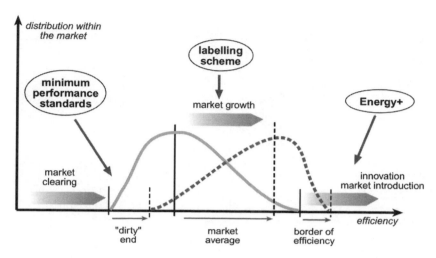

Source: Ramesohl and Kristof (2000).

Figure 15.3 The necessary mix of policy approaches to enhance market transformation towards high-efficiency appliances

modification. Energy+ was explicitly directed to bridge the time gap in between.

However, a comparison of sales of cooling appliances over Europe points at a remarkable North–South bias concerning the market shares of energy-efficient appliances (Figure 15.4). A common regulatory framework is needed to balance the still prevailing differences in environmental awareness, traditional market structures and so on, especially at the lower end of the market, where minimum performance standards are still needed to phase out the most inefficient product types.

Furthermore, the comparison underlines the importance of policy mixes. The successful case of the Netherlands with an extraordinary high share of A+ products of 14 per cent illustrates very clearly the synergies between an enlarged availability of Energy+ appliances in combination with the Dutch rebate programme for these A+/A++ appliances. Both instruments together led to a considerable growth of sales even before the start of the updated Directive. In addition, in the Netherlands public awareness on the existence and benefits of the new products and related support programmes rose to 90 per cent.

Figure 15.5 shows the assessment and scoring of the case-study's results.

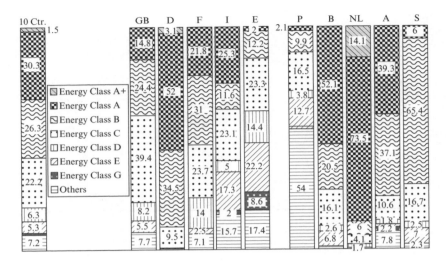

Source: Soregaroli (2003).

Figure 15.4   Overview on sales figures of cooling appliances in major European countries

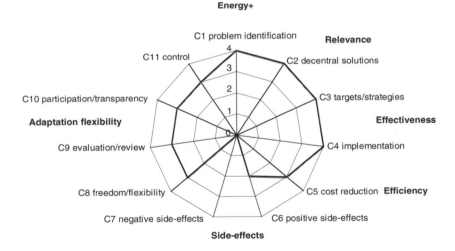

Note: 0 = no, 1 = low, 2 = moderate, 3 = above average, 4 = high action/result

Figure 15.5   Scoring chart of Energy+

NOTE

1. All information on Energy+ can be obtained at the website (www.energy-plus.org). The Wuppertal Institute acts as the national coordinator for Germany and has been involved in the initiative since the very first feasibility studies on European procurement (see Landwehr et al., 1998; Adema, 2001; Wijshoff and Attali, 2003).

16.   Responsible Care initiative: transboundary chemical network

Michael Kuhndt and Burcu Tunçer

MISSION

Established in 1985 by the Canadian Chemical Producers Association (CCPA), Responsible Care is probably the leading sectoral voluntary environmental initiative in the world. It is a chemical industry initiative concerned with continuous performance improvement at national and global level (ICCA, 2002a, p. 39). It sprang over to the USA in 1988, then to Western Europe in 1998–99 and then to the rest of the world. Today, Responsible Care is being implemented in 47 countries where more than 85 per cent of the world's chemicals (in volume) are manufactured (ICCA, 2002b, pp. 1–2).

Towards the early 1980s, the chemical industry came under continuing pressure from an increasingly sceptical public view culminating with the tragedies in Seveso, Italy in 1977 and in Bhopal, India in 1984. In Canada, marked with the leakage of a highly toxic cyanide compound at the Union Carbide plant causing the death of 3000 local residents, the chemical industry recognized the need to revisit its roles and responsibilities in society and saw the need for improvements in performance and the public image.

The Canadian chemical industries initiated the Community Awareness and Emergency Response (CAER) programme that aimed to coordinate emergency response procedures in place with local fire and police departments, which did not exist in most cases. This programme built the basis for what the Canadian Chemical Producers Association later coined 'Responsible Care', an initiative that would encompass essentially all the activities of the chemical industry. Responsible Care (RC) has become the umbrella programme for the environmentally sound management of the industry's research and development, transportation, distribution, manufacturing and hazardous waste activities (Munn, 2000, pp. 1–4).

Responsible Care is designed and managed by the industry for the industry and focuses on improving performance, communication and accountability by identifying and spreading good management practices through the publication of codes or guidance documents. The initiative promotes mutual support between companies and associations through experience-sharing and peer pressure, and tries to demonstrate the incentives to the industry to engage and work with stakeholders at local, national and international levels, to listen to and address their concerns and aspirations.

In this vein, the worldwide objective[1] of Responsible Care is mentioned as the commitment of chemical companies, through their national associations, to work together for the continuous improvement of health, safety and environmental performance of their products and processes. By covering all the activities of the industry, it aims at ethical and behavioural change: going away from a regulatory-driven approach to a proactive approach, taking into account the perceived needs of society throughout the product life, from cradle to grave.

The initiative is highly flexible and the application of codes of practice can alter significantly from one nation to another or from one company to another. While the eight fundamental features (detailed in Box 16.1) apply to all member companies, the way that they are put into practice differs drastically.

ACTORS INVOLVED AND RESOURCE-DEPENDENCY RELATIONS

The Responsible Care initiative has a multilevel structure going from the global level, then the regional and national level, to the single corporation level. At each level, different actors assume various roles to follow the eight fundamental features of the initiative (Figure 16.1).

At the global level, the International Council of Chemicals Associations (ICCA) takes the lead for the management of the initiative. In this organization, the Responsible Care Leadership Group intends to spread the implementation of RC as broadly as possible within the chemical and allied industries and to achieve new country participation. The Responsible Care Leadership Group is also responsible for the implementation of the initiative in various countries in accordance with its key elements and fundamental features, thus protecting the integrity of the initiative worldwide.

At the regional level, for example at the European level, 23 national federations participate in a Responsible Care Committee, inside the European Chemical Industry Council (CEFIC). CEFIC itself is a member of the International Council of Chemicals Associations (ICCA). In each country

---

BOX 16.1   EIGHT FUNDAMENTAL FEATURES OF THE RESPONSIBLE CARE INITIATIVE

- A formal commitment on behalf of each company to a set of guiding principles signed, in the majority of cases, by the chief executive officer.
- A series of codes, guidance notes, and checklists to assist companies to implement the commitment.
- The progressive development of indicators against which improvements in performance can be measured.
- An ongoing process of communication on health, safety and environment matters with interested parties inside and outside the industry.
- Provision of a platform in which companies can share views and exchange experiences on implementation of the commitment.
- Adoption of a title and a logo which clearly identify national programmes as being consistent with and part of the concept of Responsible Care.
- Consideration of how best to encourage all member companies to commit and participate in Responsible Care.
- Systematic procedures to verify the implementation of the measurable (or practical) elements of Responsible Care by the member companies.

Source: CEFIC (2001), p. 39.

---

there is an association of chemical companies, namely the 'national association'. While companies have their own Responsible Care programmes, it is the associations' responsibility to adapt the Responsible Care initiative to the cultural, social and legal environment of the country.

The national associations are instrumental in promoting this collective action among their members by: (1) acting as catalysts in maintaining the commitment of the industry's chief executive officers; (2) providing a mechanism for mutual assistance; and (3) coordinating joint action. The associations also produce extensive publications and foster ongoing informal exchanges of technical and management advice among company personnel and RC coordinators (Moffett et al., n.d., p. 23).

At the company level, the commitments are generally made by chief executive officers (CEOs), who are then responsible for ensuring actions by

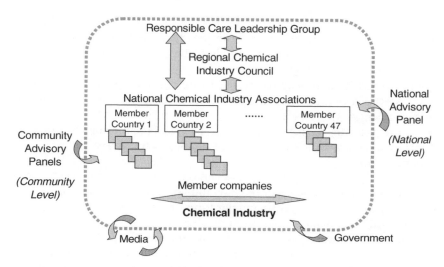

Figure 16.1   *An overview of the relationship between the actors involved with the Responsible Care initiative*

their company under the initiative and for reporting back on progress to the national and/or regional chemical industry association running the RC programme (Tapper, 1997, p. 287).

The major interaction process among member nations at the global level happens via reporting of the national-level activities to the ICCA. Each national association signed up to Responsible Care is required to submit an annual report on its progress in the implementation of Responsible Care (ICCA, 2002a, p. 34). However, the interaction scheme with the stakeholders can vary significantly at the national level. The common forms can be the National Advisory Panel (NAP) or the Community Advisory Panels (CAPs).[2]

The macro-level monitoring procedure is the peer review process developed and introduced by the Responsible Care Leadership Group in 1999 to encourage candid dialogue and constructive input among participating national associations. At national level, the national associations can carry out voluntary verification processes, for example the American Chemistry Council (ACC) conducts management system verifications (ICCA, 2002b, pp. 41–4).

Interaction with the third parties beyond advisory panels stays quite limited. It can happen in the form of monitoring government reaction and lobbying or relations with the media or occasionally through third-party verification activities.

Being an established initiative, the Responsible Care Leadership Group globally has considerable authority in the chemical sector. However, this authority has never been exercised fully, as the guiding principles stay at a generic level without any enforcement for implementation. In this regard, global authority is transferred to the national-level organizations, which can exercise their authority at different levels of ambition. For example, commitment to RC is a requirement for company membership of national chemical industry associations in Europe and North America (Tapper, 1997, p. 287), while such a requirement can be rarely observed in the developing countries.

Hence, regional and national associations are the key knowledge disseminators in the Responsible Care initiative. For example, although CEFIC's guidance on reporting under Responsible Care may not go as far as some other reporting initiatives, it does provide a general stimulus across the sector to improve information management and overall performance. However, resources of a single corporation are the determining factor in the usage and adaptation of this knowledge. Some of the large multinational corporations can go beyond sector association in terms of knowledge accumulation. Indeed, in the chemicals sector, companies with established programmes of environmental reports routinely incorporate more detail than set out in the CEFIC guidance (Tapper, 1997, p. 291).

National associations also play a major role in devising the codes of conduct and monitoring corporate activities. National associations shall be expected to have the capability to capture the national priorities, extent of flexibility, adaptability and free-rider issues. Accumulated knowledge in terms of local issues would depend on the extent of interaction of national associations with societal actors such as environmental or social NGOs or trade unions and the industry. Hence, the financial and human resources of the national associations would automatically affect the effectiveness of the applications at national levels.

Even though at the corporate level the industry is in close interaction with the societal actors, these stakeholders are not given a particular role to drive the industry forward for performance improvements. In some cases, even the resource-dependency relationships conflict with the goals of the initiative. For example, financial organizations, markets and investors, which typically focus on short-term considerations with little understanding for long-term potential of environmental investments, may not support new technology instalments or investments on site (Moffett et al., n.d., p. 9).

With respect to human resources, it is usually the case that one person in each federation is responsible for the initiative. At the company level, each site and each company shall have at least one person responsible for making RC active. CEOs of corporations shall also be actively involved in order to derive corporate ethics in the direction of RC's principles. As product responsibility is taken up in the agenda, the personnel responsible for marketing, product safety and product development can be involved in the process; currently it is engineers being involved.[3]

POLICY-RELEVANT OUTCOMES

The major policy-relevant outcomes of the RC initiative are reflected in the basic informal structures that can take the form of either internal communication documents and processes or external communication documents and processes. Internal communication in the RC initiative happens via dissemination and adaptation of principal documents such as guiding principles (GPs) and codes of practice (COPs), internal reporting or internal verification. On the other hand, external interaction can take place via third-party verifications, national advisory panels or community advisory panels. However, both outcomes demonstrate considerable differences among country-level applications,[4] while only the framework of the outcome to be produced stays common to all.

The guiding principles (GPs) refer to the responsibilities of the industry in conducting its operations, like minimizing the negative impact (and risk of impact) on the workers, environment and all other persons, which these operations may affect. Considerable variations exist in the strength and scope of the GPs, but these generally can be viewed as benchmark statements defining the fundamental ethical responsibilities and operational philosophies of the industry. The GPs entail or infer (through specific statements) pollution prevention, emergency planning, a proactive attitude towards the public and government, and the minimization of risk (to the environment, employees and the public) from all existing or proposed operations and products (Munn, 2000).

Being broad and encompassing statements of principle, the GPs do not provide a suitable framework for judging the level of progress attained by a firm. For these quantifiable requirements, RC has developed the codes of practice (COPs). Hence, within the GPs the chemical association's members indicate what they intend to do, whereas the COPs detail how these goals shall be accomplished (Munn, 2000). Within the submitted descriptions for the national Responsible Care programmes, the COPs vary significantly. As for the general form and content of the COPs, they are normally concerned with the following areas:

- plant operations;
- transportation and distribution functions;

- community awareness and emergency response and communication;
- pollution prevention;
- process safety;
- distribution;
- employee health and safety;
- product responsibility (ICCA, 2002a, p. 40).

Beyond GPs, each national association signed up to Responsible Care is required to submit an annual report on its progress in the implementation of Responsible Care. This report states for an association whether there remains much more to be done about the social and economic aspects, particularly in the developing world. Then, individual countries' Responsible Care programmes, which are at different stages of development and have different focus areas, are collected in an annual RC report.

The International Council of Chemical Associations[5] Co-ordination Group and the Responsible Care Leadership Group (RCLG), which assist in the cross-fertilization of ideas and best practice, further monitor these reports. It is recommended that the ICCA needs to follow the Responsible Care process that was based on the adoption of guiding principles, to jointly set and implement social and economic principles to improve the performance of the chemical sector. An overview of indicators communicating the performance of the chemical industry worldwide is given in Box 16.2 as cited from the Responsible Care Status Report of 2002.

BOX 16.2   PERFORMANCE RESULTS

- 28 countries have published the required codes or guidelines for implementation.
- 29 countries are reporting on a range of performance indicators such as emissions, incidents and injuries, and 20 of these are making these indicators public and discussing them with the interested parties.
- 22 countries have established a stakeholder dialogue.
- 29 countries have in place peer support and information-sharing processes.
- All countries still have significant potential for continued improvement in the area of verification.

Source: ICCA (2002b), p. 9.

All in all, Responsible Care can be described as an international initiative initiated and coordinated by the chemical industry players aiming at gaining societal trust and forecasting and influencing formal public policy by continuous improvement of health, safety and environmental performance of products and processes. As a policy network, the outcomes delivered are highly flexible, which might depend on interpretations of realizing the main principles at the national and corporate level, while complex relations prevail at international, regional, national and corporate levels. As the objective is functionalized in various forms at different levels, a concrete relationship map cannot be developed. Further detailed analyses are given in the following section.

ASSESSMENT AND EVALUATION OF PROCESSES AND OUTCOMES

The Responsible Care initiative is highly diverse in its range of forms of implementation. The country- and company-specific focus of the initiative varies considerably from one national application to another since it is up to each national chemical industry association to identify its focus areas and specific priorities for attention and the implementation of the programme's principles.

The structure of this case-study follows the organizational scheme of the Responsible Care initiative, that is, relevance, effectiveness, efficiency, side-effects and adaptation flexibility at an international, regional, national and company level. However, the main focus of the analysis lies at the regional and national level by selecting the European and the German case, represented by the European Chemical Industry Council (CEFIC) and the German Chemical Association (VCI) as examples. The analysis outcomes are based on publications and reports of the International Council of Chemical Associations (ICCA), CEFIC, VCI, scientific journals and comprehensive interviews held with various stakeholder groups of the chemical industry.

Relevance

Scientific research has shown that Responsible Care has been initiated by the chemical industry due to unsatisfactory regulation on chemical substances and planned regulative initiatives by governments (Faust and Nordbeck, 2003). At different levels, ranging from international to company level, the industry has started a number of initiatives to improve its environmental performance.

At the international level, there is no standard method identified for prioritization or identification of the important aspects of the chemical industry apart from non-systematic initiatives. A recent initiative identified has been the High Production Volume (HPV) programme to generate complete safety data files on 1000 high production volume substances by the end of 2004 and the Long-range Research Initiative (LRI) that funds research designed to find out about the effects of chemicals on human health and on the environment (ICCA, 2002b, p. 7). The creation of a knowledge database to assess the health, safety and environmental effects of chemicals is a contribution in the agenda-setting process of the initiative.

Even though the industry engages in the research of risk effects of chemicals, the scope is more subjective to the industry. Participation in Responsible Care brings up the conflict for companies of meeting a decision for long-term environmental investments in favour of short-term profit.[6] Hence, RC companies cover short-term and clearly identifiable risks for which the industry could be clearly identified and that could be claimed by the public. However, costly and long-term research on accumulating long-term risks is not considered by the industry.[7] In line with this perspective, while high production volume substances constitute the priority for the industry, they may not necessarily be the most dangerous ones. Many low production volume substances, being used in various manufacturing processes or products, can be more hazardous or toxic.[8] Whereas the industry is limiting its research to around 1000 substances, the REACH[9] initiative by the European Commission intends to address around 30 000 substances.

At the international level, several stakeholders can be identified in the process of choosing the focus areas; however, the stakeholders do not dominate the process, since they serve as a medium for consultancy. The ICCA is said to work closely with key stakeholders through events such as the UN Intergovernmental Forum on Chemical Safety (IFCS) and initiatives like the Inter-Organisation Programme on the Sound Management of Chemicals (IOMC), and the Rotterdam Convention on the Trade in Hazardous Chemicals (ICCA, 2002a, p. 2). Lately the initiative has started to address its chain by introducing RC into the activities of suppliers and customers. The greatest progress has been made in the manufacture of products. The ICCA has agreed Responsible Care Partnership arrangements with a major international organization, the International Council of Chemical Trade Associations (ICCTA).

In Europe, there is a growing tendency to consider product responsibility issues, implying that the industry is moving from a production site focus to a product chain focus (VCI, 2003, p. 11). Product responsibility and supply chain initiatives were started through CEFIC, which have since evolved into a number of Safety and Quality Assessment Systems (SQAS),[10] each related to a particular transport mode or logistic operation. These schemes are also starting to spread outside Europe (ICCA, 2002b, pp. 10–11).

So far, only a few social aspects such as safety at work and occupational health (CEFIC, 2002) have been addressed within the Responsible Care programme. Although there is an awareness of the importance of the social components within the chemical industry, the industry believes that there are some issues where the chemical industry cannot have a direct role to play. It is stated that other actors such as public organizations should take the responsibilities for the issues of wealth generation or creation of employment.[11] Moreover, the ICCA believes that the social component must be treated at a national level, before it can take a position on how to respond to the demands at the international level (ICCA, 2002b, p. 18).

At the national level, each company decides how to implement the programme, such as being consistent with the framework set by its national industry association. This allows Responsible Care to focus on the encouragement of performance improvements in relation to national and regional circumstances. Through the development of guidelines or codes of practice the initiative encourages participating companies to identify significant issues of relevance, and then to standardize principles for management and reporting in these areas. The programme motivates all companies in a country to work together and to build Responsible Care activities as elements of wider management and good neighbour policies, and by this set the agenda for action (Tapper, 1997, p. 288).

However, at the European level CEFIC is scarcely involved with stakeholder dialogue procedures and focuses on developing dissemination, implementation and review strategies of RC within its member states. At the national and company level, as the initiative's principles demand from its assigning companies that they apply a stakeholder-based policy approach, stakeholder interaction can be realized through National Advisory Panels (NAPs) and Community Advisory Panels (CAPs). The interaction schemes and degrees of influence, though, vary significantly from country to country and from company to company. For example, the VCI has implemented neither National nor Community Advisory Panels at the national level. However, the association realizes stakeholder dialogue processes through their participation in the environmental protection committee of the German Norming Institute (DIN). Besides the industry, members from trade unions, policy-makers, scientists and environmental experts are also represented in these two expert bodies. In addition, the VCI organizes 'multi-stakeholder conversation round-tables' on specific topics (for example product responsibility) (Jeder, 2004).

Wherever applied, the NAPs have emerged as an influential yet controversial aspect of Responsible Care. On the one hand, their recommendations have helped to introduce external compliance audits and to strengthen the Community Awareness and Emergency Response (CAER) Code of Practice in a number of countries. On the other hand, critics charge that the NAPs represent an attempt to control public input and there is no mechanism in place to ensure that Responsible Care members address NAP recommendations. The question therefore arises how much public input is required by an initiative that is voluntary and unilateral, but which has the guise of public policy (Moffett et al., n.d., p. 29).

Addressing the social pillar of sustainable development, the German Chemical Association (VCI) has made a first step by concluding a Social Partnership Agreement on Responsible Care in 1999 with the IG BCE (German Trade Union of the Mining, Chemical and Energy Industries) and the BAVC (Association of German Chemical Industry Employers), which has resulted in the creation of a Social Partnership Committee on RC (Jeder, 2004). This agreement states that workers and their representatives shall be involved in RC activities and be given regular status reports on its implementation (ICCA, 2002b, p. 20).

In summary, Responsible Care is concerned with the collection of information on hazardous and toxic chemical substances which pose immediate risks to the industry activities and fall under due-diligence responsibilities. However, a majority of widely used substances within chemical manufacturing processes and products are not analysed in depth in terms of their environmental and health risks. The chemical industry is not ambitious in defining the scope of its responsibility. While, through NAPs and CAPs, the industry seeks to interact with stakeholders in order to identify its priorities of action, the effectiveness of these instruments is in question. Social aspects beyond health and safety issues are slowly expanding, depending on the ambitions of national associations and corporations.

Effectiveness

Based on the findings within the Responsible Care Status Report of 2002 (ICCA, 2002b), there are no common clear and verifiable targets set to be achieved at the international level. The report mainly refers to the future challenges of the chemical industry and that it would like to reduce its impacts on human health and the environment. However, there are no certain quantified targets set up. In order to monitor, benchmark and communicate the achievements, and for possible target-setting in the future, for the first time the ICCA integrated country-by-country performance indicators in its Status Report in 2002. A common performance indicator set that can be applied by chemical industries on a worldwide basis is still missing.

At the European level, the European Chemical Industry Council (CEFIC) has started to develop a core set of quantitative indicators of performance to achieve the objective of credible performance assessment. In 2002, the safety, health and environmental performance of the industry was measured and assessed against a range of 15 indicators and it is intended to be performed annually from 2003 onwards (CEFIC, 2003, p. 5). These indicators can link into existing environmental management systems and meet requirements of management systems such as ISO-14001 and EMAS (Tappert, 1997, p. 290). CEFIC is foreseeing that in the future the chemical industry will need to formulate reduction targets (for example green-house gas emissions). Hence, CEFIC needs to improve the

---

BOX 16.3   CEFIC CORE SET OF QUANTITATIVE INDICATORS

Safety and occupational health
1. Number of fatalities
2. Number of injuries at work
3. Lost time injury rate
4. Occupational illness frequency rate
5. Number of distribution incidents involving chemicals

Environment
6. Carbon dioxide (CO_2) emissions to air
7. Sulphur dioxide (SO_2) emissions to air
8. Nitrogen oxides (NO_x) emissions to air
9. Volatile organic compounds (VOC) emissions to air
10. Chemical oxygen demand to water
11. Phosphorus emissions to water
12. Nitrogen emissions to water
13. Heavy metal emissions to water (mercury, arsenic, cadmium, lead, chromium, copper, nickel, zinc)
14. Hazardous and non-hazardous wastes to land
15. Fuel and power consumption

Source: CEFIC (2006).

European-wide indicator performance set in order to meet these reduction targets and for the purpose of national federations and companies sharing best practice and benchmarking against other countries and companies. However, it is difficult for CEFIC to develop predefined targets addressing a wider scope of action, if the national federations are not in favour of them.[12]

At the national level, in the case of Germany, the national chemical association VCI sets a yearly theme. For the year 2004/05, the focus lies on 'Integrating Responsible Care in all company-internal training and education programs' (Jeder, 2004). These goal-oriented focus initiatives are based on the concept of voluntary self-commitments of the individual member companies. The VCI defines success factors for these initiatives that can be understood as an indicator set to verify the implementation process of the yearly theme (Jeder, 2004).

VCI has also participated in the development of the CEFIC Responsible Care HSE Reporting Guidelines with indicators to be measured by all European association member companies. The majority of German companies publish these indicators and VCI has consequently published the accumulated data results to CEFIC. However, the companies are not obliged to publish these indicators. VCI organizes regional and nationwide workshops to encourage its member companies to measure and publish these indicators, to implement company-based RC programmes and to apply corresponding management tools within their business operations (Jeder, 2004, point 7).

At the corporations level, global companies interpret RC principles and some develop their own management systems and set targets for practice. For example, regarding health and safety (H&S), Dow Chemicals within the framework set by the American Chemistry Council has developed a global Discipline Management System in order to implement the security measures and to integrate Responsible Care standards into all newly acquired sites and businesses. In 1996, Dow announced a series of environmental and H&S improvement goals for the year 2005. Subsequently, the 2015 Sustainability Goals were established to reflect Dow's sustainable commitment to the principles of RC (Dow, 2007). Similarly, BASF has developed a vision for 2010. However, the extent of implementation changes according to the culture and resources of each corporation, and no clear trend can be identified.

In conclusion, there are no clear and verifiable predefined targets set at the international or regional level, while some global corporations set their own management system. Since the setting of targets and their fulfilment or non-fulfilment constitutes an essential element of voluntary approaches (OECD, 2003), the environmental effectiveness of the RC initiative is questionable. However, at the international and especially European level, indicator performance development initiatives have been initiated. Stakeholder participation in the RC process is up to the national industry associations and single companies. Whereas at the European level CEFIC mainly coordinates the RC initiative and focuses on targeting the accession countries, stakeholder involvement is only implemented on a varying level of intensity at the national and company level.

Efficiency

Evaluating the cost-efficiency of the Responsible Care initiative is difficult. A quite unclear picture exists, resulting from empirical and analytical studies of whether and under what conditions the voluntary initiative can increase economic efficiency relative to a regulatory alternative or a baseline scenario (Paton, 2000).

Even though it cannot be well calculated, at the international and the European level, a cost reduction in terms of reputation costs can definitely be observed. Other costs cannot be calculated at this level because the cost composition is very scattered.

As mentioned above, absence of clear and verifiable target-setting at the international and regional level makes it difficult to assess the cost-efficiency of the voluntary approach of RC. A recently published study on voluntary approaches by the OECD shows that these can do better in terms of efficiency than traditional 'command-and-control' regulations (OECD, 2003, p. 12). However, this is the case when targets are set because the voluntary approach allows an increased flexibility in terms of how a given target is to be met. Since no clear targets are set, calculation of costs of the RC and eventually comparing these costs to regulating procedures is hardly to be achieved.

Implementation of Responsible Care at the national level represents a considerable investment by the chemical industry. In addition to the work involved in the development of the detailed codes of practice, associations hold training workshops, publish newsletters, prepare user guides, establish a national advisory committee and, in some cases, organize regional 'leadership groups', for example in Canada, to allow member companies to share information and apply peer pressure on industry laggards. However, a wide range of possible benefits can be identified, ranging from significant savings in inputs and waste disposal costs to more intangible benefits such as strengthened communications between plant and corporate offices. RC can help to reduce costs of product R&D by helping companies to avoid costly investments in environmentally inappropriate products. Most RC participants have improved their ability to respond to emergencies, due to both improved systems and improved community relations, which enable them to avoid protracted disputes based on distrust (Moffett and Bregha, 1999, p. 9). Hence, RC membership can lead to cost savings for the firm from increased flexibility in implementation and from reduced transaction costs[13] (Paton, 2000). Hence, when communicated by the national chemical industry associations, firms are able to identify eco-efficiency improvement opportunities and realize them. These opportunities certainly constitute a source for innovation in the industry.

In the case of Germany, the VCI believes that voluntary approaches should be preferred if the expected positive outcomes of the voluntary initiative outweigh the implementation costs or the costs of regulative approaches. Based on an interview with the VCI, the association considers and assesses the costs of self-commitment approaches (Jeder, 2004). Though it is not specified how relative cost differences are assessed with respect to alternative regulative approaches, the VCI is convinced that less regulation within the chemical industry sector will improve its competitiveness performance (Jeder, 2004).

All in all, regarding the reputation costs of the chemical industry Responsible Care has achieved an enormous cost reduction. At all levels, reduction of certain costs can be anticipated but cannot be quantified. Since no actor has a built-in system to calculate costs, it is impossible to develop an international cost-calculating system. As a generic conclusion, the creation of an innovative accounting system can be foreseen. Some national industry associations at the national level are making first moves.

Side-Effects

Responsible Care has the potential to make effective use of peer pressure to minimize laggards, and determine options for improvement[14] and internal accountability by the gradual development of the programme. On the other hand, after more than two decades of existence of Responsible Care there is no clear path set for implementation of the eight fundamental features indicating the major flow of the initiative. Other positive and negative side-effects can be listed as follows.

While the objective of the initiative for building up industry credibility with government decision-makers leads to intensive lobbying activities, the precise degree to which Responsible Care has influenced policy-relevant outcomes is hard to discern. Generally, most observers and participants agree that the chemical industry now enjoys a much more cooperative and influential role with government policy-makers than before it initiated the programme (Moffett and Bregha, 1999, p. 17). However, in some cases, extended lobbying exercises by the industry can prevent continuous improvement. A recent example of this is the collective action through which it opposes common guidelines of the REACH initiative proposed by the EU Commission. This initiative is perceived as a lobbying exercise for the industry rather than an environmental improvement exercise.[15]

Lack of a clear systematic prioritization system, guidance for indicator development and an action plan causes systematic leakages such as for example free-riding. Free-riding – meaning that a firm manages to obtain the benefits related to RC (for example image improvement), while not taking on any of the associated burden – is a significant problem with the RC initiative.[16] A way to limit free-riding would be to specify environmental performance targets for the industry.

Absence of long-term targets leads to absence of continuous improvements. Although the industry regularly demands clear targets from governments, it rarely or never proposes targets itself. It is very hard to check improvements made by some innovative companies in the industry. Product Responsibility incentives are perceived to have no real improvement but likely seem to be judged by a majority as 'window dressing'. For example, an empirical study carried out by King and Lenox has shown that there is no evidence that RC has positively influenced the rate of improvement among its members. Indeed, they found evidence that members of RC are improving their relative environmental performance more slowly than non-members (King and Lenox, 2000).

The RC initiative does not include a mechanism for addressing the competency disparities between large and small companies. Large companies, in comparison to smaller companies, have been most successful at adopting initiatives like RC. This is because they have greater resources to implement the code practices, can ensure consistency across several plants and are more likely to seek to obtain positive press coverage. In addition, the RC programme has been credited with changing practices related to interaction with the local community, as well as a company's relationship with distributors and, to a lesser degree, with suppliers and customers (Solomon and Mihelcic, 2001, p. 217). Research has found that the largest firms are most likely to reduce toxic emissions subsequent to the Toxic Release Inventory data being made public. In addition, since economies of scale exist in the activities required by Responsible Care, the larger firms benefit relative to their smaller competitors (Reinhardt, 1999, p. 13).

It is worth noting that many 'specialty chemical manufacturers' and hundreds of (typically medium-sized and small) companies which blend chemicals in the process of manufacturing items such as carpets, are not represented by the initiative. Small and medium-sized enterprises are not sufficiently addressed in RC. This is to be criticized due to the fact that SMEs in general are more concerned about short-term economic performance but nevertheless, because of their number, have a high impact on the environment. In addition, small companies often have less knowledge about new 'green' technologies, and typically have fewer resources and less money available to invest in change that has little prospect of short-term payback (Moffett et al., n.d., p. 10). However, in Germany, the VCI has started to address the specific needs of SMEs and organizes workshops in which VCI experts and RC representatives from associated member companies in cooperation with SME representatives develop RC approaches for national SMEs (Jeder, 2004).

It can be assumed that RC has contributed to the implementation of new environmental management instruments and has helped progress on product responsibility. However, this development process has mainly been situated in the context of developing new ISO standards, for example ISO TC-207, ISO-14001, with clear implementation and measuring procedures. It is hard to differentiate innovative environmental management systems (EMS) and product responsibility has been a result of RC or of ISO standards (for example ISO-14062 on environmental aspects in product design and development), whose implementation is regularly demanded by regulation, is considered to be a product of the RC initiative (Jeder, 2004).

In summary, despite the peer pressure created for working on environmental and health and safety aspects of the industry, the lobbying activities of the chemical industry can be said to be counteractive against legislative bodies. The question arises as to why the industry is so much against regulating its activities, especially while research on hazardous substances is intended, for example as proposed in the REACH initiative. Legislative instances ask themselves where this behaviour is 'responsible'. As with all voluntary approaches the problem of free-riders within the RC initiative is quite significant and this problem needs to be tackled in the future.

Adaptation Flexibility

Basically, at the international level there does not exist an informal control mechanism. As the sole formal control mechanism, there is the annual Responsible Care Status Report only. Neither an evaluation mechanism nor a review mechanism exists. Transparency occurs through the Leadership Group.

RC is flexible in the way it can be adapted to the circumstances facing the chemicals industry or its component companies. It sets out principles that represent the core of the programme, but it is up to national industry associations to agree on their priorities of implementing these principles, and then for each participating company to determine its priorities within the overall national framework. RC provides a structure, through checklists, guidance or codes, for companies to use to record their progress and to identify gaps, based on a form of self-assessment or audit (Tapper, 1997, p. 288).

The flexibility of RC allows companies to work on the issues that they see as priorities because of the activities of the company, local circumstances or other factors. It provides a structure within which to systematize management practices that, for the most part, are already established in any chemical company, but which are often poorly documented. The companies being members of RC are free to develop and approach new alternatives that aim to improve their transparency, management and performance evaluation systems and verification processes (Tapper, 1997, p. 288).

At the European level CEFIC has started to collect information on the 15 indicators that it has recently developed, published by the national associations. In its Annual Report 2002, CEFIC has published the results of the accumulated indicator performance of the publishing countries for the first time (CEFIC, 2003). However, CEFIC has not installed a verification process on the published data by the national associations, which makes the collected data questionable.

As regards review or evaluation mechanisms at the national level, the VCI concentrates on collecting the 15 indicators set out in the CEFIC RC Health and Safety and Environment Reporting guidelines. However, no company is obliged to publish these data and the VCI has no verification process installed to verify the published information. Besides, the VCI has developed a 'Self-Assessment Questionnaire' for its member companies. On a regular basis the VCI organizes Responsible Care Self-Assessment Surveys in order to evaluate the state of the art of the RC initiative (Jeder, 2004).

Through the above-mentioned Social Partnership Committee on RC, the participation in various stakeholder round-table discussion groups and publication of annual RC Status Reports, the VCI aims at achieving the goal of participation and transparency. Its work is interdisciplinary in the sense that the VCI refers to external knowledge by requesting information from chemical engineers, physicians, journalists, economists and lawyers. However, control mechanisms of the implementation process of RC within the companies are rare. Since the RC programme is not provided with its own budget within the VCI (Jeder, 2004) and the activities are financed from the general budget of the VCI, which receives its funding from the companies' member fees, the implementation of independent control or sanctions mechanisms is unlikely to be foreseen.

In summary, Responsible Care is a highly flexible voluntary initiative by the chemical industry at all levels. Informal control mechanisms and verification processes do not exist at international level and depend on the engagement of the national industry associations of each country. This is highly criticized and needs to be addressed intensively by the industry and the Responsible Care initiative in the future (Tapper, 1997, p. 290). However, some countries have taken first steps in improving their formal control mechanisms, for example Canada has implemented a third-party verification within its initiative and has recently introduced a re-verification process (Moffett et al., n.d., p. 28).

CONCLUSIONS AND SCORING CHART

Being a global and sector-wide initiative, Responsible Care constitutes a unique case among all forms of schemes established for environmental improvements (see also the other cases in this study). Besides its large scale, lack of a structured process for issue identification, monitoring and continuous improvement characterizes the initiative. These properties definitely make it a difficult case for the policy-makers to evaluate its performance. As the case has implications at the international, national and company level, drawing conclusions on the strengths and weaknesses of the initiative has been relatively harder.

In line with these major observations, the type of network demonstrated by the initiative can be declared as a 'network with deliberations' rather than a 'network for deliberations'. It would be expected that a network for deliberations delivers outcomes for a given purpose. However, in the case of Responsible Care, either due to the difficulties of managing a large-scale initiative or due to the prevailing aim of maintaining a favourable image in society, structured outcomes have not been observed in our analysis. Lack of concrete and verifiable methodologies, tools, metrics and targets leads to the fact that activities and reports of the initiative have often been labelled as window dressing. Hence, the initiatives deliver several by-products, but more important questions would be whether these reports bring about continuous improvements and whether there is a common vision and mission derived from these.

For the effectiveness and efficiency of the initiative, a structured process of major issue identification, metrics development, target-setting and verification should be developed. Hence, a sector governance set-up embracing this process is foreseen (Kuhndt and Tunçer, 2004). Stakeholder involvement including the public policy actors should be carried out from the beginning in the process of identifying the issues that the initiative needs to manage. Involvement of local stakeholders is also essential for addressing intercultural differences. The range and prioritization of environmental and social aspects of the chemical industry or chemical products is perceived to be subjective to the industry. The ambition of the chemical sector to define the agenda on its own leads to ineffectiveness and criticism, as each societal actor sets its agenda independently and interaction may happen quite late only at the implementation level instead of at the common vision development stage. All in all, limitation of issues to be tackled by the initiative at the international, regional or national level needs to be carried out in a structured process. This requirement becomes more eminent as the sector becomes eager to develop a product chain perspective.

Similar to issue identification, a structured process of metrics development and verification processes are found to be missing in Responsible Care. Development of indicators for the major issues identified would enhance effectiveness by making it easier to set targets internationally, regionally or nationally. Provision of a framework of implementation is more cost-effective in terms of data collection and preventing each national association or company from developing its own indicator sets. Common indicator sets would also allow benchmarking within the sector and create a drag force for the laggards. Learnings from other sector-wide processes such as the case of sustainability indicator set development for the European Aluminium Industry (Kuhndt et al., 2002), development of key performance indicators in the cement industry (WBCSD Cement, n.d.) and development of sector supplements of the Global Reporting Initiative indicator set can be used to set up a structured process for indicator development and target-setting. The structure of the chemical sector has to be analysed in detail before developing a structure for the indicator set, as sector-specific characteristics affect the indicator selection and implementation process. For example, the high degree of vertical integration in the aluminium sector, that is, the existence of several major corporations dominating the product chain, allows relatively fast consensus development on the sustainability indicators.

Furthermore, development of verification processes is crucial for the credibility of the process. Involvement of several national associations with voluntary verification is not sufficient for the establishment of a structured process. Development of a framework for the involvement of third parties in the verification of metrics, target-setting and management processes is necessary to achieve full credibility of the Responsible Care scheme. Verification would also add in as a structural element for continuous improvement of the scheme. In the absence of an external feedback mechanism, a healthy change in the sector cannot be possible.

The role of government in such a sector governance scheme would be involvement as a stakeholder in major issue identification, indicator set development, target-setting and verification processes. It can closely

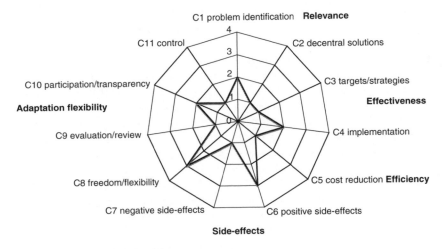

Note: 0 = no, 1 = low, 2 = moderate, 3 = above average, 4 = high action/result

Figure 16.2   Scoring chart of Responsible Care initiative

consult the sector and monitor its activities along the lines of the structured suggested above process. Instead of an aspects-driven structure, a process-driven structure needs to be in place in public administration to interact with, support and monitor more closely such sector-wide initiatives. Hence, governments should be prepared for more stakeholder involvement and organization of venues for experience-sharing between sectors.

Lastly, ignorance of the limitations of SMEs in joining the initiative has to be addressed. A rather simplified structured process can be foreseen for smaller corporations with limited financial and human resources. In order to achieve significant macro-level performance improvements beyond corporate-level achievements, active involvement of SMEs in a more struc-tured Responsible Care scheme shall be encouraged.

After almost 20 years of experience, the Responsible Care initiative deserves development of a more structured approach to environmental, health and safety improvements in the worldwide chemical industry. A responsible sector governance system supported by public policy, demand-ing the involvement of many other stakeholders such as NGOs, the financial sector and intergovernmental organizations, would pave the way to a more credible policy network.

The results of the Responsible Care initiative case-study are assessed as shown in Figure 16.2.

NOTES

1. Moffett et al. (n.d., p. 6) state the main objective of the initiative from a Canadian perspective as: 'regaining public trust and forestalling or influencing future regulatory developments by improving environmental performance of the industry as a whole and by improving community relations'.
2. For example, the Canadian National Advisory Panel brings together public interest representatives, that is, 16 individuals from across Canada who have demonstrated leadership and interest in issues related to the chemical industry (ICCA, 2002b, p. 50) while the Community Advisory Panels focus on local community dialogue.
3. Interview with R. Robson (6 January 2004), Responsible Care Contact Person at CEFIC.
4. As a country case illustration, in Canada, among the fundamental features of the initiative come the policy statement, guiding principles, the national advisory panel, a chemical referral centre, verification process and the six codes of practice with 152 individual elements covering community awareness and emergency response (CAER), research and development, manufacturing, transportation, distribution and hazardous waste management. All these features actually resemble the attributes of an environmental management system, but for a sector management level (Moffett et al., n.d., p. 1).
5. Central information body regarding Responsible Care is the International Council of Chemical Associations (ICCA). More information on RC, annual Status Reports and other relevant publications are available at http://www.icca-chem.org.
6. Such pressure usually comes from financial markets and investors, which typically have focused on short-term considerations with little understanding or appreciation for the long-term potential for environmental investments.
7. Interview with W. Mahlmann, 18 December 2003, Federal Ministry for the Environment, Nature Conservation and Nuclear Safety, Responsible for Environmental Health, Chemical Safety.
8. Interview with W. Mahlmann, 18 December 2003, Federal Ministry for the Environment, Nature Conservation and Nuclear Safety, Responsible for Environmental Health, Chemical Safety.
9. REACH stands for Registration, Evaluation and Authorization of Chemicals. For more information on REACH see http://europa.eu.int/comm/enterprise/chemicals/chempol/whitepaper/reach.htm.
10. SQAS being upgraded in 2002 enables chemical companies to have the quality and safety management systems of their logistic service providers assessed in a uniform manner, thereby avoiding multiple assessments by individual chemical companies.
11. Interview with R. Robson (6 January 2004), Responsible Care Contact Person at CEFIC.
12. Interview with R. Robson (6 January 2004), Responsible Care Contact Person at CEFIC.
13. Reputation costs are those that firms incur to construct and maintain reputation after an accident, discovery or revelation. Firms incur negotiation costs as they work to maintain discretion or autonomy through lobbying and negotiating with governmental or non-governmental actors. Firms pay search costs when they seek business partners and suppliers who are acceptable to governmental and non-governmental actors. Firms incur measurement costs as they measure the environmental effects of their behaviour or even the implementation of environmental rules. Finally, firms pay enforcement costs as they impose conformance within and beyond their organizations. Transaction costs also figure in the work of consumers and activists as they bargain with corporations, search for sustainable products and firms, measure environmental effects, and work to enforce new standards (Garcia Johnson, 2001, p. 4).
14. For example in Canada there have been institutionalized Regional Leadership Groups, comprised of the chief executive officers from each member company. These groups meet quarterly to compare notes on their progress, or lack thereof, and their difficulties, and offer each other help in approaches or expertise. Beyond providing a forum for trading

advice and reporting on progress, the group demonstrates the personal commitment of the chief executive officers and proves to be an effective means of applying peer pressure.
15. Interview with W. Mahlmann, 18 December 2003, Federal Ministry for the Environment, Nature Conservation and Nuclear Safety, Responsible for Environmental Health, Chemical Safety.
16. Interview with W. Mahlmann, 18 December 2003, Federal Ministry for the Environment, Nature Conservation and Nuclear Safety, Responsible for Environmental Health, Chemical Safety.

17. BP plc: tradeable permits at corporate level

Thomas Langrock

MISSION

BP plc is one of the largest companies in the oil and gas sector: in December 2002 115 250 employees generated US$179 billion in revenue (BP, 2004a). In total, the company owns 38 chemical sites and 24 refineries worldwide (BP, 2004a). It is divided into four business segments that cover the activities of all business units. According to BP (2004b), these are:

- Exploration and production: these segments cover all upstream and midstream activities, for example oil and gas exploration, the management of pipelines and the operation of liquefied natural gas processing facilities.
- Refining and marketing: this segment includes all activities for the supply and trading of crude oil and petroleum products. Among them is the management of almost 30 000 service stations in over 100 countries.
- Petrochemicals: this segment is responsible for the production and marketing of petrochemical products (for example ethylene, propylene, acetic acid) to bulk, wholesale and retail customers. BP is the third-largest petrochemical company in the world in terms of capacity.
- Gas, power and renewables: this relatively new segment comprises a variety of activities. Among them are the market development of solar panels and liquefied natural gas, the development of wind farms and the operation of a few gas-fired power generation plants.

Naturally, the production, transport and marketing of BP's products result in a multitude of discharges, emissions and waste. The same obviously holds true for the use of BP's products. Despite that, the company presents itself as an environmental leader. This marketing starts with the brand name and the logo. The green of the logo is translated into 'demonstrating environmental leadership' and the brand name BP is translated into 'beyond petroleum', 'reflecting [our] brand positioning today and [our] aspiration to meet the world's future energy needs' (BP, 2004c).

It is not the purpose of this case-study to judge whether this positioning is justified or not. The seemingly unlimited number of different environmental impacts of BP's operations makes such a judgement extremely difficult. Instead, the case-study will attempt to understand the approach BP has adopted versus climate change. Thus, the mission of this case-study is to combat the emissions of greenhouse gases (GHG) in the atmosphere from BP's operations as well as from the use of its products.

According to the website 'Our position', 'an integral and key element within our [BP's] strategy to address climate change' (BP, 2003c) is the commitment to control the emissions of BP's operations (see below). This commitment is accompanied by further parts of the strategy, which are enumerated in Table 17.1.

BP has been the first company in the oil and gas sector to publicly acknowledge the importance of action on climate change. In a speech delivered at Stanford University in 1997, John Browne, Chief Group Executive of BP plc, stated: 'We must now focus on what can and should

Table 17.1   BP's climate change strategy, excluding the commitment to reduce emissions from its operations

Strategy	Evidence
Promoting flexible market instruments	'We [BP] will continue to promote the flexible market instruments, including emissions trading, Joint Implementation (JI) and the Clean Development Mechanism (CDM)' (BP, 2003b)
Participating in the policy processes	'We [BP] are committed to take an active part in the climate change policy debate and to investigate innovative ways of reducing GHG emissions'(BP, 2003b)
Cooperation in order to accelerate new energy technologies	'We [BP] intend to work with other industries to advance the development of energy efficient technologies and to make these available to our customers' (BP, 2003b)
Investing in research	'BP plans to continue to invest in and support science, technology and policy research' (BP, 2003b)

be done, not because we can be certain climate change is happening, but because the possibility can't be ignored. If we are all to take responsibility for the future of our planet, then it falls to us to begin to take precautionary action now' (Browne, 1997). This speech is widely seen as the starting point of a series of activities that BP has taken in the above-mentioned direction. Today BP is perceived to be one of the pioneers of greenhouse gas mitigation in the oil and gas sector (for a comparison with other corporations in the field see van den Hove et al., 2002).

This case-study seeks to understand whether the measures BP has undertaken can be interpreted in the light of responsible corporate governance. In order to reduce the complexity of the case-study it will focus on the commitment to control BP's emissions of greenhouse gases. The approach follows the theoretical framework outlined in Part 1 and Part 2. The analysis rests on the information that BP plc publishes on its Internet site (http://www.bp.com) as well as background information that the author collected during various discussions with BP employees.

ACTORS INVOLVED AND RESOURCE-DEPENDENCY RELATIONS

On its website 'Working in Partnership' (BP, 2004a) BP enumerates a lot of partners that it works with in order to tackle its greenhouse gas emissions. However, these partners are not the only actors involved, there are of course public actors that need to be considered as well as actors from the financial community and from the critical non-governmental organization (NGO) sector. The following section describes the identified interactions with these actors and attempts to derive the resource-dependency relationships that might exist.

BP and Non-governmental Organizations

The term 'NGO' is used for a wide range of organizations. Many are non-profit entities that fulfil economic functions or provide public goods, some work as policy think-tanks and the most well-known are the critical NGOs that engage in the policy-making process through campaigning. BP maintains relations with NGOs of all three types.

BP acknowledges the cooperative work with the Nature Conservancy (BP, 2004e), an American non-profit NGO that has the mission 'to preserve the plants, animals and natural communities that represent the diversity of life on Earth by protecting the lands and waters they need to survive' (Nature Conservancy, 2006). This NGO is very active in setting up and managing natural parks, thus providing a public good. Together with BP it has set up carbon sequestration projects. In addition to that, BP sponsors the exploratory work of the Nature Conservancy, research institutes and other organizations that seek to find out how biological carbon sequestration projects can be designed in such a way that they contribute to both the conservation of biodiversity and the mitigation of climate change. On its website, BP refers to its participation in the climate and biodiversity alliance, which among many activities aims to develop an independent standard for biodiversity and restoration projects that mitigate climate change (sometimes referred to as the Blue Chip Standard).

BP further has very close relations with two American policy think-tanks: Environmental Defense and the Pew Center on Climate Change. The cooperation with Environmental Defense started in 1997 with the objective to build an internal emissions trading scheme (Environmental Defense, 1997). BP publicly acknowledges the important work that Environmental Defense has undertaken in formulating and implementing the commitment to control BP's greenhouse gas emissions. The cooperation with Environmental Defense led to further results. In October 2000 Environmental Defense together with seven big greenhouse gas emitting companies – among them BP – launched the Partnership for Climate Action (Environmental Defense, 2000). The partnership has been designed as a platform that every company can join as long as it agrees to a fixed set of objectives and common principles. Salient among these principles and objectives is the willingness of each member to declare publicly a global greenhouse gas emission limitation commitment backed by management actions, policies and incentives to achieve this (Environmental Defense, 2006).

The working relationship with the Pew Center on Climate Change is to some extent similar to that with Environmental Defense. BP has joined the Pew Center's Business Environmental Leadership Council (BELC), which is a group of 'leading companies worldwide that are responding to the challenges posed by climate change' (Pew Center on Climate Change, 2006). The website at the Pew Center states several core beliefs with regard to climate change that all members of the BELC share. The website furthermore lists the company profiles and the individual GHG reduction targets of each member of the group. The website does not contain references to concrete action of the Business Environmental Leadership Council.

BP is also a member of the International Emissions Trading Association (IETA), an NGO which strives: (1) to promote an integrated view of the emissions trading system as a solution to climate change; (2) to participate in the design and implementation of national and international rules and guidelines; and (3) to provide the most up-to-date and credible source of information on emissions trading and greenhouse gas market activity (IETA, 2004). The actual interaction between this NGO and BP that could be detected through Internet research is that a senior group advisor of BP is at the same time a director of IETA (IETA, 2004).

As has been mentioned, a variety of NGOs pursue their objectives through campaigning. The oil and gas sector has repeatedly been exposed to such campaigns. Most prominent has been Greenpeace's campaign against the dumping of the Shell oil platform Brent Spar in 1995 (Vorfelder, 1995). More recently Greenpeace demanded – based on a study conducted by the Wuppertal Institute (Luhmann et al., 2002) – that the oil and gas producing companies invest more heavily into renewable energies. At the moment Greenpeace, Friends of the Earth and People & Planet carry through a campaign in the UK that focuses on ExxonMobil's branch Esso, which operates petrol stations worldwide. It asks its UK customers to boycott Esso until ExxonMobil stops pushing its climate-sceptic position in various political arenas. The campaign further targets the political influence that ExxonMobil is supposed to exert in US foreign policy (Greenpeace et al., 2003). So far, none of the campaigns against companies in the oil and gas sector have focused on the greenhouse gas emissions from the operations. And none of the campaigns have targeted BP.

One very important interaction between BP and the NGOs is bound to remain in the shadows due to the limits of the applied research methodology. BP has a variety of relations to NGOs on a direct contact basis. On its website 'NGOs' BP states that 'early identification of key emerging issues' is one example of how BP benefits from discussions with NGOs (BP, 2004g). According to this website, 'discussing issues with people who often have very different views to your own is difficult, but often raises ideas and concerns that would not normally be considered in day-to-day business operations' (BP, 2004g).

Other Companies along the Product Chain

In his speech at Stanford, Lord John Browne announced that BP would work with engine manufacturers as well as fleet operators in order to increase energy efficiency in the transport system. Even though these energy efficiency measures occur outside BP's operations, John Browne links them with emissions of BP's operations (Browne, 2002, see below).

BP and International Law-making Bodies

The Conference of the Parties (CoP) to the UN Framework Convention on Climate Change is the law-making actor regulating greenhouse gas emissions on a global level. The Kyoto Protocol is one of the policy outcomes of this negotiation body. It was adopted in 1997 and was expected to enter into force during 2004, the entry into force depending on the ratification by the Russian Federation. The Kyoto Protocol compels the parties who are listed in its Annex B (mainly the OECD countries and the Eastern European countries with economies in transition) to limit the amount of greenhouse gases that they emit during the years 2008 to 2012.

The Kyoto Protocol as a legal document only contains provisions for subjects of international law (nation-states, the European Union, some international governmental organizations). Thus it compels nation-states to introduce policies and measures that are suitable to reduce the amount of greenhouse gas emissions from their territory. As regards BP, the CoP obviously has no mandate to establish regulation that has a direct impact on BP's operations. The only way in which BP will be affected is when governments of parties of the Kyoto Protocol implement the provisions. Due to the architecture of the Kyoto Protocol, only the countries listed in Annex B of the Kyoto Protocol are likely to do so.

As a novelty to international law, the Kyoto Protocol contains the so-called flexible mechanisms International Emissions Trading, Joint Implementation (JI) and the Clean Development Mechanism (CDM). JI and the CDM are instruments for cooperation on a project-by-project basis (the so-called CDM and JI projects) between parties of the Kyoto Protocol. These CDM and JI projects are not developed by the parties themselves but by private entities, notably private companies. The basic idea of the CDM and JI is that these entities invest in climate-friendly technologies and receive a certain amount of internationally accepted emission certificates in return. BP has announced that it wants to use the CDM and JI.

The actual interactions between BP and the international law-making bodies have, however, been informal or indirect only. Neither the websites of BP, of the UNFCCC Secretariat nor of the NGO CDM-Watch mention that BP has formally submitted a project design document of a CDM project. Thus, there are no formal interactions between BP and the international law-making bodies. Yet, BP participates in the Prototype Carbon Fund and therewith it is involved in a variety of CDM and JI projects. Thus there are indirect interactions between BP and the international law-making body.

BP and the National Governments (Restricted to the UK)

As a multinational company, BP must naturally accept the legal and economic frameworks that national governments set under their jurisdiction.

However, in the various nation-states there is only very little implemented policy that directly targets greenhouse gas emissions from industrial processes. In the United Kingdom, where the headquarters of BP are based, a number of policy instruments that directly target the operations of BP are in place (Langrock, 2001).

The business units of BP UK that belong to the chemicals operations have pledged to cut emissions in a negotiated agreement with the UK government. In exchange for delivery of the corresponding emission reductions, the business units involved will receive an 80 per cent reimbursement of the UK Climate Change Levy (an energy tax). The negotiated agreement with the UK government is not publicly available, so it is impossible to assess the proportion of BP UK total emissions that are subject to this agreement. It is further impossible to assess the magnitude of the Climate Change Levy reimbursement that BP receives in exchange.

Further parts of BP UK participate in the UK emissions trading scheme as so-called direct participants, as from 2002 onwards. BP UK entered an agreement with the UK government wherein it agreed to report its emissions from a defined set of sources of GHG during a specified commitment period. More importantly, BP UK agreed to hand in an amount of emission allowances that is equivalent to the amount of emissions by the participating business units at the end of the commitment period. As participating business units, BP mentions its refineries and the various oil and gas production sites in the North Sea as well as onshore in the UK. BP expects to realize a large magnitude of the emission reductions through reduced gas flaring at the oil and gas production sites as well as through increased energy efficiency. In exchange for a pledged reduction of 350 000 tonnes CO_2 equivalents BP UK received around €20 million incentive money from the government (Browne, 2002; DEFRA, 2006).

BP and the European Union

The European Union has adopted the directive 2003/87/EC 'establishing a scheme for greenhouse gas emission allowance trading within the community and amending Council directive 96/61/EC' (EU, 2003). The participation in EU emissions allowance trading is mandatory for certain types of industrial sites and started operating in 2005. It is important to note that the design of the EU-wide emissions trading significantly deviates from that of the UK, so that it remains to be seen whether the UK will be forced to revise its own scheme. As regards BP, the differences may be significant.

First of all, methane as well as other greenhouse gases will not be included in the EU-wide scheme and as the Directive stands now, oil and gas production sites will not be part of the scheme. Thus it is very likely that a significant share of BP's emissions in the EU member states will not be part of the EU-wide emissions trading scheme. So far it is not possible to predict whether the EU will incorporate other measures that target the operations of BP.

POLICY-RELEVANT OUTCOMES

The above research has identified a variety of joint initiatives and decisions that can be regarded as policy-relevant outcomes. The commitment to reduce and limit the greenhouse gas emissions of BP and its subsequent implementation through BP-wide internal emissions trading are policy-relevant outcomes of the cooperation between Environmental Defense and BP. Linked to this commitment are the policy-relevant outcomes that relate to the realization of CDM and JI projects. However, as the analysis has shown, only BP's participation in the World Bank's Prototype Carbon Fund can be interpreted as a tangible policy outcome. As yet, BP has not taken steps in order to register concrete CDM or JI projects. The commitment to reduce the greenhouse gas emissions of BP's operations will be evaluated more closely in the next step 'assessment and evaluation' of this case-study.

The identification of tangible policy-relevant outcomes from the cooperation with the Nature Conservancy and Conservation International is difficult insofar as the link between various joint initiatives and BP's emissions is not yet established. So far BP has not announced whether and how it will use geological or biological sinks as a means of neutralizing its own emissions.

Various policy-relevant outcomes can be subsumed under the heading of outreach and information dissemination. BP is a member of the International Emissions Trading Association (IETA), the Partnership for Climate Action and the Pew Center's Business Environmental Leadership Council.

ASSESSMENT AND EVALUATION

John Browne announced the commitment to monitor and control the greenhouse gas emissions of BP in a landmark speech delivered at Stanford University in May 1997, a few months before the adoption of the Kyoto

Protocol (Browne, 1997). This commitment was qualified in 1998: BP pledges to reduce its 'emissions of greenhouse gases by 10 per cent from a 1990 baseline over the period to 2010' (Browne, 1998). In March 2002 John Browne publicly stated: 'Now, five years on, I'm delighted to announce that we've delivered on that target. That means that our emissions of carbon dioxide have fallen to almost 80 million tonnes, 10 million tonnes below the level in 1990 and 14 million tonnes below the level that they had reached in 1998' (Browne, 2002).

In the same speech Browne announced the new target: BP will 'hold the emissions from our operations at 10 per cent below 1990 levels, through 2012, with approximately half of that coming from improvements in internal energy efficiency, and half from the use of market mechanisms, generating carbon credits' (Browne, 2002).

Of course, the two targets need further qualification as regards the system boundary and other technical details. BP provides various documents that provide clarification, among them the environmental reporting guidelines of BP (KPMG et al., 2000, 2001; KPMG LLP and DNV, 2003). All these documents primarily focus on the monitoring of BP's emissions; however, almost all include references to BP's GHG commitment. From these documents it can be deduced that the GHG commitment consists of controlling the direct equity share emissions of BP. Thus the system boundary is drawn in such a way that all emissions from sites that BP owns completely as well as an appropriate share of the emissions of those sites that BP partly owns are included.

Relevance

Climate change is one of the most widely discussed environmental problems. Although there still is considerable uncertainty in the science of climate change, the majority of scientists are convinced that climate change is occurring and can have devastating impacts. The Intergovernmental Panel on Climate Change (IPCC) is the entity that regularly assesses the knowledge about climate change. In its third assessment report, published in 2001, the IPCC concluded: 'There is new and stronger evidence that most of the warming observed over the last 50 years is attributable to human activities' (IPCC, 2001).

BP has a strong commitment to precautionary action with regard to climate change. On many websites BP explains the environmental problems associated with climate change. Its membership of the Partnership for Climate Action as well as in the Business Environmental Leadership Council includes the public acceptance of climate change as a real and pressing issue. And in his speeches on climate change John Browne makes clear that: 'we must now focus on what can and what should be done, not because we can be certain climate change is happening, but because the possibility can't be ignored. If we are all to take responsibility for the future of our planet, then it falls to us to begin to take precautionary action now' (Browne, 1997).

An evaluation of a policy-relevant outcome must include an assessment of the contribution to the mission, which is to mitigate climate change. The GHG commitment clearly is a contribution to the mitigation of climate change. Its relevance can be assessed by putting the commitment in a context with the emissions BP can theoretically control as well as with the emissions of various nation-states.

In the year 2002 BP emitted 80.5 million tonnes of carbon dioxide equivalent into the atmosphere. To put this in a perspective, this is less than 10 per cent of the emissions of Germany in 2002. Hence, a reduction of 10 per cent of BP's emissions can only contribute a little to climate change mitigation. But of course millions of different actors must contribute to the mitigation of climate change. Therefore, an assessment of the relevance of the objective should not stop at an assessment of the absolute emission reductions. In relative terms, BP's contribution is above average, that is, far above the minus 8 per cent that the Kyoto Protocol demands from the European Union or the minus 7 per cent that it stipulates from the United States of America.

Effectiveness: Targets and Strategies

It has been described above how BP defines its GHG commitment. BP has already achieved its original target: the reduction of its direct equity share emissions to 10 per cent below the 1990 level. According to the website 'Our Performance' (BP, 2003d), BP achieved this commitment in 2001 for the first time. This fact was verified by KPMG and DNV, two respected accountancy companies. BP has put the audit notes on its website (KPMG LLP and DNV, 2003; KPMG et al., 2001; KPMG and DNV 2000). Although the audit paints a comprehensive picture of the achievement of the GHG commitment (for example a lot of effort has been invested into treating acquisitions and divestments properly), it must be noted that up to 2005, there was no formal process that assesses compliance with the GHG commitment.

As noted above, a new target was taken on in 2002. The speech in which Browne announced the new target (Browne, 1998), contains a few hints as to how BP intends to achieve the commitment. BP intends to expand its business and therefore to include further emissions sources inside the system boundary. This will clearly lead to an increase of emissions inside the system boundary, if no action is taken. Browne estimated that emissions might then rise as high as 130 million tonnes. Reconciliation of this business-as-usual scenario with the GHG commitment will be done through substantial investments into emission reductions both inside and outside the system boundary. In other words, BP intends to achieve around 25 million tonnes of carbon dioxide equivalent inside and 25 million tonnes outside the system boundary. The emissions reductions outside the system boundary will then neutralize the same amount of emissions within the system boundary, that is, emissions inside the system boundary may rise as high as 105 million tonnes.

Neutralization of emissions through emissions reductions outside their own sphere of control can be regarded as an accepted principle: JI and the CDM, which are both laid down in the Kyoto Protocol, rest on the same principle. Nevertheless, neutralization poses some questions with regard to effectiveness.

Firstly, the quality of the emissions reductions must be controlled very carefully. The Kyoto mechanisms – JI and the CDM – offer a platform for producing high-quality emissions reductions; yet it is questionable whether BP can realize all the announced emissions reductions within this legal framework. Particularly, the emissions reductions it wishes to achieve by working with car manufacturers may not be eligible under these two mechanisms.

Secondly, the Kyoto Protocol stipulates so-called 'supplementarity', that is, the usage of neutralization should only be a supplement to domestic emissions reductions. One might argue that supplementarity should be applied to BP as well. Whichever way, the minimum requirement would be to report openly the amount of emissions that is neutralized.

Summing up, the inclusion of emissions reductions outside the system boundary puts the effectiveness of the GHG commitment to some degree into question. BP can easily make up for this shortcoming if it introduces a more formal compliance assessment than it has in place now. It should also state more clearly which emissions reductions outside its system boundary it wishes to include.

Effectiveness: Implementation

BP has implemented the GHG commitment through a series of activities both inside and outside the system boundary. The most important instrument inside the system boundary has been the setting up of an internal BP-wide emissions trading scheme. In 1999, a pilot scheme was introduced and during 2000 and 2001, BP-wide emissions trading took place (BP, 2003d).

In 2002, the trading scheme was abandoned in order to give room to the public emissions trading schemes that are being set up. By the nature of its construction, emissions trading only makes sure that the least-cost potential for emission reductions is tapped; the actual implementation of the GHG commitment comprises a variety of technical measures at the business sites. BP itself mentions investment into energy efficiency, reduced leaks of methane in the natural gas business, and reduced flaring and venting. With such activities inside the system boundary, BP achieved a significant emission reduction. In addition to that, BP plans to realize significant emission reductions outside the system boundary, particularly through investments in emissions reduction projects, among them CDM and JI projects (see above).

Efficiency

BP itself states that the benefits associated with the emissions reductions have so far exceeded the costs for implementation. BP states: 'The outcome was that our first target was delivered at no net cost to our business – we estimated that our reduction projects delivered over $600 million of net present value from the fuel saved' (BP, 2004i).

Summary of Evaluation and Assessment

Every evaluation of BP's GHG commitment must remain preliminary as it is running until 2012. The simplified *ex ante* evaluation above has shown that BP's commitment is clearly an above-average contribution to climate change mitigation. However, there can be no doubt that BP will need to continue the reduction of emissions far beyond 2012.

The information that BP publishes on its website provide an insight into how BP intends to implement the GHG commitment. Whether the GHG commitment will be implemented effectively crucially depends on the treatment of those emissions reductions that occur outside the system boundary. The inclusion of such emissions reductions raises questions with respect to their quality and supplementarity. Making the effective implementation of the GHG commitment visible almost certainly requires a revision of the current assessment of compliance. It may be a good idea to introduce a formal assessment of compliance instead of the audit of the GHG emissions.

This simplified evaluation has only been possible because of the extraordinary reporting policy of BP plc. The assessment has been relatively straightforward, yet there is certainly room for improvement. It could be a good idea to underline the voluntary character of the GHG commitment a little further. Incorporating a watertight formulation of the commitment as well as a formal assessment of compliance could do this, for example.

CONCLUSIONS AND SCORING CHART

BP clearly is a company that has adopted elements of responsible corporate governance, as presented in Chapter 2. The commitment to control the greenhouse gas emissions from BP's operation is a voluntary measure that BP has adopted and implemented. Access to information about the GHG strategy of BP is easy and therefore transparency can be regarded as relatively high.

The analysis of the interactions between BP and other stakeholders has resulted in the identification of a policy network for implementation, not for policy formulation. BP is involved in quite a lot of partnerships that all can be regarded as attempts to mobilize resources outside BP in order to implement the GHG commitment. Yet, the case-study could not identify interactions between BP and other stakeholders that can be regarded as significant impulses leading to the formulation of the target and the new target, respectively. This may, however, be due to the applied research methodology. Summarizing the case-study could not produce evidence as to why BP has positioned itself as a pioneer with respect to climate change.

The big picture is thus as follows. The case-study cannot answer why BP has taken up a proactive strategy towards climate change. The implementation of BP's strategy towards climate change is clearly done in a policy network for implementation. And BP undertakes a lot of effort in order to promote action for the mitigation of climate change.

The case-study therefore is a very interesting illustration of the role that companies adopting responsible corporate governance can play in the policy-making process. BP has been a key driver in the debate on emissions trading and it has actively engaged in the promotion of the idea. The knowledge generated by BP has influenced the design of the UK and EU emissions trading. Thus the importance of BP's action cannot be underestimated.

To conclude, the case-study suggests that companies adopting responsible corporate governance should be promoted, because the knowledge that they have generated is urgently needed by other companies, and also by public policy-makers. At the same time the case-study does not provide hints that a powerful policy network surrounding companies emerges that automatically drives these companies towards sustainable development.

Figure 17.1 summarizes the results of the evaluation in a scoring chart.

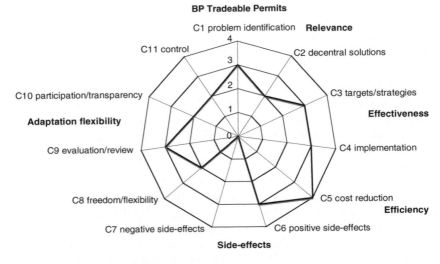

Note: 0 = no, 1 = low, 2 = moderate, 3 = above average, 4 = high action/result

Figure 17.1 Scoring chart of BP tradeable permits

18.   Dow Jones Sustainability Indexes

Oliver Karius

MISSION: THE CHALLENGE TO INTEGRATE SUSTAINABILITY IN THE FINANCIAL MARKETS

The relevance of sustainability for investors and companies alike is driven by a number of distinct trends such as rapid information exchange, increasing interconnectivity and convergence, heightened awareness for remote geographic regions, severe stress on ecosystems, regional demographic shifts and increasing transboundary interactions. In addition, the relevance of sustainability particularly for investors is driven by the relative financial outperformance of certain sustainability investments and by recent corporate scandals such as Enron, Parmalat and Ahold.

Concurrent with these shifts is the relatively new development that it is not only possible to make macroeconomic policy decisions informed by socio-environmental issues (under the assumptions of imperfect information), but that these analyses can now be complemented by a new ability to make similarly well-informed microeconomic decisions. This is due to an increase in transparency and access to a wider range of different information sources which was previously not available.

The net result of these changes is that sustainability-focused assessments are not only becoming increasingly relevant to both businesses and shareholders, but that these assessments are now also practicable and feasible while contributing to overall policy-making.

Corporate sustainability is a business approach aiming to create long-term shareholder value by embracing opportunities and managing risks deriving from economic, environmental and social developments. Corporate sustainability leaders harness the market's potential and demand for sustainability products and services while simultaneously successfully reducing and avoiding sustainability-related costs and risks.

Increasingly, investors regard forward-looking non-financial metrics as important additional indicators to provide a more realistic and comprehensive view of a company's true value. These metrics provide a broader scope of business-relevant information and insight that goes above and beyond the traditional financial analysis of companies.

Moreover, a wide range of external and internal stakeholders demands greater accountability and transparency from multinational companies on impacts and management of responsibilities to the environment and society at large.

One of the most prominent efforts to assess the sustainability performance of the world's leading companies by integrating the results into a mainstream financial index are the Dow Jones Sustainability Indexes (DJSI).

This case-study provides an overview of the main characteristics of the DJSI as financial tools that integrate sustainability into mainstream financial markets and highlights some key challenges.

ACTORS INVOLVED AND RESOURCE-DEPENDENCY RELATIONS

The success of financial instruments such as the Dow Jones Sustainability Indexes (DJSI) depends on the involvement of a number of different financially independent players. These players are interdependent due to their respective information needs.

BOX 18.1   KEY FACTS ABOUT THE DOW JONES SUSTAINABILITY INDEXES (DJSI)*

- Launched 1999
- Starting universe are the 2500 largest companies of the Dow Jones Global Index (DJGI) by free-float market capitalization
- Best-in-class methodology, contain the top 10% leading sustainability companies in each industry
- Methodology focused exclusively on corporate sustainability
- Criteria linked to value creation focusing on environmental, social and economic aspects
- Industry classification adopted from the Dow Jones Global Index (DJGI)**
- No exclusion criteria
- 308 companies in 60 industry sectors
- Benchmarking feedback to all assessed companies
- Number of licences sold 51 (July 2004)
- Performance: Over   the   last   year   (December 2002–December 2003) the DJSI World has outperformed the MSCI World by more than two percentage points. The

---

USD price index value of the DJSI World increased by 33.27% while the MSCI World rose by 30.81%.

Notes:

* For more information see www.sustainability-index.com.

** Industry sector allocation follows Dow Jones nomenclature. For a list of industry sectors see www.djindexes.com/jsp/giClassification.jsp.

The Investors

In order to satisfy market demand for a global, rational, consistent, flexible and, most importantly, investable index to benchmark the performance of sustainability investments, SAM Sustainable Asset Management[1], a Zurich-based independent asset manager founded in 1995 and exclusively focused on sustainability and asset management, entered into a cooperation with Dow Jones Indexes to launch the world's first sustainability index, the Dow Jones Sustainability Indexes, in 1999. Two years later the Dow Jones STOXX Sustainability Indexes were launched.

SAM Sustainable Asset Management employs 55 people, is headquartered in Zurich, Switzerland and is active in the Italian, Spanish, Australian, German, Austrian, US and Nordic markets. SAM has a large and experienced multidisciplinary and cross-cultural research team consisting of 20 analysts focusing on the sustainability and financial analysis of companies.

In this cooperation agreement SAM is responsible for the complete research process. This process includes among others developing, reviewing and setting the complete research methodology and criteria; analysing companies; identifying the leading sustainability companies; providing Dow Jones with a list of the index constituents; and continually monitoring all index members throughout the year. Dow Jones Indexes conducts the calculation and distribution functions for the DJSI. The two companies are financially independent, where Dow Jones Indexes generates revenue through the sale of licences.

The analysis is conducted with the support of a unique sustainability database, which contains corporate, economic, environmental and social information on over 1000 companies worldwide. The research is strengthened by an extensive international network consisting of experts from a broad diverse network including think-tanks, non-governmental organizations (NGOs), industry experts and academia, for example Transparency International (TI), Amnesty International (AI), World Wide Fund for Nature (WWF), World Resource Institute (WRI), the World Conservation Union (IUCN) and Imperial College London.

For both retail and institutional investors the index provides both a benchmark and a universe of large, global companies that embrace the concept of sustainability. Currently 56 DJSI licences are held by asset managers in 14 countries to manage a variety of financial products including active and passive funds, certificates and segregated accounts. In total, these licensees presently manage 2.8 billion euros based on the DJSI.[2]

The Companies

From a research perspective, companies are the most important stakeholder group. The largest 2500 global companies across 60 industry sectors in the Dow Jones Global Index (DJGI) form the eligible universe for the Dow Jones Sustainability Indexes. Just as sustainability is not a homogeneous concept, so the corporate executives that are dealt with are a heterogeneous group consisting of different positions within the company and of different levels of seniority, for example heads of sustainability, company secretaries, senior managers, human resource managers, environmental managers, risk officers, investor relations and corporate communication to name but a few. The overall responsibility for sustainability often rests with a member of the board of directors with clear operational responsibility delegated downwards. Furthermore, responsibility for sustainability management at a group level is increasingly linked to risk management in a company.

Global benchmarking of sustainability performance as conducted for the DJSI provides valuable insights for companies on how they rank compared to their international peers. This direct benchmarking catalyses the further development and implementation of sustainability within a company.

The Markets

As the market for socially responsible investment matures – in November 2003, the institutional market for sustainability investments stood at 336 billion euros in assets under management (Eurosif, 2003)[3] – so the need for mature, robust and reliable information about relevant sustainability issues and impacts also rises. Demand for reliable data and contextual analysis is increasing, requiring companies to disclose significant and material non-financial information that goes above and beyond the traditional reporting scope.

Mainstream socially responsible investment indices have been around since the mid-1990s. Since then, the market has grown and expanded to cover emerging markets as well with local stock exchanges introducing specific indexes incorporating sustainability, for example the Johannesburg Stock Exchange (JSE).[4] In July 2003, the JSE expanded the listing requirements to include social, ethical and environmental issues. Companies are now required to report explicitly on non-financial issues affecting their business with the aim of providing greater transparency and therefore an improved opportunity for investors to assess non-financial risks. It is likely that this trend will spread to other emerging market economies across the world.

An index tracking the performance of companies addressing sustainability is valuable when it provides insight into the future financial prospects of a company or industry that conventional analysts are unlikely to incorporate, given a lack of focus on the potential for certain social, environmental and economic issues in society to materialize and affect companies. Such an index addresses both risks and opportunities arising from sustainability in the long run. As traditional valuation metrics and historical corporate information increasingly concede importance to future-oriented, forward-looking indicators of the health of a company and its attractiveness to an investor, indexing the performance of companies addressing sustainability attempts to provide investors with the insights they are increasingly seeking (Funk, 2001). Thus, as an investment insight, equity research in relation to sustainability must be:

- forward-looking;
- based on industry-specific value drivers (as opposed to generic data);
- transparent and easily understood; and
- capable of adding value to existing valuation methods.

Assessing corporate sustainability aims to incorporate the characteristics mentioned above and offers insight across most equity asset classes and investment styles. The hypothesis for the business case for sustainability, interpreted as a portfolio of stocks, is that these stocks will be expected to outperform comparable portfolios, at least in the long run. The reasoning for this expectation can be considered sound.[5] A recent broker report produced by WestLB found that the 'DJSI was able to achieve a risk-adjusted outperformance' (Garz and Volk, 2003). The recent growth in number of new financial products integrating sustainability in their core investment strategy – on 30 June 2003 there were 313 green, social and ethical funds operating in Europe which represents a 12 per cent increase over 18 months (since the end of 2001) (SiRi Group, 2003)[6] – provided the impetus for a neutral, rigorous, transparent and easily replicable measurement of corporate sustainability. The challenge facing the indexing industry has been how to measure and quantify corporate sustainability, and how to integrate the results into an investable index that meets the needs of the investment industry while keeping on track with sustainability requirements.

SAM Research's Corporate Sustainability Assessment™ identifies the leading sustainability companies from the DJSI World investable stocks universe for each of the 60 industry sectors of the DJSI.

The DJSI is made up of 308 companies and reflects changes in valuation of a universe of companies that are leaders in terms of corporate sustainability. The universe of companies embracing sustainability is broader than the DJSI, but the DJSI comprises the leaders in corporate sustainability. Thus, the DJSI not only traces, but also implies, a universe of leading companies with regard to addressing sustainability. Within each of the 60 industry groups, a group of leading companies exist. The inclusion of these leading companies in the indexes endorses these companies publicly, it indirectly ensures access to capital and taps into the competitive nature of markets by benchmarking companies within each industry sector and thus enhances the emergence of a group of leading companies.

ASSESSMENT AND EVALUATION OF POLICY-RELEVANT OUTCOMES

The following addresses some of the major challenges encountered in conducting the research for the DJSI and how these are dealt with.

Challenge: Development of Relevant Generic and Industry-Specific Assessment Criteria

An index tracking the performance of corporate sustainability leaders first needs to define corporate sustainability and relevant assessment criteria. Criteria representing the challenges deriving from sustainability trends have to be developed and quantified so that the best-positioned companies can be measured and identified.

Selecting relevant and quantifiable criteria to assess corporate sustainability is a major challenge because the quality of the index components depends heavily on this aspect of the assessment process. Assessment criteria should be easy to measure, relevant, understandable, clearly formulated and precise. In addition to quantitative data, corporate sustainability is widely based on assessing qualitative data, so the most significant challenge is to develop quantitative proxies for qualitative data and integrate these into a system that meets the major requirements of indexing (for example, the need for replicability and objectivity). Through the thorough assessment of current and future scenarios of economic, environmental and social driving forces and trends as well as internationally recognized treaties and regulations, corporate sustainability criteria for each sustainability dimension across all industries are identified. These criteria are defined as either general criteria applicable to all industries or industry-specific criteria that are only relevant to a selection of industries. The number of industry-specific criteria varies from 1 to 14 per industry and differs between industry groups, whereas the 20 general criteria are the same for each industry group. As each industry group faces specific sustainability challenges, there is a tendency to increase the number of industry-specific criteria and their respective weightings in comparison to general criteria in the future. Where possible and feasible, criteria are developed by incorporating widely accepted standards, for example the Universal Declaration of Human Rights (UNDHR) and best-practice examples as well as extensive input from industry and regulatory experts, NGOs and consultants.

General Criteria

Based on the identification of major global sustainability challenges, general sustainability criteria are defined for each dimension and are applied to all industries. They include standard management practices and performance measures applicable to all industries, such as corporate governance, financial robustness, environmental management and performance, human rights, supply chain management, risk and crisis management, and labour practices. The general criteria are weighted 60 per cent in the assessment scheme.

Industry-Specific Criteria

Industry-specific criteria take into account the challenges and trends affecting specific industries. They reflect the economic, environmental and social forces driving the sustainability performance of a particular industry and are weighted 40 per cent in the assessment scheme.

BOX 18.2 CORPORATE SUSTAINABILITY
ASSESSMENT™ OVERVIEW CRITERIA
APPLIED IN DJSI 2003/04

The assessment is divided into three distinct sections, covering the economic, environmental and social dimensions and including answers from the questionnaire as well as the results from a Media and Stakeholder Analysis (MSA) (see below for more details on the MSA process). Each criterion has a number of sub-criteria which are not listed below but which are explained in the index rulebook:**

Economic
- Codes of conduct/compliance/corruption and bribery (MSA)
- Corporate governance
- Customer relationship management (MSA)
- Financial robustness* (MSA)
- Investor relations
- Risk and crisis management (MSA)
- Strategic planning
- Industry-specific criteria depending on industry (MSA)

Environment
- Environmental policy/management (i.e. overall responsibility for environmental issues, environmental policy and targets, public availability of targets, environmental management systems certification and organizational coverage (MSA)
- Environmental performance (organizational coverage, key performance indicators (KPI) – energy, greenhouse gases, water, waste)
- Environmental reporting* (scope)
- Industry-specific criteria depending on industry (i.e. specific manufacturing and know-how, detailed greenhouse gas emissions management, biodiversity impacts, chemicals in the environment, product stewardship, etc.)(MSA)

Social
- Corporate citizenship/philanthropy
- Stakeholder engagement (MSA)
- Labour practice indicators (MSA)
- Human capital development (MSA)
- Knowledge management/organizational learning
- Social reporting*
- Talent attraction and retention
- Standards for suppliers and supply-chain management
- Industry-specific criteria depending on industry (MSA)

Note:
* Criteria assessed based on publicly available information only.
** For a detailed listing of the sub-criteria see http://sustainability-indexes.com/htmle/assessment/criteria/html (accessed 20 October 2006).
MSA – Media and Stakeholder Analysis.
The number of industry-specific criteria varies between industries and ranges between 2 and 10 criteria in each dimension.

Challenge: Gathering Corporate Sustainability Information

A major challenge lies in developing a process to gather the correct and relevant information to measure economic, environmental and social performance, the validation of data and the choice of information sources to use. While some global companies publish corporate sustainability reports, the majority of companies are only just beginning to understand and, hence, report on the concept of corporate sustainability. More importantly, not all data are consistent, relevant or comparable.

Research for the DJSI uses four main information sources in the Corporate Sustainability Assessment™.

Company Questionnaire

Online questionnaires specific to each of the DJSI industry groups are distributed to the chief executive officers and heads of investor relations of all eligible companies in the DJSI World investable stocks universe that have agreed to participate in the annual assessment. The online questionnaire is structured along the economic, environmental and social dimension. Each dimension consists of general and industry-specific questions, which are weighted 60 per cent and 40 per cent respectively. The completed company questionnaire, signed by a senior company representative, is the most important source of information for the assessment. SAM Research conducts a major review of the overall methodology and criteria every two years to reflect best practice in each industry sector and to incorporate any major developments in the area of sustainability. It is important to note that the whole field of sustainability is not static but is in constant development. Minor optimization adjustments in the methodology, research and assessment processes are necessary and conducted annually.

The advantages of using a questionnaire-based research approach are that a structured framework and a transparent and consistent research process are applied, allowing for a rigorous and consistent assessment process. The structure allows for a detailed analysis of each criterion, which assists in the continual improvement of the research methodology and process. It is also possible to conduct regression analysis by comparing the historic sustainability performance with the current evaluations.

Company Documentation

The information in the questionnaire is checked by the industry analyst and complemented with further additional information available via publicly available and internal company documentation. Documents requested from companies include:

- sustainability, environmental, health and safety, social reports;
- annual financial reports, analyst reports;
- special reports (for example on intellectual capital management, corporate governance, R&D, employee relations);
- all other relevant sources of additional company information: for example internal documentation, brochures and website.

Media and Stakeholders

Sustainability analysts review media, press releases, articles and stakeholder commentary written about a company over the previous year. This information is integrated into the assessment system as well as serving as a basis for possible downgrading of a company through the ongoing Media and Stakeholder Analysis process in which the prevalence and severity of incidents are evaluated.

Contact with Companies

Where necessary each sustainability analyst contacts companies to clarify open points arising from the analysis of the questionnaire, company documents and Media and Stakeholder Analysis (MSA). The results are fed into the company assessment.

Challenge: Quantification of Corporate Sustainability

A key challenge in developing an index tracking corporate sustainability is how to quantify corporate sustainability. Given that sustainability trends affect each industry differently, industry-specific challenges arise. As a result, industry leaders need to be identified for each industry group, known as a 'best-in-class' approach. Sustainability leaders within each industry group need to be ranked according to their corporate sustainability performance relative to one another. In most cases, sustainability developments are qualitative in nature, so they may inherently lack easy quantification. While assessing companies' environmental performance or emission targets may seem relatively straightforward, a consistent and equally quantifiable method is not readily available for many aspects of social and economic development.

The DJSI does not exclude any sectors per se. Even if certain sectors are involved in business activities that do not have a specific positive or negative impact on the environment, the market or society, it is through the best-in-class approach with which the leading companies are identified and benchmarks are set in each sector. This approach allows the development of a methodology that is applicable across all sectors and does not make any 'values-based' or 'moral' judgements on specific business activities, products or services.

The Corporate Sustainability Assessment™ enables a sustainability performance score to be calculated for each company based on all four sources identified above. Reviewing, assessing and scoring all available information in line with the corporate sustainability criteria determines the overall sustainability score for each eligible company in the DJSI World investable universe. The objective of the Corporate Sustainability Assessment™ is to measure and verify the corporate sustainability performance of the companies in the investable universe. A company's total corporate sustainability score is calculated in SAM's Sustainability Information Management System (SIMS) based on a predefined scoring and weighting structure set by SAM Research. The specific weighting scheme reflects the strategic relevance of the issue to the industry (for example the issue of climate change is weighted higher in the automotive sector than in the chemicals or pharmaceuticals sector. This relates to SAM's view that in this sector product-related CO_2 emissions pose a higher strategic threat and/or opportunity than production-related CO_2 emissions). All questions related to each criterion receive a score. Each question has a predetermined weight for the answer, the question, and for the theme and class within the question. The total score for the question is the combination of these weights. Each score is aggregated to arrive at an overall score for each company. Based on these scores the top 10 per cent in each industry sector are selected for inclusion in the DJSI.

Once a company is selected as a member of the DJSI World, it is continuously monitored for its corporate sustainability performance. Corporate Sustainability Monitoring is a crucial and integral part of the ongoing review process.

The objective of the Corporate Sustainability Monitoring is to verify a company's involvement and management of critical environmental, economic and social crisis situations that can have a highly damaging effect on its reputation. In addition, the consistency of a company's behaviour and management of crisis situations is reviewed in line with its stated principles and policies. The Corporate Sustainability Monitoring can lead to a company's exclusion from the index regardless of how well the company performed in the yearly Corporate Sustainability Assessment™. The following issues are identified and reviewed across all industry sectors in the monitoring process:

- Codes of conduct: for example tax fraud, money laundering, antitrust, corruption, bribery.
- Corporate governance: for example balance sheet fraud, insider trading.
- Customer relationship management: for example product recall, customer complaints.
- Financial robustness: for example bankruptcy situation, access to capital.
- Risk and crisis management: for example accidents, fatalities, workplace safety issues, technical failures.
- Supply chain management: for example major price-fixing, unfair competition cases.
- Environmental management: for example ecological disasters, hazardous substances, grossly mismanaged long-term pollution.
- External stakeholders: for example cases indicative of the company systematically exploiting weak governance in emerging countries.
- Labour practice indicators: for example cases involving discrimination, forced resettlements, child labour and discrimination of indigenous people; workplace accidents and occupational health and safety.
- Remuneration, benefits, flexible working schemes: for example extensive lay-offs and strikes.

Media and Stakeholder Analysis (MSA)

Corporate Sustainability Monitoring is based on media reviews using full text database services (for example Factiva, a Dow Jones and Reuters joint venture), and analysis of stakeholder information as well as other relevant publicly available information.

Impact Evaluation

Each of the components in the DJSI World is monitored daily for crisis situations. If a crisis occurs, the impact of this is assessed. The extent of the crisis within the company, the geographic expansion and level of coverage in the media is monitored. As a result, the impact of the crisis on the reputation of the company and on its core business is assessed.

Quality of Crisis Management

If the impact of the crisis is far-reaching, covered worldwide in the media or is an important concern for the company, then an analysis of the quality of the company's crisis management is conducted. This step comprises a monitoring of how well the company communicates, informs the public, acknowledges responsibility, provides relief measures, involves relevant stakeholders and develops solutions. In this context, SAM Research weighs the severity of the crisis in relation to the company's reputation and quality of crisis management.

Review by DJSI World Index Design Committee

If deemed appropriate, SAM Research provides the DJSI World Index Design Committee with a proposal for the company's exclusion from the DJSI World. The DJSI World Index Design Committee reviews the Corporate Sustainability Monitoring results in line with the company's track record, political and cultural setting. If the crisis management of an important issue is considered poor from a sustainability point of view, the DJSI World Index Design Committee can decide to exclude the company from the DJSI World, which has not happened in the five-year history of the DJSI.

To ensure quality and objectivity, external audit and internal quality assurance procedures, such as cross-checking of information sources, are used to monitor and maintain the accuracy of the input data, assessment procedures and results. SAM Research does not explicitly verify environmental and social performance data but relies, where available, on externally verified environmental and social reports, which is reflected in the assessment scheme. External verification is viewed as an important step to ensure validity and accuracy of corporate non-financial information. Since inception of the DJSI in 1999 SAM Research's Corporate Sustainability Assessment[TM] has been verified annually by PricewaterhouseCoopers (PwC). The error margin that PwC have audited has been below 1 per cent since the launch of the indexes, providing reassurance that the rule-based assessment process is adhered to and replicable.

Challenge: Strengthening Acceptance of the Indexes

The success and acceptance of the research process depends on the quality, relevance, transparency and rigour of the research process.

To ensure transparency of the indexes, the complete methodology is publicly available through the index website[7] and is reviewed annually. As the research methodology depends on both publicly available and company-specific information, participation from companies is a crucial success factor for the indexes. Indeed, analysis of criteria such as environmental reporting collected over several years suggests a correlation between a company's sustainability performance and overall corporate transparency across all sectors. This can be applied to nearly every criterion – leading sustainability companies are generally more transparent than their peers. This transparency builds trust among the company's different stakeholders and allows the company actively to define and respond to the different information needs of its external stakeholders.

A key differentiating factor of these indexes compared with other indexes is that every assessed company receives a detailed benchmarking report highlighting the company's sustainability performance in each sustainability dimension in comparison to the industry average and the best performance in the industry.

This feedback is a crucial element in strengthening the acceptance of the indexes with companies as it is free, contains industry-specific global sustainability benchmarking information and provides the company with a detailed overview of its sustainability performance. Making this information only available to a select public, that is, participating companies, increases the incentive for companies to participate in the index assessment. As most information companies provide is readily available in the public domain, the index balances information asymmetries. Further, the feedback forms the basis for the ongoing dialogue and engagement with companies.

CONCLUSIONS AND SCORING CHART

Following the description of the main characteristics of the Dow Jones Sustainability Indexes, one can apply the proposed framework of this study to the DJSI to assess whether the DJSI can be judged an effective policy instrument that integrates sustainability into mainstream financial markets (Table 18.1).

The seventh year of existence and the fact that the index has 56 licensees, is testimony to the market success of the DJSI as a global, rational, consistent, flexible and, most importantly, investable index to benchmark the performance of sustainability investments. In addition, the DJSI meets most of the criteria in the proposed evaluation framework – an indication that the indexes are an effective policy instrument integrating sustainability into mainstream financial markets.

Concerning the methodology for assessing corporate sustainability, there are a number of key challenges that have to be addressed. The success of such a product is based on a consistent and robust assessment framework and criteria while simultaneously being flexible enough to adapt and respond to the mega-trends affecting the corporate environment and the evolution of corporate sustainability. Assessment of corporate sustainability is a nascent field and a relatively new concept, and thus a lengthy history on which to base judgements is lacking. The assessment methodology

Table 18.1   Evaluation of Dow Jones Sustainability Indexes

	Criteria	Questions for Review
Relevance	(C1) Process of problem identification; Pressure to act	Sustainability is an important concept for investors and stakeholders; the DJSI identifies the sustainability leaders in each industry
		Need to act is given by broader society and financial markets; recognition that non-financial indicators can effectively add to the traditional financial evaluation of companies
		Companies – see sustainability strategy as a source for business innovation and improved corporate resilience
		Investors – more rigorous assessment of companies
		Civil society – identification of leading companies
		Yes, the DJSI addresses its main actors; however, the process is not strictly stakeholder driven – main focus is the investors' perspective
		Yes, process incorporates global and regional trends; identification of priority areas focused strongly on issues that are linked to the financial performance of companies, i.e. criteria linked to value drivers
	(C2) Decentral solutions; Possibilities for Compensation*	Yes, decentral solution by integrating existing and proposed policy developments and market-based solutions, e.g. emissions trading
		Yes, the network is diverse and consists of a broad range of different players, e.g. NGOs, experts, think tanks
		Yes, it leads to an exchange; transparent research process requires participation and information from companies; in return companies receive a feedback in the form of benchmark reports highlighting global best practice
Effective-ness	(C3) Targets and strategies	Yes, the assessment checks both management quality and performance through clearly defined targets and goals in both general and industry-specific criteria; clear and verifiable targets are used
		Where possible criteria are based on accepted international laws and conventions; general criteria apply across industries; industry-specific criteria use industry-specific targets
		The goal of the assessment structure is to identify leading companies in a clear, reproducible and consistent manner; the structure allows for issue-specific policy deliberations

Table 18.1   (continued)

	Criteria	Questions for Review
	(C4) Implementation	Yes, as part of the annual review this is possible Ideal targets are set just above and beyond the achievable maximum to act as a positive driver for change and not as a disincentive Annual review of methodology and adaptation of criteria accordingly Assessment follows a yearly cycle of concrete steps: review, invitation, participation, analysis, launch and feedback Linked to industry-specific criteria Where possible actual performance against a criterion is tested by assessing key performance indicators Clear, transparent and publicly available rule book, which is updated regularly; these mechanisms do not entail a monitoring of costs
Efficiency	(C5) Cost reduction	Yes, streamlining and optimizing research process is crucial, e.g. automation of data gathering – however, assessment conducted by industry-specific analysts; aim to facilitate participation of companies as much as possible through technical solutions and incentives, i.e. feedback. Completion of questionnaire is resource-intensive (time, manpower) and it is crucial to demonstrate the benefits (benchmarking, logo, inclusion in index) to companies Negative environmental externalities and risks in the economic and social dimension of sustainability are considered in the Corporate Sustainability Assessment™
Side-Effects	(C6) Positive side-effects	Transparent research process and feedback to companies ensure critical evaluation of research process; identification and recognition of global sustainability leaders strengthens and fosters discussion and the ongoing development of corporate sustainability Global benchmarking as a driver for advancement; through open communication and the logo to be used in public communication Sometimes difficult to differentiate leading companies in one sector as 'low-hanging fruit' have been picked, and sustainability becomes strategic issue Balance between proprietary research and demand for fully transparent research Identification of leading companies

Table 18.1 (continued)

	Criteria	Questions for Review
		Identification of global best practice Transparent feedback and open discussion about ongoing development Expansion into emerging markets Corporate membership organizations such as the WBCSD exchange information and share knowledge
	(C7) Negative side-effects	Critical issue to provide rationale for criteria used to ensure acceptance Occasional misunderstanding between socially responsible and sustainability investment
Adaptation flexibility	(C8) Freedom and flexibility	No, the assessment scheme is set for each industry to ensure comparability and integrity of assessment scheme Full flexibility for investors is ensured as the DJSI can be used either as a benchmark or as a universe of companies of sustainability leaders in their respective industries
	(C9) Evaluation and review	Yes, industry-specific analysts evaluate all criteria for relevance, rationale has to be developed; overall methodology and questionnaire design is subjected to scrutiny from outside reviewers The evaluation is part of the role as analyst
	(C10) Participation and transparency	Participation in the annual assessment is confined to the 2500 largest companies in the Dow Jones Global Index (DJGI); all companies receive an invitation and a key fact sheet All eligible companies are invited and relevant external stakeholders are approached as required No Yes, adjusted annually
	(C11) Control	Formal control mechanism is the annual audit of the research process conducted by Pricewaterhouse-Coopers (error margin $<1\%$ in 2003) Structured weighting scheme ensures consistent application of evaluation scheme Yes, independent auditors Annual audit, transparent rule book and feedback to all participating companies Depending on severity of case identified through the Media and Stakeholder Analysis company can be downgraded or ultimately excluded from the index

Note: * This refers to Coase-type negotiation among actors, a possibility which can be seen separately from C1 (referring to a broader set of relevance criteria).

described in this chapter has to evolve continually to capture best-practice corporate behaviour, and improvements to the criteria selection and definition are made to reflect companies' performance and risk attributions better. Furthermore, regional particularities will be given increasing prominence as specialized regional and emerging market assessment approaches are developed.

Due to the above-mentioned issues, transparency of the research process and assessment methodology is of paramount importance to strengthen the reputation of the indexes among companies and investors.

Moreover, there is a distinct dearth of scientific back-up to many of the tenets of the sustainability-investing hypothesis and approach. Increased collaboration among academia, science and business should be promoted to close this gap. This cooperation between the sciences and the private sector will also provide the background for the much-needed standardization of corporate sustainability reporting.

However, in its relatively short history the DJSI has demonstrated that it is an effective mechanism to introduce and integrate sustainability into the mainstream financial markets.

The scoring chart in Figure 18.1 summarizes the results of the case-study above and scores all 11 criteria.

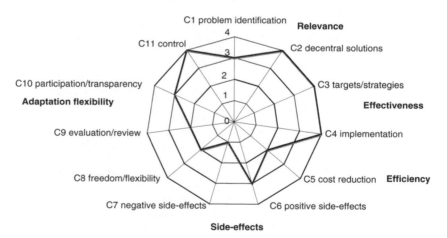

Dow Jones Sustainability Indexes

Notes: 0 = no, 1 = low, 2 = moderate, 3 = above average, 4 = high action/result

Figure 18.1   Scoring chart of Dow Jones Sustainability Indexes

NOTES

1. For more information see www.sam-group.com/
2. http://www.sustainability-indexes.com/htmle/news/monthlyupdates.html
3. http://www.eurosif.org/publications
4. http://www.jse.co.za/sri/
5. Companies embracing global sustainability trends are likely to achieve a higher return on equity (ROE) and/or a lower required rate of return (RRR) than companies that ignore these trends. Higher ROE may result from a better understanding of investment opportunities or from lower non-operating cost, because of a better understanding of risks. Higher ROE may also result from social pressure groups channelling demand into sustainable products. A lower RRR may result from a better understanding and management of risks. The RRR is a function of both operating and financial risks. Companies embracing sustainability trends may reduce their operating risks and, thereby, lower their equity costs. It presumably would also result in lower borrowing costs, leading to lower costs of capital and, again, to higher ROE. Lower borrowing costs may also be the result of investors considering other parameters than just risk and return. High ROE and low RRR result in free cash flow that can be invested profitably when embracing sustainability trends (Flatz, 2001). A portfolio, or an index composed of this type of company, thus will appreciate faster than a portfolio or an index of companies not embracing theoretically profitable investment opportunities. Investments in companies embracing sustainability thus promise higher returns and, due to lower business risk, better risk–return ratios. Based on this hypothesis, better performance can also be expected on a risk-adjusted basis (Flatz, 2001).
6. http://www.siricompany.com/
7. http://www.sustainability-index.com/htmle/djsi_world/methodology.html

PART 4

Conclusions

19. Conclusions for policy analysis and the empirical assessment of corporate environmental networks, for policy-makers and corporate actors

Raimund Bleischwitz and Bettina Bahn-Walkowiak

CONCLUSIONS FOR POLICY ANALYSIS

The present study has pointed out several characteristics of responsible corporate governance for sustainable development: in this concept, corporate and civil society action co-evolve with policies. The resulting governance processes facilitate the development of markets for eco-efficient services and other goods. They also lead to increasing energy and resource productivity of economies. With its emphasis on stakeholder consultations, our concept of corporate governance also involves organizational learning both from outside and within an organization.

Knowledge creation, therefore, is a key feature of those co-evolutionary governance processes. This kind of knowledge generation goes beyond reporting schemes and formalized procedures in that it actively pursues cost reduction, innovation and organizational improvements above a level that is usually thought of as optimal: co-evolutionary governance processes can make exploration into the unknown more beneficial than exploitation of existing skills. Knowledge creation permanently transcends the borders of the organization in question as knowledge generated externally is transformed through processes of mutual learning that involve actors from inside and outside. Networks align current core competences of their members to future tasks of acquiring new skills and market development.

The claim can be made that such co-evolutionary processes can even achieve an endogenous internalization of externalities because they exploit not only the low-hanging fruit of efficiency improvements but also seek for incremental and radical improvements. The involvement of stakeholders outlined in our concept of responsible corporate governance also forms a sound basis from which business can develop a more strategically oriented corporate social responsibility (CSR, see Davis, 2005).

Both the analytical framework and the case-studies indicate that self-enforcing contracts and soft incentives are important steering tools for the micro- and meso-levels of action, even if actor groups are heterogeneous and their members do not share a common set of preferences or interests. From such a perspective, governance processes would formulate phased approaches starting with a mission as well as with short-term and well-defined tasks added by performance review processes, which together increase the responsibility of corporate actors over time. Such an approach provides for flexibility and allows for gradual legal and political attempts of revising framework conditions later on.

Contracts, incentives and rules, however, do not eradicate the importance of individuals. In distinction to a bias in favour of institutions, our analysis confirms that people matter. Individual involvement, motivation and the related organizational dynamic are vital. In particular, driver functions and creative adaptation depend on individual factors much more than on rules. Actors and rules are interdependent in the sense that rules set the mindset for actors and stabilize their activities once they have begun; individual involvement is indispensable for pioneering activities as well as for reorientation when uncertainties and external novelties result in the failure of the stabilizing function of rules.

The governance processes observed are characterized by corporate action where the public interest is represented through:

- stakeholder participation (Ecoprofit, Dow Jones Sustainability Indexes [DJSI], Energy+);
- public supervision (Burnside eco-industrial park, climate funds); or
- public initiatives prior to corporate action respectively 'in the shadow of the law' without formal rules (BP tradeable permits, DJSI, Responsible Care initiative).

Analysis on governance processes and its actors at the micro- and meso-levels can therefore be seen as a necessary complement to analysing formal rules at the macro-level. The case-studies reveal that governance processes develop a dynamic that mobilizes support for pioneers, early adopters and early majorities and – as a result – facilitate policy formulation, implementation and compliance procedures. Such driver functions are especially visible in the case of DJSI and BP, where corporate activities trigger international market processes and help policy-makers to pursue their goals without being directly involved in corporate activities. Attempts to accomplish responsible corporate governance therefore can be seen to serve a public interest. It should be noted however that other case-studies do not entirely support the thesis of a general driver function. Responsible Care and eco-industrial parks may be seen as examples for an initial dynamic losing drive over time. It thus seems that governance processes at the micro- and meso-levels need additional incentives for those periods when the initial dynamic slows down or when more challenging tasks need to be accomplished. This is when policies should kick in again, providing for adaptive flexibility and long-term orientation (Bleischwitz, 2004; Rammel and v.d. Bergh, 2003).

Stakeholder processes, certainly a characteristic feature of governance, differ in scope and in function. Ideally, they give specific impetus, serve as scouting processes for innovation, and increase the dynamic capability of an organization. Seen as a specific form of interaction, they generate trust among interest groups that do not necessarily have shared concerns. In a stepwise development, stakeholder consultations can be transformed into deliberations, that is, processes of formalized consultation where power relations are balanced, different interests are negotiated, and solutions are implemented.

Our case-studies, however, reveal more specific and, in some instances, more basic forms of stakeholder involvement. BP's scheme of tradeable permits, for example, is not driven (or implemented) by stakeholder consultations. Instead, the Environmental Defense Fund, a green NGO, has been hired as a consulting agency. In other cases a review mechanism (DJSI) has been put in place, or a limited number of stakeholders is permanently involved in a supervisory function (climate funds, Energy+, eco-industrial parks). Ecoprofit, the local initiative active in parts of Central Europe, can perhaps be seen as coming closest to what stakeholder processes could mean.

The data suggest however that stakeholder consultations can hardly replace politics. In particular, poorly organized interests (such as basic rights, future generations, weak or vulnerable groups) will continue to rely on politics and the law. Though this poses limits to the function of stakeholder processes in governance for sustainable development, the benefits of stimulating innovation and market evolution that they bring make them worthwhile. Policy analysis should therefore identify which legal provisions set a framework helpful to these decentralized processes of knowledge generation, and how democratic processes of decision-making co-evolve with them. Liability and access to information are key issues in those policies.

As regards sustainability indicators and targets, our book features a flexible, mid-term approach where a set of core indicators and targets is preferred against any single-issue approach or against a voluminous handbook of complex performance measurements. Though our overall focus is on the environmental dimension, the social dimension, that is, equity and fairness, becomes increasingly important. In both dimensions, the case-studies identify highly diverse degrees of transparency, measurability and harmonization. Indicators and targets, in general, emerge gradually during governance processes. The overall result in our case-studies, however, is that these processes are slow and lead to incomparable approaches. Heterogeneous actor groups and processes hamper the definition of targets and indicators in governance processes. This is especially visible where public actors are not directly involved (DJSI, BP), where a great variety of actors exist (Ecoprofit), or where institutions and corporations of different sizes, cultures and values have to collaborate (Responsible Care). In assessing such processes one must keep in mind that governance processes are often driven by a high degree of uncertainty and curiosity.

Our conclusion calls for a stepwise approach where indicators and targets can be developed over time, that is, are not formulated at the beginning of a policy cycle. Governance processes improve as public authorities take up the relevant themes while decentralized processes are running. A clarification on indicators and targets can be derived from other governance processes (that is, horizontal diffusion) and scientific expertise, as well as from an integrated assessment of possible leakages (externalities, problem shifting). Governance processes therefore profit by politically binding agreements on core indicators and measurement methodologies. Again, policies kick in later on and lower transaction costs via selecting best practices and harmonizing efforts.

In relation to contemporary policy analysis, our book cuts across the distinction between economic and legal instruments. Economic and legal incentives alike spur the learning processes, which are involved in governance approaches. Serious price distortions and legal leakages can be seen as major obstacles, which policy-makers will have to address. After a first assessment, any instrument or set of instruments needs to be evaluated against its potential to increase problem-solving knowledge where it is necessary. This step complements traditional cost–benefit analysis (allocation efficiency) and distributional effects. Our conclusion favours a combination of economic and legal incentives. This is because price mechanisms can hardly be considered to cover all necessary information; legal provisions on access to information, accounting procedures and methodologies as well as on stakeholders' rights lower the transaction cost of learning and facilitate the generation of new knowledge. The plea for a variety of instruments is supported, for example, by Faure and Skogh (2003).

Governance processes as analysed in our book go beyond what are called 'voluntary agreements'. Though the dramatic increase in the use of voluntary agreements since the early 1990s can be seen in parallel with governance processes and may have been triggered by similar forces, there are clear differences. Voluntary agreements are most often made in efforts to implement pollution abatement where policy-makers either fail to decide on appropriate instruments or find voluntary approaches superior. The difference is that voluntary agreements can be related to a specific problem where scientific evidence is high and compliance costs are relevant, whereas governance processes aim at lowering the complexity and transaction costs of market development via learning and knowledge creation. For that reason, the literature on voluntary agreements emphasizes the need for a strong regulatory power, reliable monitoring and incentives for participation (Alberini and Segerson, 2002, p. 177; Carraro and Lévêque, 1999). As described above, our governance approach does not include explicit elements of regulatory power, and monitoring tasks are focused on measurement methodologies and transparency rather than on meeting certain targets. Incentives for participation are similarly expressed.

Table 19.1 summarizes selected 'good and bad practices' of governance processes of sustainability at the meso-level along the criteria of our assessment methodology.

METHODOLOGICAL CONCLUSIONS FOR EMPIRICAL ASSESSMENTS OF CORPORATE ENVIRONMENTAL NETWORKS

Corporate environmental networks can be interpreted as knowledge-generating and capacity-building governance structures emerging in reaction to and/or anticipation of market failure and lack of political governance. They occur at all conceivable policy and governance levels, combining and using these levels in modern ways and embracing a wide range of various actors. Their policy-relevant outcomes are as different as their ambitions, and so are their results regarding sustainability and their status of institutionalization. It should be noted that corporate environmental networks are not policy networks in a general sense – which emphasize the involvement of political actors – but rather work in a particular yet wide policy field: sustainable development.

Eight case-studies of corporate environmental networks were carried out in Part 3 in order to illustrate the emergence, appearance, multifaceted functioning and development status of co-evolutionary governance structures that follow our concepts of 'responsible corporate governance' (Chapter 2) and evolutionary competition (Chapter 3). Responsible corporate governance can be understood as an emerging business strategy

Table 19.1　'Good and bad practices' of governance processes of
sustainability

Criteria	Good practice	Bad practice
(C 1) Process of problem identification; Pressure to act	Translates challenges into missions and tasks for private actors	Remains rather general, does not constitute responsibilities
(C 2) Decentral solutions; Possibilities for compensation*	Proactive strategies at micro- and meso-levels, coordinated at a higher level, dissemination	Isolated action without learning from outsiders
(C 3) Targets and strategies	Develops a roadmap with targets and performance review beyond existing regulation	Focuses on compliance with existing regulation
(C 4) Implementation	Develops measurement systems and aligns those with individual responsibility	Leakage effects and unclear responsibilities favour weak and insufficient implementation
(C 5) Cost reduction	Comprehensive scheme for full cost monitoring (incl. social costs, transaction costs etc.)	Focuses on one type of cost reduction (e.g. compliance costs) while leaving business operations untouched
(C 6) Positive side-effects	Addresses radical innovation and Factor-X	Stagnation and inertia
(C 7) Negative side-effects	Monitoring provided by research in order to reduce or avoid negative side-effects	Generates new externalities, shifts burden to developing countries
(C 8) Freedom and flexibility	Freedom to choose tools for implementation, exploration and experiments towards improvements	Either freedom is misused to opt out of governance processes or action is restricted by bureaucracy
(C 9) Evaluation and review	Regular evaluation by outsiders added by internal reviews.	Reports are designed to conceal insufficient action, 'window dressing'

Table 19.1 (continued)

Criteria	Good practice	Bad practice
(C 10) Participation and transparency	Full access to core information, participation open for stakeholders on demand	Strategic cooperation with selected stakeholders supports existing business plans
(C 11) Control	Budget controlling by independent accounting firms, general control by public authorities, trust between actors	Control is thought of as superfluous

Note: * This refers to Coase-type negotiation among actors, a possibility which can be seen separately from C1 (referring to a broader set of relevance criteria).

whose conception serves as a starting basis for corporate action and learning processes, but whose results and policy-relevant outcomes differ and cannot be determined in advance. When conclusions are to be drawn from the case-studies, this subtle but important aspect needs to be taken into consideration. Responsible corporate governance thus needs to be assessed against criteria which explicitly link business concerns with public interests.

Part 2 introduced the evaluation methodology for policy networks and adapted it to the analysis of networks that do not necessarily feature political actors but corporate actors. Five criteria from the policy network analysis (relevance, effectiveness, efficiency, side-effects, adaptation flexibility) were classified into 11 sub-categories that each covered a set of questions for the empirical exploration of the selected networks. New branches of economics such as evolutionary and new institutional economics have been utilized to support an assessment. The networks were selected with the proviso that they together represent a broad field of policy and governance levels, a wide range of various actors, and different modes of interaction within the scope of our book.

For exploration five steps were concerted: (1) identification of the mission; (2) identification of the actors involved and resource-dependency relations; (3) identification of the policy-relevant outcomes; (4) assessment and evaluation of the policy-relevant outcomes; and (5) conclusions.

The abdication of a mere targets–instruments evaluation and the turn towards a performance-based assessment instead can be considered a strength of our approach as it opens up new vistas for dynamic effects and knowledge generation. Also, the claim can be made that our approach can capture processes of market dynamics rather well. Empirical practice has shown, however, that real network processes are complex and not easily explored with criteria that usually operate with a clear number of actors integrated in widely constant hierarchies. Access to data and scoring of qualitative aspects are evident cases in point. Accordingly, the empirical analysis produced some findings that are not simply compared, evaluated and assessed. In order to contribute to the further development of the network analysis, the following section will discuss some of the criteria that have raised questions throughout the empirical phase.

Criteria 1 'process of problem identification and pressure to act' and 2 'decentral solutions and possibilities for compensation' aim at illustrating the relevance of the networks' outcomes. In our study, however, it seemed difficult to distinguish between the network's relevance and the relevance of the network's policy-relevant outcomes in a precise way. Both of them may show the same direction but they do not necessarily so. Consequently, some case-studies expose a sort of 'diffusion relevance' (due to strong or frequent corporate involvement) (for example Ecoprofit); others refer to the status of internal and external documents and institutionalization (for example Responsible Care initiative). Second, the inspection of the case-studies clearly indicated that the term 'decentral' had left a too-wide scope for interpretation. Hence, at least four different interpretation patterns of decentral turned up:

- policy-driven top-down (for example Energy+, PIUS);
- corporate-driven bottom-up processes (for example BP);
- purely regional approaches (for example proKlima, eco-industrial parks); and
- transboundary, but institutionally decentral (for example Responsible Care initiative) processes.

This could even go into more detail. However, all four may evolve different effects regarding 'relevance'.

Criterion 5, 'cost reduction', raised problems concerning data. At least half of the case-studies (for example Ecoprofit, PIUS, eco-industrial parks, proKlima) were able to prove cost effects with figures and can be updated by research continuously.

Positive and negative side-effects (criteria 6–7) are by their nature not easily assessed during running processes. This is notably true for system leakages which was asked for as a negative side-effect. Thus, most of the case-studies give rather general impressions of potential and previous side-effects, while some document clear attestable effects. In particular those networks that do not provide any figures yet had to remain theoretical concerning the side-effects. One should also note that the selection process for the case-studies featured those aiming at eco-efficiency improvements with minimum negative effects.

Criterion 10 showed that participation and transparency are not easily assessed at the same time and without a precise definition of what is meant by 'participation' and 'transparency' respectively. Are internal or external processes of participation and transparency addressed? Both of them may have different characteristics. Transparency may be high when participation is low, and the other way round – they do not necessarily imply a correlation. The case-studies showed that this is not only difficult to handle during analysis, but it could also cause an average and less-significant value for the final evaluation through web graphs. In addition, our observation is that the notion of adaptation flexibility – a core element of our analysis – is not fully understood outside a few research strands (such as evolutionary economics). It requires explanation and guidance throughout the whole assessment process, which in turn may bias the results.

For future analysis, it could be advisable to inspect some of the criteria discussed above in more detail and adapt them for a network analysis that is – above all – characterized by highly variable constellations of stakeholders, corporate actors, organizations, institutions and, finally, political governance structures. Precise definitions of the criteria themselves and well-elaborated questions relating to those are preferable.

Accordingly, scoring processes conducted in the final stage of our analysis may raise concerns about subjectivity and biased results. Those who assess therefore bear responsibility, and they need experience in order to compare and weigh. The authors of this book share much experience and have compared findings and results. We believe that any review of a first scoring is necessary and can eliminate at least a few drawbacks and biases. Further research will lead to better competences on such scoring metrics and assessment methodologies. For applied research this implies two interesting frontiers: being involved in those activities in order to disseminate best practices from others and reflecting on assessment methodologies and drawing conclusions for research.

Having concluded on some critical aspects, the empirical analysis also reveals that the structure the corporate environmental network analysis followed here gains a lot of useful information about the differences, dynamics and mutability of networks as visualized by the web graphs. It also contributes to the question of how governance structures evolve from corporate–stakeholder cooperation, how governance structures can induce corporate–stakeholder cooperation once they are set, and the interactions between structures and actors. Our claim, thus, is that comparative analysis and assessments are a useful if not indispensable part of research.

CONCLUSIONS FOR POLICY-MAKERS AND CORPORATE ACTORS

The cases analysed in our book of course represent only a small part of the whole picture. Today, governance processes including private actors form a core element of sustainability strategies, a fact that is underestimated in analyses focusing exclusively on formal governmental policies. It is perhaps the most striking conclusion from our book that methods derived from policy and assessment analysis can be applied to processes of responsible corporate governance. Driven by like-minded actors and appropriate rules, governance processes especially attract early adopters, thus actively enlarging the market share of sustainable production and consumption.

In some cases (for example Energy+, climate funds), governance processes tackle specific barriers, for example information and adaptation deficits. It may be an important conclusion for policy analysis that these processes rely on a diversity of actors (pioneers and laggards, and different groups in between). Governance processes as described here seem especially suitable for purposes of early adaptation and diffusion at a point when technological inventions have been made, demonstration projects have been accomplished and markets for sustainability need to be created. In this context, the main advantage of governance processes over political intervention can be seen in their flexibility: how, where and when decisions are taken is up to firms, markets and societal stakeholders rather than bureaucrats. At the other end of the spectrum, late majorities and laggards can hardly be reached by those governance systems and are candidates for any impulse programme (see Figure 19.1) and a tougher regulation kicking in later on. These laggards also include firms whose asset-specific investments prevent rapid change; in such cases governance systems can prepare negotiations about new investments, but can hardly replace formal decisions and political responsibility.

Looking ahead, responsible corporate governance will become more visible and even stronger in future years as both regional governance structures and international regimes gain importance. Not only the sustainability issue, but also the subsidiarity principle of the EU Amsterdam Treaty and the EU Governance White Paper clearly indicate a general shift in the way public concerns are handled. All cases analysed contribute to the vertical and horizontal diffusion of policies, helping to lessen the need for supranational structures via action at the meso-level and forms of dissemination. Any deficits or negative side-effects of governance processes can therefore be assessed against the hypothetical effects of a stronger regulation with more bureaucracy and less flexibility.

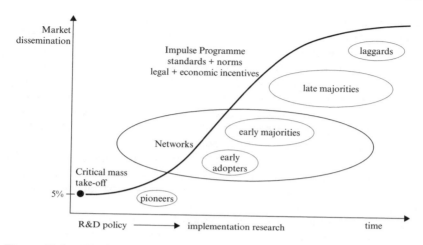

Figure 19.1 Market dissemination of new technologies and strategies

Our assessment methodology suggests that corporate governance processes can still be improved and need to be analysed with a view to improving regulation too. Regions with weaker legislations that as yet lack an effective environmental policy are challenged to set a framework to define minimum conditions and guarantee stability. In other regions (for example the EU) where an *acquis communautaire* of legislation has already been achieved, the political transaction costs of reforming framework conditions can be weighed against incentives for a more decentralized approach where corporate activities play a major role. Any better regulation may consist of long-term targets supported by technology platforms and information exchange.

The question is whether one can expect responsible corporate governance approaches to flourish without further support from politics. Why should corporate actors not ask for a share in the societal benefits or positive externalities occasioned through their activities? Our book reveals that most corporate actors continue their activities even in hard times because they still expect benefits, be it in the form of cost reduction, innovation, staff motivation or reputation. In addition, they may expect a loss of reputation if they opt out of these governance processes (see, for example, the case-study on Responsible Care). This factor is especially important for corporate activities beyond 'window dressing': as soon as action is announced publicly, concerns for accountability will be made.

Despite these self-enforcing mechanisms it seems that additional incentives for RCG are essential provided policy is interested in enlarging the share of active firms.. 'Benefit-sharing' between corporate, societal and political actors certainly is important for the future agenda. Our book focuses the general issue of benefit-sharing onto the following question: 'Which governance path would encourage corporate accountability in the global markets?' The responsibilities that arise from global product chains and the new economic set-up require incentive systems to aim at finding strategies or new pathways for external stakeholders to establish linkages between responsible corporate activities and benefits for a given corporation. They need to prepare a favourable environment for the corporation to assume all responsibilities (without leading to problem-shifting or new externalities across different jurisdictions). Thus, reporting requirements and producer responsibility remain on the agenda for regulatory reforms. Publishing the use of materials, for instance, would boost market search for both cost reduction and resource productivity improvements.

The area of application for corporate governance in a co-evolutionary perspective seems vast. Policy areas like climate, energy, mobility, agriculture, waste and housing are obvious areas of application. In promoting such perspective, policy analysis will have to rethink individual sectoral approaches and prevailing regulatory tools. Relaxation on some carefully defined regulations can be legitimate as long as progress in other areas can be achieved through RCG. Companies undertaking pioneering efforts in one area or internationally will certainly want less pressure from traditional regulation (see, for example, the BP case-study). Our book suggests that domestic efforts can open up cross-sectoral markets, and also includes some criteria toward a compensation scheme for assessing cross-sectoral approaches. Beyond the areas mentioned, our governance approach is also helpful in broader areas like economic policy, technology policy, trade policy and development cooperation. Given our remarks on weak and strong legislations, it seems especially applicable for industrialized countries and countries in transition. In a broader vein, one may also find some areas of application in managing the commons and services in the general interest.

In summary, the book reveals the following strengths of corporate governance approaches in a co-evolutionary perspective:

- they stimulate innovation and continuous improvements;
- they activate early adopters and early majorities in market development;
- they contribute to the formation of actor coalitions beyond established market participants;
- they may also overcome path-dependencies and inertia (stepwise);
- thus contributing to the creation of markets for sustainable development.

On the other hand, deficits may be seen in the following:

- A slow diffusion due to difficulties related to approaching the early majority, not to mention late majorities and 'laggards'.
- Slow processes of horizontal diffusion where good practice needs to be integrated into other branches of industry and other sectors of society.
- Difficulties in monitoring performance, where priorities are not made visible. When priority-setting is not transparent, monitoring for both insiders and outsiders becomes impossible.
- Underdeployment of overall potentials, economies of scale and scope because governance processes may lack the ultimate authority that states normally possess.

It thus becomes evident that corporate governance approaches in a co-evolutionary perspective need good partners from civil society and policy-makers. Beyond giving feedback and pushing pioneers, civil society and policy-makers are essential for overcoming persisting lock-ins and for long-term clarity. In the short run, policy can set up a programme designed to facilitate low-cost materials efficiency improvements, thus moving the dissemination frontier from early adopters to majorities (see Box 19.1).

BOX 19.1 POTENTIAL COMPONENTS OF AN IMPULSE PROGRAMME (PILOT PHASE)

- Loan programme for PIUS Checks: 5000–10 000 euros for pre-feasibility studies; refunding in the case of demonstrable economic efficiency, otherwise lost grant.
- Performance-based investment grant: Up to 50% of investment costs depending on scale of material and energy saving; development of evaluation methods and concept for a control authority.
- Start-up support for local eco-industrial parks: Municipal support; performance standards developed at regional, national or EU levels; revolving funds to promote resource efficiency in public services ('intracting').
- Promotion of local training and job-creation initiatives ('Eco-profit'): Local and regional incentives addressing small and medium-sized (trade and craft) businesses through information meetings, start-up financing; integration of business

and industry through targeted promotion of PIUS Checks and local job-creation schemes.

- Development of regional resource efficiency profile, development of new system solutions: Clusters, networks, and R&D efforts promoted in the scope of regional eco-efficiency concepts; especially in new industrial estate models (zero-emissions operations; up-cycling).
- Grants for additional costs of integral planning for non-dwelling buildings: Up to 50%; a considerable part of future life-cycle cost can be prevented through integral construction and project planning; this also applies for more comprehensive planning.
- Promotion of operational alliances for employment and resource efficiency: Minimum standards for employee and stakeholder participation; mediation and information transfer; trainings for experts.
- Call for bids for a resource-efficiency award: Co-financing from private sources, announcement of a new award: concepts ready for diffusion receive professional support at lowest possible costs (free of charge; e.g. Wuppertal Award).
- Incentives for engineering offices and contracting companies for further development of eco-efficiency contracting; backing and flexibly available funds for training, additional costs, risks of eco-efficiency contracting; certification of contracting bidders; coaching for potential contracting clients.
- Communication concept / multiplier events: Promotion of targeted marketing campaigns and events; involvement of important multipliers and participants (also from financial markets).
- Network of resource-efficiency agencies: Synergies emerge as organizations link up at various levels of national and local government.
- Promotion of initiatives for resource efficiency and employment: Programmes at national (or EU) level for start-up financing for impulse consulting, network developing, pioneer projects, public awareness-raising campaigns, evaluation plus publications; checklists, assessment and rating criteria, manuals, development of revolving funds on the basis of profit-sharing.
- Development and certification of a pool of experts: Comprehensive training programmes in universities, institutes of applied sciences, including organizations of advanced education and training, financial markets.

- Wage grant for resource-efficiency agents and resource managers: Employment and vocational retraining programme for unemployed managers; alternatively the costs for a six-month manager training programme are refunded if the company hires a long-term unemployed person.
- Developing an integrated R&D–market diffusion network (comparable with the Swiss RAVEL programme); e.g. organizational processing, developing consensus, material for further education, courses, workshops, manuals, checklists, software.

As other governments reluctant or unwilling to act scrutinize policy itself, any policy facilitating corporate action in the ways described here will also shape the slow progress of international policy-making – again a case for corporate governance approaches in a co-evolutionary perspective.

References

Ademe (French Agency for the Environment and Energy Management) (2001), 'Energy+: Aggregated Purchase of Energy Efficient Refrigerator-Freezers at Europan Level', Final Report, Paris.

ADL (Arthur D. Little GmbH) / Wuppertal Institute for Climate, Environment, Energy / ISI (Fraunhofer Institute) (2005), 'Studie zur Konzeption eines Programms für die Steigerung der Materialeffizienz in Mittelständischen Unternehmen', Abschlussbericht, available online at http://www.bmwi.de/BMWi/Redation/PDF/Publikationen/Studien/studie-konzeption-eines-programms-steigerung-materialeffizienz,property=pdf,bereich=bmwi,sprache=de,rwb=true.pdf (2006-07-13).

Adriaanse, A., S. Bringezu, A. Hammond, Y. Moriguchi, E. Rodenburg, D. Rogich and H. Schütz (1997), *Resource Flows: The Material Basis of Industrial Economies*, Washington, DC: World Resource Institute.

Adrian, L. (2003), 'Regionale Netzwerke als Handlungskonzept: Erfolg versprechender Weg einer innovationsorientierten Regionalentwicklung?' Berlin: Deutsches Institut für Urbanistik (Difu).

Ahrens, J. (2002), *Governance and Economic Development: A Comparative Institutional Approach*, Cheltenham, UK and Northampton, MA, USA: Edward Elgar.

Alberini, A. and K. Segerson (2002), 'Assessing Voluntary Programs to Improve Environmental Quality', *Environment and Resource Economics*, **22**(1/2), pp. 157–84.

Ayres, I. and J. Braithwaite (1992), *Responsive Regulation: Transcending the Deregulation Debate*, Oxford: Oxford University Press.

Backhaus, J. (1999), 'The Law and Economics of Environmental Taxation: When Should the Ecotax Kick in?', *International Review of Law and Economics*, **19**, pp. 117–34.

Beckenbach, F. (1998), 'Socio-technological Innovation and Sustainability', in S. Faucheux, J.M. Gowdy and I. Nicolaï (eds), *Sustainability and Firms: Technological Change and the Changing Regulatory Environment*, Cheltenham, UK and Northampton, MA, USA: Edward Elgar, pp. 99–129.

Berg, R. v.d. (2000), 'Regulatory Competition in Europe', *Kyklos*, **53**, pp. 435–66.

Bergh, J.C.J.M. van der and S. Stagl (2003), 'Coevolution of Economic Behavior and Institutions: Towards a Theory of Institutional Change', *Journal of Evolutionary Economics*, **13**, pp. 289–317.

Berkhout, F., M. Leach and I. Scoones (eds) (2003), *Negotiating Environmental Change: New Perspectives from Social Science*, Cheltenham, UK and Northampton, MA, USA: Edward Elgar.

Bleischwitz, R. (2003a), 'Governance of Eco-efficiency in Japan: An Institutional Approach', *Internationales Asienforum / International Asian Quarterly*, **34**(1–2), pp. 107–26.

Bleischwitz, R. (2003b), 'Cognitive and Institutional Perspectives of Eco-efficiency', *Ecological Economics*, **46**, pp. 453–67.

Bleischwitz, R. (2004a), 'Evolutorische Wirtschaftspolitik als Institutionen-reform' in Lehmann-Waffenschmidt, M., A. Alexander Ebner and D. Fornahl (eds), *Institutioneller Wandel, Marktprozesse und Dynamische Wirtschaftspolitik: Perspekiven der Evolutorischen Ökonomik*, Marburg: Metropolis.

Bleischwitz, R. (2004b), 'Governance of Sustainable Development: Co-Evolution of Political and Corporate Strategies', *International Journal of Sustainable Development*, 7 (1), pp. 27–43.

Bleischwitz, R. (2005), *Gemeinschaftsgüter durch Wissen generierende Institutionen: Ein evolutorischer Ansatz für die Wirtschaftpolitik*, Marburg: Metropolis.

Bleischwitz, R. and P. Hennicke (2004), *Eco-Efficiency, Regulation and Sustainable Business*, Cheltenham, UK and Northampton, MA, USA: Edward Elgar.

Bleischwitz, R. and U.-M. Schubert (2000), 'Gemeinsames Umwelt-management in Unternehmensnetzwerken: Das Beispiel der Eco-Industrial Parks', *Zeitschrift für Angewandte Umweltforschung*, **13**(3/4), pp. 457–68.

Börzel, T. (1997), 'What's so Special about Policy Networks: An Exploration of the Concept and Its Usefulness in Studying European Governance', European Integration Online Paper (EIoP), **1**(16), available online at http://eiop.or.at/eiop/texte/1997-016a.htm (accessed 30 June 2006).

BP (2003a), 'Climate Change: Greenhouse Gas Audit', London: BP plc, available online at http://www.bp.com/environ_social/environment/clim_change/greenhouse.asp (2003-11-05).

BP (2003b), 'Climate Change: Our Performance', London: BP plc, available online at http://www.bp.com/environ_social/environment/clim_change/perform.asp#f (2003-11-05).

BP (2004a), 'BP at a glance', London: BP plc, available online at http://www.bp.com/sectiongenericarticle.do?categoryId=3&contentId=2006926 (2006-06-30).

BP (2004b), 'An Overview of BP', London: BP plc, available online at http://www.bp.com/sectiongenericarticle.do?categoryId=14&contentId =2002063 (2006-06-30).

BP (2004c), 'BP', London: BP plc, available online at http://www.bp.com/ genericarticle.do?categoryId=9&contentId=2002350 (2006-06-30).

BP (2004d), 'HSE', London: BP plc, available online at http://www.bp.com/ genericarticle.do?categoryId=27&contentId=2000432 (2004-01-13).

BP (2004e), 'Working in Partnership', London: BP plc, available online at http://www.bp.com/genericarticle.do?categoryId=27&contentId=20 00432 (2004-01-13).

BP (2004f), 'NGOs', London: BP plc, available online at http://www. bp.com/sectiongenericarticle.do?categoryId=802&contentId=2001461 (2004-01-16).

BP (2004g), 'Products and the Environment', London: BP plc, available online at http://www.bp.com/sectiongenericarticle.do?categoryId=57& contentId=2000094 (2004-01-16).

BP (2004h), 'Climate Change: Overview', London: BP plc, available online at http://www.bp.com/genericarticle.do?categoryId=55&contentId= 2004291 (2004-01-15).

Bressers, J.Th.A., D. Huitema and S.M.M. Kuks (1995), 'Policy Networks in Dutch Water Policy', in J.Th.A. Bressers, L.J. O'Toole and J.J. Richardson (eds), *Networks for Water Policy: A Comparative Perspective*, London: Frank Cass, pp. 24–51.

Brown, L.D. (1993), 'Development Bridging Organisations and Strategic Management for Social Change', *Advances in Strategic Management*, **9**, pp. 381–405.

Browne, J. (1997), 'Addressing Climate Change', speech by John Browne, Group Chief Executive, BP, delivered at Stanford University, California, 19 May, available online at BP plc, http://www.bp.com/genericarticle.do? categoryId=98&contentId=2000427 (2006-07-18).

Browne, J. (1998), 'Leading a Global Company: The case of BP', John Browne, Group Chief Executive, BP, Yale School of Management – Perspectives of Leadership, 18 September London: BP plc, available online at http://www.gasandoil.com/goc/reports/rex84717.htm (2006-07-18).

Browne, J. (2002), 'Beyond Petroleum. Business and the Environment in the 21st Century', speech by John Browne, Group Chief Executive, BP, hosted by Stanford Graduate School of Business, 11 March, London: BP plc, available online at http://www.bp.com/centres/press/stanford/ highlights/index.asp (2006-07-18).

Buchanan, J.M. and R.A. Musgrave (1999), *Public Finance and Public Choice: Two Contrasting Visions of the State*, Cambridge, MA: MIT Press.

Budzinski, O. (2000), *Wirtschaftspolitische Implikationen evolutorischer Ordnungsökonomik: Das Beispiel ordnungskonformer ökologischer Wirtschaftspolitik*, Marburg: Metropolis.

Budzinski, O. (2003a), 'Cognitive Rules, Institutions, and Competition', *Constitutional Political Economy*, **14**(3), pp. 213–33.

Budzinski, O. (2003b), 'Pluralism of Competition Policy Paradigms and the Call for Regulatory Diversity', Philipps-University of Marburg, Volkswirtschaftliche Beiträge No. 14/2003, available online at http://ssrn.com/abstract=452900 (2006-06-30).

Budzinski, O. (2004a), 'Die Evolution des internationalen Systems der Wettbewerbspolitiken', in O. Budzinski and J. Jasper (eds), *Wettbewerb, Wirtschaftsordnung und Umwelt*, Frankfurt a.M.: Lang, pp. 81–100.

Budzinski, O. (2004b), 'The International Competition Network: Prospects and Limits on the Road towards International Competition Governance', *Competition and Change*, **8**(3), pp. 243–66.

Busch, T. and T. Orbach (2003), 'Zukunftsfähiger Finanzsektor: die Nachhaltigkeitsleistung von Banken und Versicherungen', Zukunfts fähige Unternehmen (8). Wuppertal Papers No. 128, Wuppertal.

CACG (Commonwealth Association for Corporate Governance) (2003), 'CACG Guidelines', available online at http://www.cacg-inc. com/documents/publications/draft-cpg-for-annuel-reporting-in-the-commonwealth.pdf (2006-06-03).

Carlsson, L. (2000), 'Policy Networks as Collective Action', *Policy Studies Journal*, **28**(3), pp. 502–20.

Carraro, C. and F. Lévêque (eds) (1999), *Voluntary Approaches in Environmental Policy*, Dordrecht: Kluwer.

CCPA (Canadian Chemical Producers Association) (2000), 'Through Our Critics' Eyes: Responsible Care', Annual Performance Report 2000.

CEFIC (European Chemical Industry Council) (2001), 'Responsible Care Status Report Europe 2000', Brussels.

CEFIC (2002), 'Responsible Care 2002', Status Report, Brussels.

CEFIC (2003), 'Responsible Care', Status Report Europe 2002, Brussels.

CEFIC (2006), 'List of Core Parameters', available online at http://www. cefic.be/activities/hse/rc/guide/02.htm (2006-07-12).

Chertow, M.R. (1999), 'The Eco-Industrial Park Model Reconsidered', *Journal of Industrial Ecology*, **2**(3), pp. 8–10.

Christensen, J. (1999), 'Proceedings of the Industry and Environment Workshop', Ahmedabad, India: Indian Institute of Management.

Clark, J.M. (1961), *Competition as a Dynamic Process*, Washington, DC: Brookings Institution.

Cleaner Production Center Austria (2006a): 'Ökoprofit®; Sustainable Economic Development through Eco-Efficiency in Public–Private Partnerships – Structure and Organisation', available online at http:/www.cpc.at/oeko/download/E_2.pdf (2006-06-30).

Cleaner Production Center Austria (2006b), 'Training and Structure of the ÖKOPROFIT® Program', available online at http://www.cpc.at/oeko/oe_1-2_htm (2006-10-20).

Clinch, J.P., K. Schlegelmilch, R.-U. Sprenger and U. Triebswetter (eds) (2001), *Greening the Budget: Budgetary Policies for Environmental Improvements*, Cheltenham, UK and Northhampton, MA, USA: Edward Elgar.

Clinch, P.J., L. Dunne and S. Dresner (2006), 'Environmental and Wider Implications of Political Impediments to Environmental Tax Reform', *Energy Policy*, **34**(8), pp. 960–70.

Coase, R.H. (1960), 'The Problem of Social Costs', *Journal of Law and Economics*, **3**(1), pp. 1–44.

Corporate Watch (2001), 'Greenwash Fact Sheet', available online at http://www.corpwatch.org/article.php?id=242 (2006-07-03).

Coté, R.P. and E. Cohen-Rosenthal (1998), 'Designing Eco-Industrial Parks: A Synthesis of Some Experiences', *Journal of Cleaner Production*, **6**(3), pp. 181–8.

Cowe, R. (2000), 'Measuring eco-efficiency: a guide to reporting company performance', Geneva: WBCSD.

Dalkmann, H., D. Bongardt, K. Rottman and S. Hutfilter (2005), 'Review of Voluntary Approaches in the European Union'. Feasibility Study on Demonstration of Voluntary Approaches for Industrial Environmental Management in China. Wuppertal: Wuppertal Report No. 2.

Davis, I. (2005), 'The biggest contract: On Corporate Social Responsibility', *The Economist*, 2005-05-26.

De Beer, J. (1998), 'Potential for Industrial Energy-Efficiency Improvements in the Long Term', habilitation thesis, University of Utrecht.

De Soto, H. (2002), *The Mystery of Capital*, New York: Basic Books and London: Random House.

DEFRA (Department for the Environment and Rural Affairs) (2006), 'UK Emissions Trading Scheme: Frequently Asked Questions', London, available online at http://www.defra.gov.uk/Environment/climatechange/trading/uk/faq.htm (2006-07-03).

Delphi International Ltd. and Ecologic GmbH (1997), 'The Role of Financial Institutions in Achieving Sustainable Development', Report to the European Commission.

Denzau, A.T. and D.C. North (1994), 'Shared Mental Models: Ideologies and Institutions', *Kyklos*, **47**(1), pp. 3–31.

Desroches, P. (2001), 'Eco-Industrial Parks: The Case for Private Planning', *Independent Review*, **3**, pp. 345–71.

Deutscher Bundestag der 14. Wahlperiode (ed.) (2002), 'Enquete Commission on Sustainable Energy Supply Against the Background of Globalisation and Liberalisation: Summary of Final Report', Berlin: Deutscher Bundestag.

Dixit, A.K. (2000), *The Making of Economic Policy: A Transaction-Cost Perspective*, Cambridge, MA: MIT Press.

Dow Jones Sustainability Indexes (2006), 'Keyfacts', Available online at http://www.sustainability-indexes.com/06_htmle/other/faq.html#keyfacts (2007-01-23).

Dow (2007), Corporate Website. Available online at http://www.dow.com/commitments/goals/index.htm (2003-01-23).

Dror, Y. (2001), *The Capacity to Govern: A Report to the Club of Rome*, London: Frank Cass.

Dulbecco, P. and V. Dutraive (2001), 'The Meaning of Market – Comparing Austrian and Institutional Economics', in P. Garrouste and S. Ioannides (eds), *Evolution and Path-Dependence in Economic Ideas*, Cheltenham, UK and Northampton, MA, USA: Edward Elgar, pp. 41–70.

Dunn, B.C. and A. Steinemann (1998), 'Industrial Ecology for Sustainable Communities', *Journal of Environmental Planning and Management*, **41**(6), pp. 661–72.

EfA NRW (Effizienz-Agentur Nordrhein-Westalen) (2006), 'Die Effizienz-Agentur NRW: Zahlen und Fakten 2006', Duisburg, available online at http://www.efanrw.de/downloads/publikationen/EFA-ZuF-06.pdf (2006-10-20).

Eggertson, T. (1997), 'The Old Theory of Economic Policy and the New Institutionalism', *World Development*, **25**(8), pp. 1187–203.

Egidi, M. and S. Rizzello (2003), 'Cognitive Economics: Foundations and Historical Evolution', Università di Torino, Working Paper 04/2003.

Ehrenfeld, J. and N. Gertler (1997), 'Industrial Ecology in Practice: The Evolution of Interdependence at Kalundborg', *Journal of Industrial Ecology*, **1**(1), pp. 67–79.

Elkington, J. (1998), *Cannibals With Forks*, Gabriola Islands, BC: New Society Publications.

Elliott, S.R., R. Godby and J.B. Kruse (2003), 'An Experimental Examination of Vertical Control and Cost Predation', *International Journal of Industrial Organization*, **21**(2), pp. 253–81.

EM (Swedish National Energy Administration) (1998), 'Procurement for Market Transformation for Energy-Efficient Products: A Study under the SAVE Programme', Report ER 15:98.

ENDS Report (2003), 'Sustainable Consumption Strategy', Environmental Data Services, 345, pp. 22–6.

Energy+ (2004), 'Europe's Most Energy-efficient Refrigerators and Freezers', Final brochure of the Energy+ procurement project.

Environmental Defense (1997), 'British Petroleum Announces Plan to Measure and Report Greenhouse Gas Emissions; to Set Targets; and to Practice Emissions Trading', Washington: Environmental Defense (News Release; 9/30/1997), available online at http://www.envir onmentaldefense.org/pressrelease.cfm?ContentID=1931 (2006-06-30).

Environmental Defense (2000), 'Global Corporations and Environmental Defense partner to reduce Greenhouse Gas Emissions: Partnership Pioneers Real-World Solutions', Environmental Defense (News Release; 10/17/2000), Washington, available online at http://www.environmen taldefense.org/article.cfm?contentid=503 (2006-06-30).

Environmental Defense (2006), 'The Partnership for Climate Action' (PCA), Environmental Defense: New York, available online at http:// www.environmentaldefense.org/subissue.cfm?subissue=3 (2006-07-13).

Europäische Gemeinschaft / Wuppertal Institut (1998), 'Procurement for Market Transformation of Energy Efficient Products: A Study under the SAVE Program', Eskilstuna: Swedish National Energy Administration.

European Commission (EU) (2001), 'Promoting a European Framework for Corporate Social Responsibility', Green Paper, COM(2001) 366 final, Brussels.

European Commission (EU) (2002), 'Amended Proposal for a Directive of the European Parliament and the Council establishing a scheme for greenhouse gas emission allowance trading within the community and amending Council directive 96/61/EC', Doc. 14935/02, Council of the European Union, Brussels.

European Parliament (2003), 'Directive 2003/87/EC of the European Parliament and of the Council of 13 October 2003 for establishing a scheme for greenhouse gas emission allowance trading within the community and amending Council Directive 96/61/EC', Brussels.

Eurosif (European Social Investment Forum) (2003), 'Socially Responsible Investment among European Institutional Investors 2003 Report', Paris: Eurosif.

Fabian Society (2003), 'Fabians Attack Consumer Choice', available online at http://www.fabian-society.org.uk/press_office/display.asp?id=177% type=new&cat=24 (2006-06-30).

Faure, M. and G. Skogh (2003), *The Economic Analysis of Environmental Policy and Law*, Cheltenham, UK and Northampton, MA, USA: Edward Elgar.

Faust, M. and R. Nordbeck (2003), 'European Chemicals Regulation and its Effect on Innovation: An Assessment of the EU's White Paper on the Strategy for a Future Chemicals Policy', *European Environment*, **13**, pp. 79–99.

Field, A.J. (1979), 'On the Explanation of Rules Using Rational Choice Models', *Journal of Economic Issues*, **13**(1), pp. 49–72.

Field, A.J. (1984), 'Microeconomics, Norms, and Rationality', *Economic Development and Cultural Change*, **32**(4), pp. 683–711.

Flatz, A. (2002), 'Corporate Sustainability and Financial Indexes', in Esty, D.C and P. Cornelius (eds), *Environmental Performance Measurement: The Global Report 2001–2002*. New York: Oxford University Press, pp. 66–81.

Fleig, A.-K. (2000), 'Eco-Industrial Parks: A Strategy towards Industrial Ecology in Developing and Newly Industrialised Countries', GTZ, Eschborn.

Forrest, C.J. and R.H. Mays (1997), *The Practical Guide to Environmental Community Relations*, New York: John Wiley.

Freeman, C. (1998), 'The economics of technical change', in D. Archibugie and J. Michie (eds), *Trade, Growth and Technical Change*, Cambridge: Cambridge University Press, pp. 16–54.

Freeman, R.E. and J. McVea (2001), 'A Stakeholder Approach to Strategic Management', Charlottesville, VA: Univ. of Virginia, Darden Business School Working Paper No. 01-02.

Frey, B. (1997), *Not Just for the Money: An Economic Theory of Personal Motivation*, Cheltenham, UK and Northampton, MA, USA: Edward Elgar.

Frey, B. and M. Osterloh (eds) (2002), *Successful Management by Motivation: Balancing Intrinsic and Extrinsic Incentives*, Berlin: Springer.

Friedman, M. (1962), *Capitalism and Freedom*, Chicago, IL: Chicago University Press.

Funk, K. (2001), 'Sustainability and Performance: Uncovering Opportunities for Value Creation', London: Cap Gemini Ernst & Young Center for Business Innovation.

Gabel, H.L. and B. Sinclair-Desgagné (1998), 'The Firm, its Routines and the Environment', in T. Tietenberg and H. Folmer (eds), *The International Yearbook of Environmental and Resource Economics 1998/99*, Cheltenham, UK and Northampton, MA, USA: Edward Elgar, pp. 89–118.

Garcia Johnson, R. (2001), 'Certification Institutions in the Protection of the Environment: Exploring the Implications for Governance', Paper prepared for the 23rd Annual Research Conference of the Association for Public Policy, Analysis and Management, Washington, DC.

Garner, A. and G.A. Keoleian (1995), 'Industrial Ecology: An Introduction', University of Michigan, National Pollution Prevention Center for Higher Education, Ann Arbor.

Garz, H. and C. Volk (2003), 'Inside SRI: Update, More Pain than Gain', WestLB Equity Markets.

Geels, F.W. (2005), *Technological Transitions and System Innovation: A Co-evolutionary and Socio-technical Analysis*, Cheltenham, UK and Northampton, MA, USA: Edward Elgar.

Gege, M. (1997), *Kosten senken durch Umweltmanagement: 1000 Beispiele aus 100 Unternehmen*, München: Vahlen.

Grant, R.M. (1996), 'Toward a Knowledge-Based Theory of the Firm', *Strategic Management Journal*, **17**, pp. 109–22.

Greenpeace (1996), 'Greenpeace Brent Spar Protest in the North Sea', Amsterdam: Greenpeace International, available online at http://archive.greenpeace.org/~comms/brent/brent.html (2006-06-30).

Greenpeace, Friends of the Earth (FoE) and People & Planet (2003), 'Don't Buy Esso', http://www.greenpeace.org.uk/climate/climatecriminals/esso/index.cfm (2006-06-30).

Grossekettler, H. (1996), 'Öffentliche Finanzen', in D. Bender et al. (eds), *Vahlens Kompendium der Wirtschaftstheorie und Wirtschaftspolitik*, München: Vahlen, pp. 483–628.

Grossekettler, H. (1997), *Die Wirtschaftsordnung als Gestaltungsaufgabe. Entwicklungsgeschichte und Entwicklungsperpektiven des Ordoliberalismus nach 50 Jahren Sozialer Marktwirtschaft*, Münster: Lit Verlag.

Gunderson, L.H. and C.S. Holling (2002), *Panarchy: Understanding Transformation in Human and Natural Systems*, Washington, DC.: Island Press.

Harrison, N.E. and G.C. Bryner (eds) (2004), *Science and Politics in the International Environment*, Lanham, MD: Rowman & Littlefield.

Hart, O. (2003), 'Incomplete Contracts and Public Ownership: Remarks, and an Application to Public–Private-Partnerships', *Economic Journal*, 113, pp. 69–76.

Hart, S.L. (1995), 'A Natural-Resource Based View of the Firm', *Academy of Management Review*, **20**(4), pp. 996–1014.

Hayek, F.A. (1937), 'Economics and Knowledge', *Economica*, **4**(1), pp. 33–54.

Hayek, F.A. (1945), 'The Use of Knowledge in Society', *American Economic Review*, **35**(4), pp. 519–30.

Hayek, F.A. (1948), 'The Meaning of Competition', in F.A. Hayek (ed.), *Individualism and Economic Order*, Chicago, IL: Chicago University Press, pp. 92–106.

Hayek, F.A. (1952), *The Sensory Order*, Chicago, IL: Chicago University Press.

Hayek, F.A. (1967), 'The Results of Human Action but not of Human

Design', in F.A. Hayek (ed.), *Studies in Philosophy, Politics and Economics*, Chicago, IL: Chicago University Press, pp. 96–105.

Hayek, F.A. (1968), 'Competition as a Discovery Procedure', in F.A. Hayek (ed.) (1978), *New Studies in Philosophy, Politics, Economics and the History of Ideas*, Chicago, IL: Chicago University Press, pp.179–90.

Hayek, F.A. (1973), *Law, Legislation and Liberty – Vol. 1: Rules and Order*, Chicago, IL: Chicago University Press.

Hayek, F.A. (1975), 'The Pretence of Knowledge', *Swedish Journal of Economics*, **77**(4), pp. 433–42.

Héritier, A. (ed.) (2002), *Common Goods: Reinventing European and International Governance*, London: Rowman & Littlefield.

Hooge, L. and G. Marks (2003), 'Unravelling the Central State, but How? Types of Multilevel Governance', *American Political Science Review*, **97** (2), pp. 233–43.

Horwitz, S. (1993), 'Spontaneity and Design in the Evolution of Institutions', *Journal des Economists et des Etudes Humaines*, **4**(4), pp. 571–87.

ICCA (The International Council of Chemical Associations) (2002a), 'Industry as a Partner for Sustainable Development: Chemicals', Nairobi: UNEP.

ICCA (2002b), 'Responsible Care Status Report', Brussels: CEFIC, available online at http://www.icca-chem.org/rcreport2002/Respcare.pdf (2006-06-03).

ICGN (International Corporate Governance Network) (1995), 'Draft ICGN Statement on Global Corporate Governance Principles', available online at http://www.icgn.org/issues/2005/consultations/cgp/index.php (2006-06-30).

IETA (International Emissions Trading Association) (2004), 'About IETA', International Emissions Trading Association, Geneva, available online at http://www.ieta.org/ieta/www/pages/index/php?IdSiteTree=2 (2006-06-30).

ILO (International Labour Organization) (1999), 'Responsible Care and Related Voluntary Initiatives to Improve Enterprise Performance on Health, Safety and Environment in the Chemical Industry', Working Paper by Kevin Munn, Geneva.

Innovest Strategic Value Advisors (2002), 'Value at Risk: Climate Change and the Future of Governance', Boston, MA: Coalition for Environmentally Responsible Economies (CERES), available online at http://www.ceres.org/pub/docs/Ceres_value_at_risk_0418.pdf (2006-07-03).

Innovest Strategic Value Advisors (2003), 'Carbon Disclosure Project: Carbon Finance and the Global Equity Markets', London: CDP.

International Right to Know (2003), 'Empowering Communities through Corporate Transparency', January, http://www.amnestyusa.org/justearth/lrtk.pdf.

IPCC (Intergovernmental Panel on Climate Change) (2001), 'Climate Change 2001. Impacts, Adaptation and Vulnerability. Contribution of the Working Group II to the Third Assessment Report of the Intergovernmental Panel on Climate Change', Cambridge: Cambridge University Press, available online at http://www.grida.no/climate/ipcc_tar/wg 2/ (2006-07-03).

Jacobsen, N.B. (2003), 'The Industrial Symbiosis in Kalundborg, Denmark: An Approach to Cleaner Industrial Production', in E. Cohen-Rosenthal and J. Musnikow (eds), *Eco-Industrial Strategies. Unleashing Synergy Between Economic Development and the Environment*, Sheffield: Greenleaf Publishing, pp. 270–75.

Jänicke, M. and K. Jacobs (2002), 'Ecological Modernization and the Creation of Lead Markets', FFU rep 02-03. Berlin: Free University.

Jaffé, A.B., Newell, R.G. and R.N. Stavins (2002), 'Environmental Policy and Technological Change', *Environmental and Resource Economics*, **22** (1–2), pp. 41–69.

Jeder, P. (2004), 'Verband der chemischen Industrie e.V. (VCI)', Wissenschaft, Technik und Umwelt, Bereich Produktsicherheit und Grundsatzfragen, Interview Questionnaire (2004-01-14).

Jeucken, M. (2001), *Sustainable Finance and Banking: the Financial Sector and the Future of the Planet*, London: Earthscan.

Jordan, A., R.K.W. Wurzel, and A.R. Zito (2003), ' "New" Instruments of Environmental Governance? National Experiences and Prospects', *Environmental Politics*, **12**(1), pp. 201–24.

Kahneman, D. (2003), 'A Psychological Perspective on Economics', *American Economic Review*, **93**(2), pp. 162–8.

Kahneman, D. and A. Tversky (2000), *Choices, Values, and Frames*, New York: Sage.

Kaisla, J. (2003), 'Choice Behaviour: Looking for Remedy to Some Central Logical Problems in Rational Action', *Kyklos*, **56**(2), pp. 245–62.

Kenis, P. and V. Schneider (1991), 'Policy Networks and Policy Analysis: Scrutinizing a New Analytical Toolbox', in B. Marin and R. Mayntz (eds), *Policy Network: Empirical Evidence and Theoretical Considerations*, Frankfurt: Campus Verlag, pp. 25–59.

Kerber, W. (1994), 'Evolutorischer Wettbewerb', habilitation thesis, Freiburg.

Kerber, W. (1997), 'Wettbewerb als Hypothesentest – Eine evolutorische Konzeption wissenschaffenden Wettbewerbs', in K. von Delhaes and U. Fehl (eds), *Dimensionen des Wettbewerbs – Seine Rolle in der Entstehung und Ausgestaltung von Wirtschaftsordnungen*, Stuttgart: Lucius & Lucius, pp. 29–78.

Kerber, W. (2006), 'Competition, Knowledge, and Institutions', *Journal of Economic Issues*, **40**(2), pp. 457–64.

Kerber, W. and O. Budzinski (2003), 'Towards a Differentiated Analysis of Competition Laws', *ZWeR Journal of Competition Law*, **1**(4), pp. 411–48.

Kerber, W. and N. Saam (2001), 'Competition as a Test of Hypotheses: Simulation of Knowledge-Generating Market Processes', *Journal of Artificial Societies and Social Simulation*, **4**(3), pp. 1–34.

King, A.A. and M.J. Lenox (2000), 'Industry self-regulation without sanctions: the chemical industry's responsible care program', *Academy of Management Journal*, **43**(4), pp. 698–716.

King Committee on Corporate Governance (2002), 'King Report on Corporate Governance', available online at http://www.cliffedekker.co.za/files/CD_King2.pdf (2006-06-30).

Korten, D.C. (2001), 'The Responsibility of Business to the Whole', in R. Starkey and R. Welford (eds), *Business and Sustainable Development*, London: Earthscan, pp. 230–41.

Kovach, H., C. Neligan and S. Burall (2003), 'Power Without Accountability? The Global Accountability Report No. 1', London: One World Trust.

KPMG LLP and Det Norske Veritas (DNV) (2003), 'BP's 2002 Greenhouse Gas Emissions: Independent Greenhouse Gas Audit Report, 3 March 2003', available online at http://www.bp.com/liveassets/bp_internet/globalbp/STAGING/global_assets/downloads/G/Greenhouse_gas_audit_of_2002_data_KPMGDNVICF.pdf (2006-07-13).

KPMG, Det Norske Veritas and ICF Consulting (2001), 'BP's Greenhouse Gas Emissions: Audited 2000 Data, 28 February 2001', available online at http://www.bp.com/environ_social/downloads.asp (2003-10-31).

Kuhndt, M. and B. Tunçer (2004), 'Sector Governance Systems: Elements and Case Analysis', unpublished.

Kuhndt, M., B. Tunçer, S. Andersen and C. Liedtke (2004), 'Responsible Corporate Governance: An Overview of Trends, Initiatives and State-of-the-art Elements', Wuppertal Institute Papers No. 139, Wuppertal.

Kuhndt, M., J. von Geibler and C. Liedtke (2002), 'Towards a Sustainable Aluminium Industry: Stakeholder Expectations and Core Indicators – Final Report', Wuppertal, available online at http://www.pius de/dokumente/docdir/wupp/praxis_info/pdf/WI-0803-SustainAlu.pdf-info. (2006-07-03).

Lachmann, L.M. (1963), 'Wirtschaftsordnung und wirtschaftliche Institutionen', *ORDO – Jahrbuch für die Ordnung von Wirtschaft und Gesellschaft*, 14, pp. 63–77.

Lafferty, W.M. and J. Meadowcroft (2001), *Implementing Sustainable Development: Strategies and Initiatives in High Consumption Societies*, Oxford and New York: Oxford University Press.

Landwehr, M., S. Thomas, G. Wohlauf and K. Ostertag (1998), 'Procurement as a Means of Market Transformation for Energy Efficient Products. Task A: Country Survey for Germany; Report within the EU SAVE Project', in Cooperation with Wuppertal Institute for Climate Environment Energy. Karlsruhe, Wuppertal: Fraunhofer ISI and Wuppertal Institute.

Langlois, R.N. (ed.) (1986a), *Economics as a Process*, Cambridge: Cambridge University Press.

Langlois, R.N. (1986b), 'Rationality, Institutions, and Explanation', in R.N. Langlois (ed.), *Economics as a Process*, Cambridge: Cambridge University Press, pp. 225–55.

Langlois, R.N. (1994), 'The Market Process: An Evolutionary View', in P.J. Boettke and D.L. Prychitko (eds), *The Market Process*, Aldershot, UK and Brookfield, USA: Edward Elgar, pp. 29–37.

Langlois, R.N. (1998), 'Rule-Following, Expertise, and Rationality: A New Behavioral Economics?' in K. Dennis (ed.), *Rationality in Economics: Alternative Perspectives*, Dordrecht: Kluwer, pp. 55–78.

Langlois, R.N. (2001), 'Technological Standards, Innovation, and Essential Facilities: Towards a Schumpeterian Post-Chicago Approach', in J. Ellig (ed.), *Dynamic Competition and Public Policy*, Cambridge: Cambridge University Press, pp. 193–228.

Langlois, R.N. and P.L. Robertson (1995), *Firms, Markets, and Economic Change: A Dynamic Theory of Business Institutions*, London: Routledge.

Langrock, T. (ed.) (2001), 'Emissions Trading and Joint Implementation as a Chance for CEECs', Berlin: Federal Ministry of the Environment, Nature Protection and Nuclear Safety.

Leonard-Barton, D. (1995), *Wellsprings of Knowledge: Building and Sustaining the Sources of Innovation*, Boston, MA: Harvard Business School Press.

Litvin, D. (2003), *Empires of Profit: Commerce, Conquest and Corporate Responsibility*, New York and London: Texere.

Loasby, B.J. (1993), 'Institutional Stability and Change in Science and the Economy', in U. Mäki, B. Gustafsson and C. Knudsen (eds), *Rationality, Institutions, and Economic Methodology*, London and New York: Routledge, pp. 203–21.

Loasby, B.J. (2000), 'Market Institutions and Economic Evolution', *Journal of Evolutionary Economics*, **10**(3), pp. 297–309.

Lowe, E.A. (2001a), 'Eco-Industrial Parks', available online at http://www.indigodev.com/Ecoparks.html (2006-07-03).

Lowe, E.A. (2001b), 'Introduction to Eco-Industrial Parks and Networks', Konferenzpapier, New Strategies for Industrial Development. An International Conference and Workshop, Manila, Philippines, 3–6 April.

Lowe, E.A., S.R. Moran and D.B. Holmes (1998), *Eco-Industrial Parks: A Handbook for Local Development Teams*, Emeryvill, CA: RPP International.

Luhmann, H.-J., E. Müller, J. Nitsch and H.-J. Ziesing (2002), 'Oil Corporations and the Destruction of the Climate: How Investment can be Diverted into Renewable Energies to Protect the Climate', Hamburg: Greenpeace Germany.

Majone, G. (1998), 'From the Positive to the Regulatory State: Causes and Consequences of Changes in the Mode of Governance', *Journal of Public Policy*, **17**(2), pp. 139–67.

Mantzavinos, C. (2001), *Individuals, Institutions, and Markets*, Cambridge: Cambridge University Press.

March, J.G. (1999), *The Pursuit of Organizational Intelligence*, Oxford: Blackwell.

Marsh, D. and M. Smith (2000), 'Understanding Policy Networks: towards a Dialectical Approach', *Political Studies*, **48**, pp. 4–21.

Martin, S., H.-T. Normann and C.M. Snyder (2001), 'Vertical Foreclosure in Experimental Markets', *Rand Journal of Economics*, **32**(3), pp. 466–96.

Matthews, E. et al. (2000), 'The Weight of Nations: Material Outflows from Industrial Economies', Washington, DC: World Resource Institute.

Meier, A. and T. Slembeck (1998), *Wirtschaftspolitik – Ein kognitiv evolutionärer Ansatz*, Munich and Vienna: Oldenbourg Verlag.

Metcalfe, J.S. (1998), *Evolutionary Economics and Creative Destruction*, London: Routledge.

Metcalfe, J.S. (2001), 'Institutions and Progress', *Industrial and Corporate Change*, **10**(3), pp. 561–86.

Mistra (The Foundation for Strategic Environmental Research) (2001), 'Screening of the Screening Companies. Social Responsible Investment, SRI – an assessment of the quality of existing products/services', Miljöeko AB, in cooperation with SustainAbility, available online at http://www.innovestgroup.com/pdfs/MISTRA.pdf (2006-07-03).

Moffett, J. and F. Bregha (1999), 'Responsible Care: A Case Study of a Voluntary Environmental Initiative', in R. Gibson (ed.), *Voluntary Initiatives*, Peterborough: Broadnew Press.

Moltke, K. and O. Kuik (1998), 'Global Product Chains: Northern Consumers, Southern Producers and Sustainability. Part 1 Global Product Chains and the Environment', Institute for Environmental Studies Vrije Universiteit, UNEP Programme.

Mueller, D.C. (2000), 'Capitalism, Democracy and Rational Individual Behaviour', *Journal of Evolutionary Economics*, **10**(1–2), pp. 67–82.

Müller, U. (1974), *Wettbewerb, Unternehmenskonzentration und Innovation*, Göttingen: Vandenhoek.

Munn, K. (2000), 'Responsible Care and Voluntary Initiatives to Improve Enterprise Performance on Health, Safety and Environment in the Chemical Industry', International Labour Office Geneva, Sectoral Activities Programme, Working Paper, available online at http://www.ilo.org/public/english/dialogue/sector/papers/respcare/ (2006-06-30).

Munton, R. (2003), 'Deliberative Democracy and Environmental Decision-making', in F. Berkhout, M. Leach and I. Scoones (eds), *Negotiating Environmental Change: New Perspectives from Social Science*, Cheltenham, UK and Northampton, MA, USA: Edward Elgar, pp. 109–36.

Murphy, D.F. and J. Bendell (1999), 'Partners in Time? Business, NGOs and Sustainable Development', UNRISD Discussion Paper No. 109, Geneva.

National Economic and Social Forum, Ireland (2003), 'The Policy Implications of Social Capital', Forum Report No. 28, Dublin: NESF, available online at http/www.nesf.ie/dynamic/docs/nesf_28.pdf (2006-07-03).

Nature Conservancy (2006), 'How We Work', available online at http://nature.org/aboutus/howwework/ (2006-06-30).

Nelson, R. (2002), 'The Problem of Market Bias in Modern Capitalist Economies', *Industrial and Corporate Change*, **11**(2), pp. 207–44.

Nelson, R. and B.N. Sampat (2001), 'Making Sense of Institutions as a Factor Shaping Economic Performance', *Journal of Economic Behavior and Organization*, **44**, pp. 31–54.

Nilsson, H. and C.-O. Wene (2001), 'Best Practices in Technology Deployment Policies', presentation at Workshop on Good Practices in Policies and Measures, 8–10 October 2001, Copenhagen, available online at http://unfccc.int/files/meetings/workshops/other_meetings/ application/pdf/nilsson.pdf (2006-07-03).

Nonaka, I. and R. Toyama (2002), 'A Firm as a Dialectical Being: Towards a Dynamic Theory of a Firm', *Industrial and Corporate Change*, **11**(5), pp. 995–1009.

Nonet, P. and P. Selznick (1978), *Law and Society in Transition: Towards Responsive Law*, New York: Harper & Row.

North, D.C. (1990), *Institutions, Institutional Change and Economic Performance*, Cambridge: Cambridge University Press.

North, D.C (1998), 'Five Propositions about Institutional Change', in Knight J. and I. Sened (eds), *Explaining Social Institutions*. Ann Arbor: University of Michigan Press, pp. 15–26.

O'Rourke, A. (2002), 'A New Politics of Engagement: Shareholder Activism for Corporate Social Responsibility', *The Greening of the Industry Conference*, June 23–26, Göteborg.

OECD (Organisation for Economic Co-operation and Development) (1999), 'OECD Principles of Corporate Governance', Paris: OECD.

OECD (2000), 'OECD Guidelines for Multinational Enterprises: revision 2000', Paris, available online at http://www.oecd.org/dataoecd/56/36/ 1922428. pdf (2006-06-30).

OECD (2003), 'Voluntary Approaches for Environmental Policy: Effectiveness, Efficiency and Usage in Policy Mixes', Paris.

OECD (2004), 'OECD Principles of Corporate Governance', Paris, available online at http://www.oecd.org/dataoecd/32/18/31557724.pdf (2006-06-30).

Okruch, S. (2003), 'Knowledge and Economic Policy: A Plea for Political Experimentalism', in P. Pelikan and G. Wegner (eds), *The Evolutionary Analysis of Economic Policy*, Cheltenham, UK and Northampton, MA, USA: Edward Elgar, pp. 67–95.

Olson, M. (1965), *The Logic of Collective Action*, Cambridge, MA: Harvard University Press.

Olson, M. (1982), *The Rise and Decline of Nations*, New Haven and London: Yale University Press.

Olson, M. (1996), 'Big Bills Left on the Sidewalk: Why Some Nations are Rich, and Others Poor', *Journal of Economic Perspectives*, **10**(2), pp. 3–24.

Osterloh, M. and B. Frey (2000), 'Motivation, Knowledge Transfer, and Organizational Forms', *Organization Science*, **11**(5), pp. 538–50.

Ostertag, K. (2003), 'Evaluation of the pilot procurement project in Germany', Time to turn down energy demand, proceedings of the 2003 ECEEE Summer Study, Paris: European Council for an Energy-Efficient Economy, pp. 623–9.

Ostertag, K. and C. Dreher (2002), 'Cooperative Procurement. Market Transformation for Energy Efficient Products', in P. Clinch, K. Schlegelmilch, R.U. Sprenger et al. (eds), *Greening the Budget: Budgetary Policies for Environmental Improvement*, Cheltenham, UK and Northampton, MA, USA: Edward Elgar.

Ostrom, E. (1998), 'A Behavioural Approach to the Rational Choice Theory of Collective Action', *American Political Science Review*, **92**(1), pp. 1–22.

Ostrom, E. et al. (1999), 'Revisiting the Commons: Local Lessons, Global Challenges', *Science*, **284**, pp. 278–82.

Patel, M. (1999), 'Closing Carbon Cycles: Carbon Use for Materials in the Context of Resource Efficiency and Climate Change', habilitation thesis, University of Utrecht.

Paton, B. (2000), 'Voluntary Environmental Initiatives and Sustainable Industry', *Business Strategy and the Environment*, **9**, pp. 328–38.

Pelikan, P. and G. Wegner (eds) (2003), *The Evolutionary Analysis of Economic Policy*, Cheltenham, UK and Northampton, MA, USA: Edward Elgar.

Persson, A. (2004), 'Environmental Policy Integration', Stockholm: Stockholm Environment Institute.

Pew Center on Climate Change (2006), 'BELC Company GHG Reduction Targets', available online at http://www.pewclimate.org/companies_leading_the_way_belc/targets/index.cfm (2006-07-20).

Popper, K.R. (1987), 'Das Elend des Historizismus'. Tübingen: Mohr Siebeck Verlag.

Popper, K.R. (1997), 'Tribute to the Life and Work of Friedrich Hayek', in S.F. Frowen (ed.), *Hayek: Economist and Social Philosopher: A Critical Retrospect*, London: MacMilllan, Houndmills, pp. 311–13.

Porter, G. (1999), 'Trade Competition and Pollution Standards: "Race to the Bottom" or "Stuck at the Bottom"', *Journal of Environment and Development*, June, pp. 133–51.

Posen, A.S. (1998), 'Do Better Institutions Make Better Policy?', *International Finance*, **1**(1), pp. 173–205.

ProKlima (1999), 'Partnership Contract proKlima of 8 June 1998 with the Supplementary Agreement of 6 October 1999', certified translation into English, Stadtwerke Hannover AG, Hanover.

ProKlima (2001), 'The Partnership Contract "proKlima" as a Model for Cooperative Climate Protection', information brochure, Stadtwerke Hannover AG, Hanover.

ProKlima (2002), 'proKlima – der enercity-Klimaschutzfonds, Jahresbericht 2001', Stadtwerke Hannover AG, Hanover.

ProKlima (2003), 'proKlima – der enercity-Fonds, Jahresbericht 2002', Stadtwerke Hannover AG, Hanover.

Ramesohl, S. and K. Kristof (2000), 'Voluntary Agreements – Implementation and Efficiency: the German Country Study – an Evaluation of the Updated Declaration of German Industry on Global Warming Prevention (1996)', Wuppertal: Wuppertal Institute.

Rammel, C. and van den Bergh, J.C.J.M. (2003), 'Evolutionary Policies for Sustainable Development: Adaptive Flexibility and Risk Minimising', *Ecological Economics*, **47**, pp. 121–33.

Reijnders, L. (1998), 'The Factor X Debate: Setting targets for Eco-efficiency', *Journal of Industrial Ecology*, **2**(1), pp. 13–22.

Reinhardt, F. (1999), 'Market Failure and the Environmental Policies of Firms', *Journal of Industrial Ecology*, **3**(1), pp. 9–21.

Reinicke, W. and F. Deng (2000), 'Critical Choices: The United Nations, Networks, and the Future of Global Governance', Ottawa: International Development Research Centre.

Rip, A. and R. Kemp (1998), 'Technological Change', in S. Rayner and E.L. Malone (eds), *Human Choice and Climate Change*, Vol. 2, Columbus and Ohio: Battelle Press, pp. 327–99.

Ritthoff, M., H. Rohn and C. Liedtke (2002), 'Calculating MIPS: resource productivity of products and services', *Wuppertal Spezial* **27** Wuppertal: Wuppertal Institute for Climate, Environment and Energy.

Rizzello, S. (1999), *The Economics of the Mind*, Cheltenham, UK and Northampton, MA, USA: Edward Elgar.

Rodrik, D. (2000), 'Institutions for High-Quality Growth: What They Are and How to Acquire Them', *Studies in Comparative International Development*, **35**(3), pp. 3–31.

Sabatier, P.A. (ed.) (1999), *Theories of the Policy Process*, Boulder, CO: Westview Press.

Scharpf, F.W. (1997), *Games Real Actors Play: Actor-Centred Institutionalism in Policy Research*, Boulder, CO: Westview Press.

Scharpf, F.W. (2001), 'Notes towards a Theory of Multilevel Governing in Europe', *Scandinavian Political Studies*, **24**(1), pp. 1–26.

Schlarb, M. (2001), 'Eco-Industrial Development: A Strategy for Building Sustainable Communitites', Cornell University.

Schmidt-Bleek, F. (1994), 'MIPS and Factor 10 for a Sustainable and Profitable Economy', Wuppertal: Wuppertal Institute.

Schneider, S.H. and J. Sarukhan (2001), 'Overview of Impacts, Adaptation, and Vulnerability to Climate Change', in *Climate Change 2001 – Impacts, Adaptation, Vulnerability. Contribution of Working Group II of the Third Assessment Report of the Intergovermental Panel on Climate Change*, Cambridge: Cambridge University Press, pp. 75–103.

Searle, J.R. (1995), *The Construction of Social Reality*, London: Penguin Press.

Searle, J.R. (2001), *Rationality in Action*, Cambridge, MA: MIT Press.

Simon, H.A. (1992), *Economics, Bounded Rationality and the Cognitive Revolution*, Cambridge, MA and London: MIT Press.

SiRi (Sustainable Investment Research International) (2002), 'Green Social and Ethical Funds in Europe 2002', Milan, available online at http://www.avanzi-sri.org/pdf/SRI%20Funds-Complete%20report%2020002.pdf (2006-07-13).

SiRi Group, Avanzi SRI Research (2003), 'Green, Social and Ethical Funds in Europe 2003', Milan, available online at http://www.avanzi-sri.org/pdf/Complete%20report%202003_final.pdf (2006-07-13).

Smith, A. (1761), *The Theory of Moral Sentiments*, Glasgow.

Smith, A. (1776), *The Wealth of Nations*, Glasgow.

Smith, A. (1997), *Integrated Pollution Control: Change and Continuity in the UK Industrial Pollution Policy Network*, Studies in Green Research,

Aldershot, Brookfield USA, Singapore, Sydney: Ashgate Publishing Company.

Solomon, B.D. and J.R. Mihelcic (2001), 'Environmental Management Codes and Continuous Environmental Improvements: Insights from the Chemical Industry', *Business Strategy and the Environment*, **10**, pp. 215–24.

Soregaroli, M. (2003), 'Evolution of sales of domestic appliances in Western Europe', 3rd International Conference on Energy Efficiency in Domestic Appliances and Lighting – EEDAL'03, Torino, Italy, 1–3 October.

Stiglitz, J. (1998), 'The Private Use of Public Interests: Incentives and Institutions', *Journal of Economic Perspectives*, **12**(2), pp. 3–21.

Stiglitz, J. (1999), 'Knowledge as a Global Public Good', in I. Kaul, I. Grunberg and M. Stern (eds), *Global Public Goods: International Cooperation in the 21st Century*, New York: Oxford University Press, pp. 308–25.

Stiglitz, J. (2000), *Economics of the Public Sector*, New York and London: Norton & Company.

Stockmann, R. (2000), 'Evaluationsforschung: Grundlagen und ausgewählte Forschungsfelder', Opladen: Leske+Budrich.

Sullivan, R. and P. Frankental (2002), 'Corporate Citizenship and the Mining Industry: Defining and Implementing Human Rights Norms', *Journal of Corporate Governance*, **7**, pp. 79–91, Autumn.

Sykes, A.O. (2000), 'Regulatory Competition or Regulatory Harmonization? A Silly Question', *Journal of International Economic Law*, **3**, pp. 257–64.

Tapper, R. (1997), 'Voluntary Agreements for Environmental Performance Improvement: Perspectives on the Chemical Industry's Responsible Care Programme', *Business Strategy and the Environment*, **6**, pp. 287–92.

ToBI (Task Force on Business and Industry) (1997), 'Minding Our Business: The Role of Corporate Accountability in Sustainable Development', an NGO Report to the UN Commission on Sustainable Development, available online at http://isforum.org/tobi/reports/minding/index/html (2006-06-30).

Trachtman, J.P. (2000), 'Regulatory Competition and Regulatory Jurisdiction', *Journal of International Economic Law*, **3**, pp. 331–48.

UBA (Umweltbundesamt) (2002), 'Langfristszenarien für eine nachhaltige Energieversorgung', Studie des Wuppertal Instituts für Klima Umwelt Energie und des Deutschen Zentrums für Luft- und Raumfahrt (DLR, Institut für Thermodynamik) im Auftrag des Umweltamts, Forschungsbericht 200 97 104, UBA Climate Change 02/02.

UNEP (United Nations Environment Programme) (2002), 'Industry as a Partner for Sustainable Development UNEP's Finance Industry Initiatives'.

United Nations (2006), 'Global Compact Governance', available online at http://www.unglobalcompact.org/AboutTheGC/stages_of_development. html (2006-07-03).

Utting, P. (2000), 'UN–Business Partnerships: Whose Agenda Counts?' Paper presented at seminar on Partnership for Development or Privatisation of the Multilateral System? North South Coalition, Oslo, Norway.

Van den Bergh, J.C.J.M. and S. Stagl (2003), 'Coevolution of Economic Behaviour and Institutions: Towards a Theory of Institutional Change', *Journal of Evolutionary Economics*, **13**(3), pp. 289–317.

Van den Hove, S., M. le Menestrel and H.-C. de Bettignies (2002), 'The Oil Industry and Climate Change: Strategies and Ethical Dilemmas', *Climate Policy*, **2**(1), pp. 3–18.

Van Kersbergen, K. and F. van Waarden (2001), 'Shifts in Governance: Problems of Legitimacy and Accountability', Dutch Organisation for Scientific Research (NWO), Background Report NOW, 77.

Vanberg, V.J. (1994), *Rules and Choice in Economics*, London: Routledge.

Vanberg, V.J. (1999), 'Markets and Regulation: On the Contrast between Free-Market Liberalism and Constitutional Liberalism', *Constitutional Political Economy*, **10**(3), pp. 219–43.

Vanberg, V.J. (2002), 'Rational Choice vs. Program-based Behavior: Alternative Theoretical Approaches and their Relevance for the Study of Institutions', *Rationality and Society*, **14**(1), pp. 7–53.

Vanberg, V.J. and W. Kerber (1994), 'Institutional Competition Among Jurisdictions: An Evolutionary Approach', *Constitutional Political Economy*, **5**(2), pp. 193–219.

VCI (Verband der Chemischen Industrie) (2003), 'Responsible Care: The Chemical Industry's Data on Safety, Health and Environmental Protection', Frankfurt a. Main.

Voet, E. van der, L. van Oers and I. Nikolic (2003), 'Dematerialisation: Not just a Matter of Weight', Leiden: Centre of Environmental Science, CML report 160.

Voet, E. van der, L. van Oers, S. Moll, H. Schütz, S. Bringezu, S. de Bruyn, M. Sevenster and G. Warringa (2005), 'Policy Review on Decoupling: Development of Indicators to Assess Decoupling of Economic Development and Environmental Pressure in the EU-25 and AC3 Countries', CML Report 166, Leiden: Centre of Environmental Science, CE Delft, Wuppertal Institute.

Vogel, D. (2000), 'Environmental Regulation and Economic Integration', *Journal of International Economic Law*, **3**, pp. 265–79.

Vorfelder, J. (1995), 'Brent Spar oder die Zukunft der Meere. Ein Greenpeace Report', München: Beck.

Waddell, S. (2000), 'Complementary resources: the win–win rationale for partnership with NGOs', in J. Bendell (ed.), *Terms for Endearment: Business, NGOs and Sustainable Development*, Sheffield: Greenleaf Publishing.

Walker, W. (2000), 'Entrapment in Large Technological Systems: Institutional commitment and Power Relations', *Research Policy*, **29**, pp. 833–46.

Wang, Z., C. Wu and G. Wang (2002), 'Comparative Research on the Two Industrial Symbiosis Patterns in Eco-Industrial Parks', conference paper, 12th International Conference on Comparative Management, 1–2 November.

WBCSD (World Business Council for Sustainable Development) (ed.) (2000a), 'Eco-efficiency: Creating more value with less impact', Geneva.

WBCSD (ed.) (2000b), 'Corporate Social Responsibility: Making Good Business Sense', Geneva.

WBCSD Cement (n.d.), 'Substudy 5: Determination of Key Performance Indicators for SD and the Cement Industry', available online at http://www.wbcsdcement.org/pdf/progress_report_5.pdf (2006-06-30).

Weber, M. and J. Hemmelskamp (eds) (2005), *Towards Environmental Innovation Systems*, Heidelberg: Springer.

Wegner, G. (1996), *Wirtschaftspolitik zwischen Selbst- und Fremdsteuerung*, Baden-Baden: Nomos.

Wegner, G. (1997), 'Economic Policy From an Evolutionary Perspective: A New Approach', *Journal of Institutional and Theoretical Economics*, **153**(3), pp. 485–509.

Wegner, G. (2003), 'Evolutionary Markets and the Design of Institutional Policy', in P. Pelikan and G. Wegner (eds), *The Evolutionary Analysis of Economic Policy*, Cheltenham, UK and Northampton, MA, USA: Edward Elgar, pp. 46–66.

Weidner, H. (1996), 'Umweltkooperation und alternative Konfliktregelungsverfahren in Deutschland. Zur Entstehung eines neuen Politiknetzwerkes', Schriften zu Mediationsverfahren im Umweltschutz Nr. 16, Discussion Paper; FS II 96-302, Berlin: Wissenschaftszentrum Berlin.

Weizsäcker, E.U., A. Lovins and H. Lovins (1997), *Factor Four: Doubling Wealth – Halving Resource Use*, London: Earthscan.

Westling, H. (1996), 'Cooperative Procurement: Market Acceptance for Innovative Energy-Efficient Technologies', Report for NUTEK, Energy, Stockholm.

Wijshoff, L. and S. Attali (2003), 'Energy+ cold appliances beyond the A-label, thanks to pan-European procurement', Time to turn down energy demand; proceedings of the 2003 ECEEE Summer Study Proceedings, 2–7 June, St Raphael, France, Vol. 2, Europ. Council for an Energy-Efficient Economy, Paris, pp. 761–4.

Williamson, O.E. (1999), 'Strategy Research: Governance and Competence Perspectives', *Strategic Management Journal*, **20**(12), pp. 1087–108.

Witt, U. (2003), *The Evolving Economy: Essays on the Evolutionary Approach to Economics*, Cheltenham, UK and Northampton, MA, USA: Edward Elgar.

World Bank/OECD (2006), 'Global Corporate Governance Forum', available online at http://www.valuebasedmanagement.net/organizations_worldbank.html (2006-07-03).

Worrel, E. (1994), 'Potentials for Improved Use of Industrial Energy and Materials', habilitation thesis, University of Utrecht.

Young, O. (1999), *Governance in World Affairs*, Ithaca and London: Cornell University Press.

Zadek, S. (2002), 'Third Generation Corporate Citizenship: Public Policy and Business in Society', London: Foreign Policy Centre in Association with AccountAbility.

Zerbe, R.O. (2001), *Economic Efficiency in Law and Economics*, Cheltenham, UK and Northampton, MA, USA: Edward Elgar.

Zollinger, P. (2001), 'The Social Bottom Line of Sustainable Development', in E.U. Weizsäcker et al. (eds), *From Eco-efficiency to Overall Sustainable Development in Enterprises*, Wuppertal Spezial 18, Wuppertal: Wuppertal Institute, pp. 151–7.

Index